To SABRINA –
GOOD FISHING ALWAYS)
BEST,

Larry Bay...

Larry Bozka's

SALTWATER STRATEGIES™:

How, When and Where

to Fish the Western Gulf Coast

Larry Bozka's

SALTWATER STRATEGIES™:

How, When & Where

to Fish the Western Gulf Coast

By Larry Bozka

Texas Fish & Game
Publishing Co., L.L.C.

7600 W. Tidwell, Suite 708
Houston, Texas 77040
713-690-3474
Website: www.fishgame.com

Published by

Texas Fish & Game
Publishing Co., L.L.C.

7600 West Tidwell, Suite 708
Houston, Texas 77040
Phone: 713-690-3474
Fax: 713-690-4339
Website: www.fishgame.com

First Edition

Cover illustration from a photo by Mary Bozka.

Cover illustration by Mark Mantell.

All photos by the author unless otherwise noted.

Foreword by Shannon Tompkins.

Edited by Judy Rider.

ISBN:0-929980-00-X

This book is dedicated to the memory of my father,
William D. Bozka, Sr.
His advice was invariably sound.
He did a lot of things for me and my brothers that other
fathers do for their children every day.
But most of all, he took us fishing.
For that, I will remain eternally grateful.

Contents

Foreword

Fire in the Belly: A Burning Desire to Inform

One of the greatest challenges writers face is maintaining a passion about their subject.

It's impossible to write anything of substance or usefulness unless the author cares deeply about the topic on which he focuses.

But passion takes a writer only so far. Experience with the topic is as necessary an ingredient, as is a gnawing need to know and understand the subject on a personal level.

And then it takes the skill learned by practicing the craft—the profession, really—of journalism. Research, and lots of it. Search out the experts. Know what questions to ask. Ask them. And ask them again.

Then pull it all together, cobbling a cohesive, understandable and entertaining read that seems like it just fell together with no effort.

That's the trick.

It's like fishing for speckled trout.

You don't consistently catch trout (or reds or flounder or even sheepshead) with a halfhearted approach to the subject.

You need that fire in the belly, that drive that leads to soaking up every nuance of wind, weather, tide and season. There's so much to learn—biology, gear, geography, topography.

And you have to ferret out the people who know the subject better than you. Be willing to listen and learn from them. Be open to questioning your own beliefs and tactics, be willing to approach things from a different angle, to try something different, if for no other reason than to learn from the experience.

And you have to come to grips with the fact that you will never know everything. No angler will ever in his life have all the answers, just as no writer will ever author the perfect, complete work.

But there is honor and self-satisfaction in both efforts.

This book combines those elements. It's the work of a journalist who fishes. Or maybe it's the work of an angler who writes.

Either way, it works.

I knew Larry would do this book, and I believe I knew it almost 25 years ago.

Our meeting and subsequent friendship was pure serendipity. Probably the only two journalism students at the University of Houston who owned fishing gear ended up thrown together in the same classes.

It didn't take us long to find each other and discover our mutual passion for fishing.

And it was immediately clear to me that this tall, slim (it was a long time ago) Czech boy from Pearland was "eat plum up" with coastal fishing. Between classes, he'd talk about fishing for bull reds off the beach near San Luis Pass, or how his father, whom it was obvious he adored, held the state record for amberjack. We'd talk about writers we admired, and the kind we wanted to be.

Larry wanted to be an "outdoor writer." Fishing, mostly. Coastal fishing.

Our professors were brutally frank. They told us how very, very few of us journalism students would ever make a living as writers or reporters of any sort. The competition was fierce, jobs scarce, the pay abysmal and the burnout factor higher than the casualty rate for helicopter door gunners.

But I never doubted Bozka would make it. He had that fire in his belly—ambition to spare, and the guts to pursue it in the face of odds only a young person could ignore.

And I knew he'd pursue his passion for coastal fishing with the same relentless drive.

This book is one of the results of all those things coming together.

"Saltwater Strategies™" is a years-long labor of passion and craft and burning desire to inform, entertain and explain the science and art of coastal fishing.

And now that it's completed, maybe Larry will take the time to waste a day fishing with an old friend.

But probably not. He'll be too busy spending time with people who know how to actually CATCH fish.

Shannon Tompkins   Houston, Texas, June 1998

Introduction

Show Me
The Stringer

The old cliché comes up just about every time a group of fishermen encounters a lousy day on the bay. It goes something like this:

"If you caught 'em every time, they'd call it 'catching,' not 'fishing.' Heck, it'd get boring if you caught fish every time you went out."

Let's get this on the record, up front and straight. If I caught fish every time I hit the water, I would be one very happy man.

Of course, I don't. And neither does anyone else, despite what he or she may tell you. Show me an angler who scores on every outing, and I'll show you either a liar or a magician.

There are, nonetheless, individuals who manage to succeed more often than not when pursuing gamefish. Some call them "lucky." I dare not downplay the importance of Lady Luck, having benefited from her gracious intervention on many occasions in the 25-plus years that I've been so ridiculously obsessed with the sport of coastal angling. Still, there's much more to the consistent success of these highly revered saltwater sportsmen than sheer good fortune.

Foremost, they recognize the pieces of the puzzle, and intimately understand the almost mystic mix of environmental variables that collectively set the scene for a killer fishing trip. Furthermore, they head for the water—without either hesitation or a tinge of "I oughta be working instead" guilt—when the pieces finally come together.

No doubt, catching fish is tremendous fun. But over the years, I've come to believe that the enjoyment of saltwater fishing encompasses much more than driving a hook barb into the yellowed jaw of a big speckled trout. As my wife and fishing partner, Mary, puts it, "It's the going and the doing."

Half the thrill of a fishing trip rests in the preparation. What better way to anticipate a trip than to meticulously construct a list of things that need to be done, gear that needs to be packed and tackle that needs to be rigged? For the saltwater fishing enthusiast, though, this fishing foreplay goes even further.

Back to those "environmental variables."

Look in the back yard, see a pretty day, and that's just what you have—a pretty day and little else. It takes much more than sunshine and clear skies to create good fishing conditions along the Gulf Coast. A good day for golf is not necessarily a good day on the Gulf. Matter of fact, some of the best fishing I've ever experienced has occurred in the midst of drizzling rain and gunmetal-gray skies—the kind of stuff that confines ardent duffers to the country club bar.

No, it's the stuff you can't see that counts. The wind, its direction and intensity. The tides, their frequency and degree of flow. The temperature, not only of the air but also the water. These factors and others make or break a day of saltwater fishing, and they are as unforgiving and fickle as the meanest sorority girl on campus.

I wrote my first story for the Houston Post (may she rest in peace) back in 1976. It had to do with a trip to Matagorda, fishing with the Talasek brothers out of River Bend Bait Camp and Tavern on the Colorado River. These guys were—and still are—verified "old salts."

In the decades since, I have fished with literally hundreds of anglers who also merit that ranking. I've conducted hundreds of interviews, and written hundreds of stories. So, if there's any credit to be given for the knowledge and advice which follows herein, it goes to the guides (and persons who could be guides if they wanted to) who have so kindly allowed me space and time on their fishing boats since I opted to devote my life to writing about God's great outdoors.

Others deserve acknowledgment as well. My father, who put me on my first fish (a mighty hardhead catfish landed off the docks below the Kemah Bridge) at the age of five. My friends in the outdoor writing fraternity—most notably the late A.C. Becker, Jr., of Galveston, with whom I published a series of saltwater-oriented books from 1989 through 1991, and several others who have passed on—Houston Post outdoor writer Stan Slaten, San Antonio Express-News outdoor writer Dan Klepper, Dallas Morning News outdoor writer Andy Anderson, San Antonio radio personality Charly McTee and Texas Parks and Wildlife magazine senior editor Jim Cox. My friends in the Texas Outdoor Writers Association. The many industry personnel with whom I have learned about everything from baitcasting reels to broken-back plugs. And, certainly not least, the thousands of readers who have so generously shared their ideas and experience since my first word made print.

The list, quite literally, is much too extensive to comprehensively cover. You know who you are, and you have my heartfelt thanks.

It's my sincere hope that what you learn in the following pages plays a mentionable role in your future on-the-water successes. Good fishing, and— what the heck; it can't hurt—

Good Luck.

Larry Bozka   Seabrook, Texas

Chapter One

An Open Book: Reading the Water

SEVERAL YEARS AGO, DURING AN AFTER-GAME television interview, a leading college quarterback explained the reason for his phenomenal junior year. "When I was a freshman," he said, "I could only see to the 30-yard line. When I was a sophomore, I could see to the 50. Now," he concluded with a smug grin, "I can see the whole field."

Saltwater fishing, strange as it seems, is little different.

The ability to "read the water" is an invaluable asset to the coastal angler. In a bay or on the beachfront, an aptitude to discern the subtle signs that betray the presence of gamefish makes the difference between a weightless stringer and success.

SEEING IT IN THE SURF

From the dying breakers of the first gut to the rising swells of the third bar and beyond, the surf is an open book—but only to those who over the years have come to understand the language.

To many, "reading the water" seems a mysterious process, and rightfully so. The saltwater guru is part meteorologist, part biologist, part analyst and part prophet, a unique and perceptive breed of fisherman who not only looks, but sees,

When the birds are "working," the fisherman had best get to working as well. Diving flocks of seagulls, homing in on pods of shrimp driven to the surface by feeding gamefish, are sure-fire indicators of quality fishing waiting to happen.

interprets and reacts. The signals, though often elusive, are relatively simple.

The biggest challenge in surf fishing, many will tell you, is patience—waiting out the weather. There is no saltwater spot anywhere more vulnerable to the whims of wind and temperature than the first few hundred yards of the Gulf of Mexico. The beachfront is, at best, one extremely fickle fishing hole.

Sight-feeding gamefish require reasonably clear water, and in turn, favorable winds. As a rule, that translates to south, or preferably, southeast. Whoever penned the old adage "When the wind is out of the west, fishing is best" was obviously much more into rhyming words than catching fish. To a bay fisherman a westerly breeze is very bad news. For the surf wader, it's an outright curse.

Westerly winds approach the beachfront at a coarse angle which in essence knocks the tops off of the nearshore bars and sends the sand and sediment flying in roiling, wave-borne clouds. It takes very little time for a west wind to completely wipe out quality surf waters. In a favorable scenario, however, with a southerly shift in the wind, light velocities and substantial and repeated tide flow, the same waters can once again become "trout green" in a matter of a half-day or so.

Amazingly, both surf and bay waters can sometimes, in fact, become too clear. Transparent, see-your-shoelaces conditions create a glass house in which roving trout and reds can literally see everything—especially you. Anything in the "sandy-green" category will suffice, providing adequate clarity for artificial lures while retaining just enough cloudiness to mask the wader's presence.

The magic thermometer mark of 55 degrees, which usually comes in about the last week of February, triggers the black drum run. That's when whopper drum kick off their annual spawn and bring rod-bending life to the surf and adjacent passes and jetties. Roughly two months later, the advent of 70-degree water prompts the debut of both redfish and speckled trout, along with a wide and colorful variety of "bonus" species such as Spanish mackerel, pompano, bluefish, ladyfish, blacktip sharks, jack crevalle and even an occasional tarpon.

Though wintertime isn't especially conducive to catching gamefish from the surf, it nonetheless provides a wonderful window through which to check out bare bottom terrain that for the rest of the year is covered up by surging waters pushed in from predominantly southerly breezes. Sand bars and bottom areas which would normally be submerged become delightfully visible, yielding a wealth of information to the trained eye. Those armed with hand-held GPS units should duly save the satellite coordinates (a.k.a. "waypoints") of any substantial structure variances, and return to those spots come springtime with gold spoons and Mirr-Olures in hand.

On the whole, the surf appears to be little more than a continuous progression of wave-carved underwater sand dunes. Yet, viewed up close, one small stretch of sand at a time, the differences begin to appear. Some—for instance a patch of shell along the waterline or on the bottom, or maybe a sunken tree trunk—are fairly obvious. Others, like breaks between the sandbars and shallow holes within the guts, are a bit tougher to discern. Either way, they're easiest to see when you're fresh on the heels of a sandblaster cold front.

High tides mean deep water, and as such allow the fish to range extremely close to shore. In the surf, this tendency is especially prevalent. Of all the mistakes made by beginning beachfront waders, one of the worst is the proclivity to ignore shallow water. Steam past the first gut without a cast and you may well be blowing the best fishing of the day.

Expect, too, to encounter the best surf plugging while the sun is still working its way over—or, to a lesser degree, back down—the horizon. I've enjoyed some great beachfront fishing in the glow of summertime sunsets, but nothing compared with the regularity that often greets the dawn patrol. The warmer the surf waters become with the passage of summertime, the more this general rule of thumb becomes apparent.

If you miss the cold-weather chance to see the sandbars unveiled, all is not lost. Aside from the clarity and color hue of the water (darker color indicates deeper water), the height of the incoming breakers will divulge the location and depth of the troughs.

Watch the wave closely as it breaks over the bar. Determine the distance from the curl to the crest. With only a small degree of variance, that distance will equal the depth of the trough. And the trough, without exception, is the target area for your bait or lure.

On a broader scale, the best area to begin fishing is within fairly close proximity of a major pass. If beachfront troughs are the highways, then the passes and jetty channels which connect the bays with the surf are the entrance and exit ramps of roving sportfish.

Remember, though, that the same tidal surge which makes the fishing in

Only 50 feet away, a distinct "slick" erupts in front of the approaching wade fisherman. Never take slicks for granted—especially the small, fresh ones.

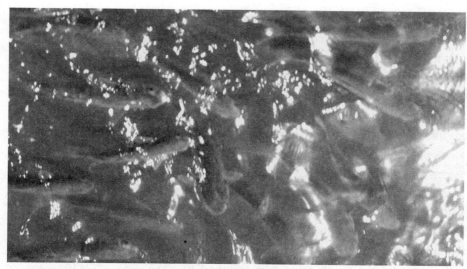

Seeing is believing. At top, a surfaced pod of mullet viewed without the glare-cutting advantage of a polarized lens. Below, the same basic shot, but with polarization. It's easy to understand why polarized shades are so important. Spend the money for good ones, and use them.

these areas so productive is also a potential killer. The only thing more dangerous than an undertow is one that's magnified by the constricted and rapidly jettisoned waters of a tide-swollen pass. It cost me a dear friend years ago—a friend who, sadly, refused to wear a life jacket.

Where the water changes color, it's a pretty sure bet that a change in the bottom contour made it happen. The beachfront guts are in essence thoroughfares for fish, and when they become irregular or wallowed-out, the traveling predators stop for a look. The deeper waters of the guts and troughs offer refuge to marauding gamefish and the forage species they pursue. Holding near the bottom, the fish get a break from the mega-powered beachfront elements, protected by a wave-stopping wall of sand. There, they suspend and conserve energy. They also take advantage of an easy meal. The infinite and continuous onslaught of currents and waves pounds the tops of the sandbars, in the process unearthing countless marine worms and small crustaceans.

A pair of quality polarized fishing glasses is as essential to the surf and bay wader—and the bay drifter and offshore angler as well—as a fighting belt to a marlin troller. The angler who assesses the surf without a good pair of glare-cutters is at a definite disadvantage, not unlike the hunter who attempts to shoot long ranges without the aid of a quality rifle scope. Good polarized shades such as those made by Costa Del Mar, Hobie, Ocean Wave and others are essentials, not options.

The reduced toll on eyes alone is well worth a hundred-dollar-plus investment in first-rate shades. With glare minimized, baitfish become much easier to see. So do surface slicks and color changes. Color changes, again, are valuable indicators not only along the beachfront but also within the confines of inland estuaries.

It doesn't take an entire flock of seagulls to merit an angler's attention. The "signs" that lead to quality fishing are often as subtle as a single laughing gull or jumping finger mullet.

Small inlets and coves that cut into saltwater shorelines are every bit as enticing to coastal wade fishermen as they are to avid bassers on freshwater lakes.

INLAND INSIGHTS

Bay waters, fortunately, are not nearly so unforgiving as the surf when it comes to sheer vulnerability. Perhaps the biggest difference between the bays and beachfront, however, is that whereas surf structure is almost always invisible, fish-attracting structure in the bays can be seen either visually or—in deeper waters—with the aid of a depthfinder.

Pier pilings, oyster reef islands, spoil bank ledges and sunken wrecks with barnacle-encrusted masts protruding through the surface are dead-on and easy-to-see gamefish giveaways. With the depthfinder, though, a bay fisherman can slowly scan an area and discern the location of bottom breaks, holes, sunken debris and—perhaps most precious of all—shell pads left behind by vacated gas production platforms. The biggest advantage of the latter is that unlike fishing the visible stuff, the angler who jigs shrimptails or soaks live croakers over an abandoned well pad isn't likely to be competing with many other boaters. It's also another situation in which the possession of a GPS unit becomes a major plus.

It's often the most subtle of signs—color changes, the gentle twitch of mullet tails, tidal rips and perhaps a feeding egret, cormorant or heron on a near-by shore—that are the most valuable to a bay angler who's trying to read saltwater signals. All the same, there are three primary scenarios that are wonderfully reliable and, for the novice, delightfully easy to detect with the assistance of the aforementioned polarized shades—slicks, working birds, and mud boils.

Fresh slicks—small, oily patches on the surface sporting a bright sheen that results from oils emitted by feeding gamefish—are critical signs for fish-hunting bay anglers. The tell-tale "watermelon smell" of a fresh trout slick is enough to up the pulse rate of even the most experienced coastal bait-caster. (Personally, if I ever came across a watermelon that smelled that way I'd toss it in the trash can.)

The best slick is a small slick. Why? Because it's a fresh one. A large, spread out slick isn't nearly so dependable as one that's about the size of a garbage can lid. You can bet, without question, that where there is a slick there are going to be feeding fish below. The catch, however, is that those fish are not always the desired speckled trout or, less often, "slicking" redfish.

During the summer months, gafftopsail catfish move into the bays in big numbers. A foraging school of gafftops can pop a slick that looks like something produced by a ruptured tanker. Gafftops, though incredibly slimy and somewhat of a hassle to clean, are nonetheless great eating fish. If you want a fresh batch of catfish fillets, cast natural baits into a gafftop slick and hold on. You'll usually catch all you want.

Spanish mackerel will also create slicks, most often in deeper waters off of jetty channels or within the surf. Again, if it's mackerel you'll know it. They have teeth that'll sever 30-pound-test mono leader like it's not even there. The good news is that they're excellent fighters and, promptly cleaned and iced, wonderful eating. You'd just best have some flat black steel leader on hand if you hope to bring one in.

Likewise, if it's speckled trout you're after, you'll know in seconds flat if they are indeed there. Rare is the occasion when stoked-up specks beneath a fresh slick will ignore an erratically retrieved soft plastic shadtail or sinking plug.

There is another false alarm when it comes to fishing slicks, and to turn it on you need look no further than the nearest crab trap. There's hardly a bay system on the Gulf Coast that's not littered with box-shaped chicken wire crab traps. Freshly baited with chicken parts, cut baitfish or fish carcasses, they'll cough up slicks that you can see from a mile away. Always check out a slick when you see it, but if a crab trap appears on further inspection, keep on moving.

Equally visible, and just as reliable on coastal bays, are working flocks of seagulls. Bird action generally occurs between mid-April and the end of October—

the same period of time when the bays are host to large pods of white and brown shrimp. The hapless crustaceans become sandwiched between feeding trout below and wheeling flocks of gulls which pick them off from above. When this exciting phenomenon occurs, there's hardly a lure that can't be tossed into the midst of the fray without immediate results.

"Bird trout" tend to be small, school-caliber fish that don't make the minimum legal measurement. That isn't however, an absolute rule. The only absolute rule of saltwater fishing, after all, is that there are no absolute rules. I've seen more than a few occasions when trout under birds all measured better than 21 inches. A recent fall trip to East Matagorda Bay with guides Tony Casarez and Rick Kersey produced the most incredible big-trout bird action I've ever witnessed. None of the fish measured less than 22 inches, and two of them tipped the scales at better than 5 pounds.

If you're selectively after bigger fish holding beneath working gulls, think deep. The bigger speckled trout get, the more fat and lazy they become. Their smaller and much more energetic brethren do a great job of stunning more food than they need. The opportunistic big fish patiently wait below and partake of a

During spring and fall—and during mild seasons, even early winter—the fisherman who ignores the actions of resident gulls is at a real disadvantage.

slow-sinking meal that they didn't have to twitch a fin to collect.

As opposed to slicks and working birds, it takes a sharpened eye to detect mud boils—especially when the water is off-colored to begin with. Mud boils— cloudy puffs of exploded aquatic dust that are left behind when a spooked game- fish is either bottom feeding or, suddenly disturbed, engages its tail, and heads posthaste for less threatening surroundings—are particularly endemic to feeding redfish. However, they can also be caused by not only speckled trout, flounder and black drum but also fleeing mullet. Usually, when it's a redfish making the boil you'll know it. Bottom-grubbing redfish eat about as daintily as rooting feral hogs.

The fish probe the bottom with their big, blunt noses and extract every-

When approaching a flock of "working" birds, always remember that the smallest speckled trout will usually be the ones nearest the surface. The bigger specks—fat, lazy and unwilling to expend any more energy than absolutely necessary to procure a meal—are prone to hold below the frenzied "pencil trout" above. Therefore, in-the-know anglers always try to keep their baits deep for bigger fish. The trick is to cast the lure—in this case a Rapala Weedless Minnow Spoon rigged with a pink bucktail—beyond the surfaced school, let it sink and then begin a slow, wobbling retrieve. Lead-headed shrimptail and shadtail jigs will get the job done equally well, though you might want to rig them with a heavier jig head—say, 3/8-ounce—in order to both cast farther and get the bait down as quickly as possible. (Illustration by Mark Mantell)

Mary Bozka casts a shrimptail into the fray while working seagulls go after surfaced pods of shrimp in the Land Cut. It doesn't get much faster than this.

thing from shrimp and worms buried in the mud to skittering blue crabs. It's this behavior which in very shallow waters creates the "tailing" scenario that inshore sight casters so anxiously anticipate.

All things considered, the most influential element of all is one that's invisible—the ebb and flow of the tides. No single factor influences the behavior and migrations of marine creatures more dramatically than the direction and intensity of tidal currents.

Fortunately, tides can be predicted with a great degree of accuracy (for the benefit of Texas coastal anglers they're listed in every issue of *Texas Fish & Game®*, as well as within the pages of the magazine's *Texas Lakes & Bays®* map annual). Times of peak rise and fall are provided, along with correction tables that allow for the gradual "time delay" which takes place when the waters of the surf begin to move up or down the coastline.

Of all the variables encountered by the surf wader, tides are the easiest to anticipate. Key in on four-tide days whenever possible. Make it a point, too, to begin fishing a given area around an hour in advance of the predicted tidal peak. As a rule, fishing inside of coastal passes is best during incoming tidal phases, and angling outside of those passes is superior when the tide is running out. Most important, though, is the fact that the tide is moving. Some degree of current is essential no matter where you are or how you're fishing.

Almost as easy to discern and every bit as critical to productive fishing is the presence of baitfish. Clarity and current become moot points when the surf is devoid of mullet, shrimp and crabs. All three are most scarce when the tide is standing. Accordingly, the same holds true for predator species.

Surface-running pods of mullet are always a good sign, but when the fleeing baitfish get nervous it's almost a cinch. It takes a good reason, most often the likelihood of being attacked and eaten alive, to send an entire school of mullet rocketing from the surface in a dozen different directions. When the mullet come unglued, get a bait in front of them and do it fast. If you are emotionally attached to the lure you're tossing, don't throw it. You may well never see it again.

Within the bays, a change in water color affords predator species a belly-filling opportunity, a deadly "hide-and-go-seek" game that takes place on the fringes between clear and dingy water. Tidal rips often create distinct color lines, and they should never be ignored. Redfish and trout lurk on the outside clear edge of the change. There, they wait for mullet, menhaden, glass minnows and crabs to unwittingly venture out of the dirty stuff and into the open. At that point, the predators make a fast attack and then retreat to await a re-run of the process.

There is, finally, one last factor that ultimately determines the long-term success or failure of an aspiring old salt—his or her work schedule. Time won't wait, and neither will the surf and bays. When it all comes together, there are no guarantees that the magic combination will outlast the next tide. Any way you look at it, the precarious nature of the situation puts the nine-to-fiver at a real disadvantage. The "best" saltwater angler in any given area is invariably a person who can grab a rod and run when opportunity beckons.

When in doubt, stop and cast. Trust your instincts. Anticipate conditions, and go prepared to meet those conditions. Any fisherman around can score once in a while, just on the merits of good fortune and the occasional "fish signs" that are virtually impossible to miss. Interpret the subtleties, though, with an open mind and keen eyes, and unlike many of your peers, you'll soon find yourself playing the whole field.

Chapter Two

Interpreting Tides: The Rise and Fall of the Angling Empire

Since time immemorial, the moon-driven ebb and flow of coastal waters has dictated the harvest of fishermen. Waters rise, waters fall, and as the state of the aquatic habitat changes, so do the movements of the denizens which inhabit the bays.

The degree to which the movements of forage species, and in turn, gamefish, are influenced varies from place to place. In the flooded marshes of Louisiana and the bays of the Upper to Middle Texas Coast, the tides play a rather critical role. Conversely, in the Upper Laguna Madre, Baffin Bay and the flats south to Port Isabel, the tidal variance tends to be much less significant. Either way, it pays to know the ways of the water if you intend to catch coastal gamefish on a consistent basis.

Tide, in essence, is the vertical rise and fall of saltwater in accordance with the gravitational pull of the moon and the sun. Said rise and fall, coupled with the intensity and direction of the wind, results in the horizontal element of the equation—the current.

As if that's not enough to consider, predicted tidal heights should be considered those expected under average weather conditions. The direction and strength of the wind can wreak absolute havoc on tide predictions. A blustery south or southeast wind along the Western Gulf Coast can push anticipated high

Tidal flows are greatly magnified in the vicinity of coastal passes—in this case mile-wide San Luis Pass, situated between Galveston and Freeport. Well-known Texas angler Robert Tucker caught this 6-pound trout while free-shrimping "The Pass" during a photo shoot we conducted back in late spring of 1981.

tides from 6 inches to well over a foot above predicted levels. Conversely, a screaming howler out of the frigid north can rapidly render a normally calf-deep saltwater slough into a bare mud flat. Either scenario can at times work to the angler's advantage.

Take the south wind first. Combined with a substantial high tide, a powerful south wind can push enough water into a normally inaccessible flat to suddenly create a redfish stalking haven. The "phantom lakes" of Matagorda and San José Islands off the middle and southern coasts of Texas are excellent examples. Fishermen either pole super-shallow-draft hulls into these soft-bottomed tidal pools or wade their way in when flood or "bull" tides inundate the relatively small lagoons. Some are as diminutive as a fair-sized living room; others cover several acres or more. Regardless, when a powerful high tide stand pushes in water, plankton and forage species such as mullet, glass minnows and shrimp, predators—primarily redfish—are sure to follow.

When, you might well wonder, can a drop in water levels be good news? Look no further than the Texas flats from Rockport-Fulton south to the Upper Laguna Madre. In this area, where bay waters are considerably more shallow than you'll encounter along the Upper Coast, a high tide can actually scatter the gamefish and make pinpointing their locales a much more difficult proposition. When fall arrives and the first cold fronts of the year couple with low tide phases, the reduced water depth concentrates predator species in what are often indistinct guts and holes. Almost invariably, such a hole will be located near a deep-water escape route.

Here, as in many other situations, there is a distinct parallel between fishing for saltwater gamefish and freshwater largemouth bass. The structure may vary, but whether it's an oyster reef or a hydrilla bed, the fish stay close to its edges. For both creatures, a drop-off situated within easy swimming distance of both shallow flats and a deeper ledge serves as a primary ambush point from which to attack unsuspecting prey on the move.

Along the Texas Coastal Bend, from Port O'Connor south to the Lower Laguna Madre, wind is a year-round culprit. Furthermore, from April through as late as May there's always the very real possibility that an errant cold front will rudely interrupt a choice period of calm conditions and clear waters.

Rockport-area guides in particular enjoy much more protection than is afforded their counterparts on the Upper Texas Coast. Gusts up to 15 mph are commonplace, nothing to worry about. They can, strange as it seems, actually work to the angler's advantage by creating current flow in waters that are otherwise only slightly affected by tidal fluctuations.

"You learn to cope with the wind, and even use it to your advantage," says my good friend Capt. Lowell Odom. "In the Rockport area, shallow as the water is, you actually *need* some degree of wind to help create currents. The water is still cool in early spring, when your odds of snagging a big speckled trout are much better than average. Being cool, it will clear up fairly fast."(Cool water is more dense than hot water, and also carries much less phytoplankton. Both factors contribute significantly to the traditionally clearer waters of fall, winter and early spring.)

"If it's not just a terribly strong norther, it will sometimes push the water up on a south shoreline as opposed to blowing it out," Odom explains. "In the process, it'll also push the bait up on the shoreline while simultaneously adding a bit of oxygen content. It'll dirty the water enough to create a color change, which creates a zone in which the trout and reds can ambush the bait. And despite the way it looks and seems to the average fisherman," he notes, "it can actually create a quality fishing opportunity."

One trip in particular comes to mind. It was April of '96. Wife Mary, son Jimmy and I had joined Odom for two days of wade fishing and shooting footage for the upcoming *Texas Fish & Game* Video Library. True to trips past, conditions were superb until the day of our arrival, at which point the wind kicked into gear like a wild horse jabbed in the flank with a cattle prod.

"No problem," Odom told us as we pulled away from the boat ramp at Goose Island State Park. "I deal with this stuff all the time."

We ran, and then we ran some more. Nothing but coffee-colored saltwater for miles on end, except for the ivory-colored hue of whitecaps frothing across the wind-blasted bay surface. Then, without warning, Odom throttled back the big Mariner and nosed the boat toward a small cove that sliced its way back into the far recesses of Matagorda Island.

"Water's better here," he announced with confidence. "There's bait in here, too."

Sure enough, small pods of mullet skittered across the mouth of the grass-fringed slough. And though the water was still a long way from clear, in comparison to the surrounding area it looked like a Chub Cay bonefish flat.

That morning, in around two hours of casting, we snagged limits of keeper speckled trout on Producer Ghost topwaters—baits that, according to popular belief, are only productive when bay waters are at least sandy green. We got our video, and kept a few of the smaller trout for the freezer. And we pulled it off because the very wind I had cursed that morning had, by pushing water back into the marsh, created an "artificial tide" of sorts.

Several days following the passage of a front, the situation changes. This change can again—in the right spot—make for a productive scenario.

"The water that was pushed back into the marsh will begin to fall out," Odom explains. "On that same shoreline, the sloughs that flow into the bay become primary targets. I call them 'feeders,' because when they back-wash into the bay with a falling tide they jettison the baitfish back into the open water. For the gamefish in the area, it's almost like a deer feeder going off. The trout and reds

Capt. Gerald Bryant shows off the bronze-backed bounty of the marsh bayous located near Cocodrie, La. Houston Chronicle outdoor writer Doug Pike and I had a ball on this particular early-May afternoon, sight-casting small topwater plugs to hungry, shore-hugging redfish that couldn't help but give away their locations via the watery swirls of gently waving, blue-tinged tails. After one trip to Cocodrie, Mary and I decided to visit Cocodrie Charters at least once a year. From food to fishing, the place will outright spoil you.

know that the current will carry the mullet and baitfish back out, and they wait at the mouths of the sloughs and within the guts beyond those mouths until the bait shows up."

According to Odom, anglers can find sloughs of this sort all the way down the shorelines of Matagorda and San José Islands. "The water doesn't typically stack up as high on St. Jo as it does on Matagorda," he says. "Sometimes it'll stack the water up on the west shoreline of San Antonio Bay. It'll also stack up back into Swan Lake, on the far west end of Copano Bay, and Port Bay, on the south side of Copano. But it's a scenario," he adds, "which applies up and down the entire Gulf Coast, anywhere you find tidal marshes and lagoons. Study a map," he advises, "and you'll find 'feeder' areas like this most anywhere you go."

As you'd expect, waters on the protected north shorelines flow out immediately with the arrival of a late-season norther. "As it blows out on the first day of the front, you can also find gamefish intercepting bait on the outside shores of the north side," Odom points out. "It's largely a matter of timing, and being familiar with the area you're fishing and how it reacts to the wind."

Wife Mary shows off a 28-inch speckled trout caught on an Excalibur Super Spook while wade fishing with Matagorda, Texas pro Capt. Bill Pustejovsky, Capt. Mel Talasek and friend Robert Williams of Seabrook. When the tides run, so do the gamefish.

As a rule, when the tide falls out, bay fishermen are well advised to do the same. Conversely, when tides are exceptionally high—and especially when the inward flow is coupled with a strong southerly wind (a northerly wind blows the water out)—feeding gamefish can often be caught up against the banks.

Back to the tides: Most often, there are two high tides and two low tides per day, a.k.a. "semi-diurnal tides." Two-tide days, properly referred to as "diurnal tides," are less than ideal for obvious reasons. Half the tide movement results, in many areas, in half the fish feeding activity. A worthwhile side note: As a general rule of thumb, tides tend to occur roughly an hour later with the passing of each day.

During the new and full moon phases, the sun and moon are in alignment. The in-line placement of the two celestial bodies results in higher high tides (spring tides) and lower low tides (neap tides). As a rule, neap tides occur in consequence with the first- and third-quarter moons, producing what is generally an average degree of rise and fall.

Spring tides, however, sometimes referred to by old salts as "bull tides," are harbingers of top-notch fishing action during the spring and autumn gamefish migrations. Spring heralds the speckled trout spawn in shallow estuaries. Come fall, heavyweight and sexually mature red drum laden with tens of thousands of eggs move in toward the mouths of major coastal passes and drop their cargo. Fertilized by the males, the tiny fry wash with the tide into grassy shallows where they

eventually grow out to the fingerling stage and spend their first several years.

Point is, the bull tides created by the aforementioned full moon alignment provide the makings of bullish fishing for bigger-than-average fish. It's a point, I learned, which can be proven outright.

Better than a decade ago, when I was working as editor of *Texas Fisherman* magazine (which later merged with *Texas Fish & Game*®), assistant editor Matt Vincent took it on himself to study the correlation between new and full moon phases and the catching of state-record gamefish. Turned out, roughly three-fourths of the state record fish taken from Texas waters had been caught within a four-day window of the new and full moon phases.

For trophy hunters that was, and still is, something worth keeping in mind.

Chapter Three

Lunar Landings: Effects of the Moon

It was late May, around 15 years ago, when guide Jimmy West called to let me know that some heavyweight speckled trout had moved onto the south shoreline of East Galveston Bay. There was, he told me, no need to hurry. The moon phase was full, and the fish, he predicted, would hit right at dark.

"Bring plenty of mosquito repellent," West advised. "We're gonna be out there a while, and with the wind as light as it is there's going to be a bunch of 'em flying around on the edges of the marsh grass."

Indeed there were. Nightmarish hordes of the salt-crazed aerial bloodsuckers hovered around us as the fading sun gently settled over Galveston Island. It would have been downright unbearable, were it not for the fact that we were sufficiently coated with bug dope to keep the bugs at bay and, just as important,

As the moon phase changes, so do the activities of saltwater gamefish. Though some will argue just how much lunar changes impact fishing action, there is no doubt that they do—and in a big way.

the promise of putting a hook in the yellow-fringed jaw of a mount-worthy sow trout hung in the evening air like a protoplasmic fog bank.

Sure enough, our topwater plugs went unmolested for the two hours prior to dark. Baitfish were thick, with dense, milling schools of finger mullet gasping at the surface in continuous living rows that stretched for a mile, dappling the mirror-like bayshore all the way with tiny but shimmering waves.

The water clarity was tinged a perfect hue of speckled trout green. Loop knots draped lazily from the plugs' metal-ringed noses, allowing the cigar-shaped lures to dance right and left in classic "walk-the-dog" fashion. A narrow sliver of soft, pale light finally appeared on the darkened bay water. I peered over my left shoulder to watch the gently glowing lunar orb majestically rise like a huge and radiant ballroom chandelier over the open and untamed waters of the Gulf of Mexico.

Another two casts with carefully calculated retrieves, and the moon had hurdled the horizon. Still, it was plenty dark. A few hundred yards to the south, the monotonous but powerful drone of growling diesel tugboat engines pushing a barge up the Intracoastal Waterway crudely harmonized with the high-pitched whine of a million frustrated mosquitoes and the gentle splash of waves slapping the shore. Then, a sudden cacophony of saltwater, not altogether unlike the plunging sound of a flushed commode, and the 6-1/2-foot popping rod bent down and forcefully leveraged the short cork handle square into my lower gut.

There was no time to set the hook. Nor was there any need.

It's a bizarre feeling, duking it out in the dark with a powerful and furious gamefish that you can't even begin to see while standing chest-deep in the same inky bay water it calls home. You consciously drag your feet as you pivot with the fish, praying that you'll harmlessly nudge any nearby stingrays out of your way as you shuffle along. Nervously, you back off the drag, wondering fearfully if the big trout's jaw is carrying the entire treble hook or merely the bare and tenuous tip of a single, disengaged barb.

You feel everything the fish does like you have never felt it before, every furious shake of its silvery head, every surge of thrusting pectoral fins and defiant kick of the tail. You feel the fish sound, your thumb senses the line sputtering fast off the spool as it runs and, finally, you hear the trout surface. And the whole time, you wonder just how far the fish is from your shaking and expectant hands.

You remember to put your legs together, to close the vulnerable and inviting gap between the knees that has opened the door for the embarrassing getaway of so many big specks hooked and lost by unprepared and unsuspecting wade

This 27-inch East Galveston Bay speckled trout, caught while wade fishing near "Fat Rat" Pass under a full moon with a bone-colored Rebel Jumpin' Minnow in spring of '85, remains my biggest after-dark trout to date. (Photo by Genie Bolduc)

fishermen. Deeply immersed in the surreal and incredibly humid soup of darkness and moonlight, you imagine the magnificent creature's length and girth while sweat drops the size of Red-Hots roll down your forehead and burn into your tearing eyes.

Could it really be that big? Or maybe, instead, a small one that's either foul-hooked or just a whole lot stronger than it's supposed to be? Certainly not. Hopefully not, anyway.

One thing's for sure. You *know* it's not a red. Redfish don't go back to the surface like that, time and time again, and their runs are more deliberate and linear. If the redfish is a bulldog, then the speckled trout is a ballerina. It's that street-fighting, in-your-face and on-the-top persona that makes the speck the number-one choice of millions of saltwater fishermen, and keeps them coming back to the Gulf Coast year after year after year.

The fish circles, you follow, and in the corner of your eye—now a bit more accustomed to the dark—you see the moon shining above, just a touch higher than it was a few moments before.

Minutes pass, then what seems like eons, before you hear the watery swirl of the defiant and unbeaten gamefish beneath your heaving chest and catch your first glimpse of its broad, glistening shoulders. Unconsciously, you begin the merry-

Capt. Jim West of Bolivar Guide Service works a topwater plug while the full moon rises over the southeast shore of East Galveston Bay. Night wading is a unique experience—perhaps not one for everyone, but certainly one that every serious—and adventurous—coastal fisherman should add to his or her list of experiences.

go-round revolutions that lead the trout into a steady circular track and position it in a direct but moving line immediately ahead of the horribly trembling right hand that tentatively follows its every move and twitch.

You wait to strike; you wait some more. Then, with moonlight bathing the purple-tinged scales and the sweet spot behind the slowly pulsing gill plates in clear view, you make the grab as if you're snatching a dropped Rolex watch from the water.

You spear your hand downward, hold tight, and clutch the thrashing sow speck to your chest. Her paddle-like tail droops and hangs beneath your cocked right elbow; the needle-sharp hooks of the big surface plug dangle precariously below your little finger. You secure the still-resisting trout, keeping the hook barbs at bay.

Your heart pounds like a sledge, so hard and so fast that you can hear it thud. You realize at that precise moment that you have her, and relish the fact that you've experienced yet another priceless pinnacle in a lifetime of outdoor experience. You'll forget your first kiss before you forget what it was like to catch this fish.

And, what it was like to release it.

A quick scan at the Rod-Rul-R and I can see that the trout measures just over 27 inches. She's the biggest I've caught since the Legendary 29-inch Freeport Jetty 9-pounder of Spring '74 (more on her later). Come next spring, right about the time the CCA S.T.A.R. Tournament kicks off, she may well be bigger than that.

One barb has completely penetrated the upper jaw, just to the side of the right canine. I pop the hook free and admire her for a moment while my friend Genie Bolduc shoots a few quick flash photos and then I carefully slide the magnificent fish back into the water. She catapults out of my violently shaking hands and, in an instant, is gone.

I had to leave shortly thereafter. She was the only fish I caught that night, but West called the trip right on the money. He said there would be a brief but spectacular window of opportunity, a fleeting moment of transition between sun and moon when the bay's bigger speckled trout would move up onto the shallow shoreline to feed. He said that they'd hit just as soon as the moon cleared the horizon. Had we been able to stay longer, I'm sure we would have caught more—provided my cardiovascular system could have withstood the pressure.

An experience like that makes you wonder.

Ever narrowly avoided a major car accident and then waited a full 15 minutes for your heartbeat and nervous system to return to normal? That's what it was like catching that trout.

I realized that night the full impact of the moon on saltwater fishing, though no one will ever fully understand the relationship between the earth's closest rock and the remarkable effect it has on everything from sow trout to speckle-bellied geese to white-tailed deer. That relationship, make no mistake, is profound.

There is much debate among seasoned anglers as to the merits of the full and new moon phases. For what it's worth, I take a simplistic viewpoint on the matter.

When the moon is full, Mother Nature's residents are active at night and, to a lesser degree, the middle of the day. When the moon is "new," invisible in the sky, and nights are dark, the traditional feeding periods of early morning and late evening are at their peaks.

Admittedly, this is a gross generality at best. That theory and a $10 bill will buy you a quart of shrimp. Nonetheless, it's one that over several decades of fishing with some of the best fishermen in the states of Texas and Louisiana has proven itself to be true time and time again. And I have a hard time arguing with history.

Don't let the moon—or any other solitary factor—dictate everything you do in the outdoors. Likewise, never disregard or discount its importance in the overall scheme. The more we learn about fish and game, the more we come to understand that it's largely the duration of light—not simply the air temperature or the barometric pressure or any other climactic variable—that governs the seasonal activities and patterns of God's incredibly fascinating creatures.

It only makes sense that the duration of the night, and the amount of light which pierces through the sky between sunset and sunrise to illuminate the waters and woods, is likewise a factor the serious outdoorsman should never underestimate or ignore.

Chapter Four

Wind:
It's Not Always a Breeze

My father always operated on the simple but indisputable adage that one cannot catch fish unless one's line is in the water.

It was with this principle in mind that Port O'Connor fishing guide Capt. Cody Adams and I approached San Antonio Bay on one of the most ridiculously windy days ever dedicated to the sport of Texas coastal fishing. Had the wind velocity been much higher, the National Weather Service would likely have given it a name. I'd already given it a few of my own—none of which can be printed here.

So, cussing the conditions as Adams wheeled his big Ford pickup down Highway 35, I asked him if he felt we had a snowball's chance in hell of catching fish. Ever optimistic, the former rodeo cowboy shifted his sizable frame, peered out the east-side window of the truck toward Lavaca Bay's frothing waters and smiled.

"Well," he finally replied, "at least it isn't out of the southwest." Boy, did that make me feel better.

An hour later, engine tilted up and anchor inside, we found ourselves being pushed at a remarkable rate of speed parallel to the eroded banks of a slender island finger that melded with an expansive and shallow oyster reef. Marked by a distinctive green-to-brown color change, the shoreline break plummeted sharply for several feet before leveling out flat over a dense carpet of broken shell, pebbles and sand. Tightly grouped schools of finger mullet raced along that change, following the thin ribbon of saltwater as if it were a one-way road through the wilderness.

It was there, right on the green/brown fringe, where we unleashed our baits—long, white jumbo shrimp that snapped their big tails like spike-loaded whips beneath the orange-and-green plastic Alameda floats. Immediately below the jagged horns that adorned their thin, transparent helmets, the menacing points of coffee-colored Mustad wide-gap single hooks stuck out like minuscule daggers.

Given the assist of a near-gale-force wind that squalled and howled like a stray cat with its tail slammed in a car door, it wasn't too hard to make Olympic-distance casts. A word of warning, though: Unless you have an hour or so to spend sorting through hopelessly tangled piles of exploded fishing line, you don't "whip" a heavy float like the Alameda. You launch it. Deliberately, delicately, with the force-gathering rhythm and glass-smooth follow-through of a slow-motion golf club. A stout, medium-action blank with a fast, sensitive tip takes the place of a 9-iron—and on a day like this, can achieve almost as much distance.

Incredibly, we got several strikes in the first 10 minutes. Trouble was, the wind was pushing our monofilament so hard to the left that it was all but impossible to take out enough slack to set the hook. But on his third hit, with a dramatic, world-class hookset that almost cost him his balance and put him flat on his back, Adams finally pulled it off.

Riding Brahma bulls for all those years, I surmised, must have taught the big cowboy something about staying upright in a bucking boat—in this case, a 24-foot El Pescador center console. Custom-built in Victoria, Texas, and designed by Port O'Connor resident Davis Gordon, the high-bowed, wide-beamed El Pescador handles rough water better than any shallow-water hull I've ever ridden in. Still, on a day like this, the bucking bull comparison was not at all inaccurate. That fish were biting in such absurd conditions, 3-foot waves and all, seemed little shy of a miracle.

We needed one, too. The deadline for the *Texas Lakes & Bays* map annual was approaching, and we were in serious need of a good-quality photo of a bigger-than-average speckled trout.

But on a day like *today*?

"It ain't much," Adams said with his trademark western drawl, "but at least it's a fish." When the trout suddenly realized it was hooked and turned seaward, Adam's expression—and tone of voice—immediately changed. "*Get the net!*" he shouted, at which point I looked to the heavens and thanked the Good Lord Almighty for what in light of the day's downright obscene conditions was apparently nothing short of the miracle for which we'd been hoping. A few very nervous minutes later, I slipped the heavy-gauge webbing of a wide-mouthed Frabill landing net beneath the vibrant purple body of a pot-bellied 26-1/2-inch speck.

Sandblasting us at a little better than 20 mph, the northeast wind had now pushed the already low tide to the max. Water so brown it made root beer look like club soda had cut visibility to near-zero. And despite it all, a bragging-size speckled trout once again went to prove my father's basic but brick-solid philosophy in regard to the virtues of unfazed and unyielding persistence.

We got our photo.

Fortunately, as noted in Chapter 2, wind is sometimes the fisherman's friend. It is, of course, a prerequisite to drift fishing. No wind, no drift.

"It even plays a positive role when you're wade fishing," Adams pointed out later that evening over a cold mug of beer at Gordon's POC waterfront lodge. "A dead-flat, glass-calm day can be great if all the conditions are right—a strong moving tide, good water conditions and plenty of bait around. But in the absence of all that, especially on a slack tide, the wind can be a big help.

"It'll provide some kind of current movement in the bays and the shallow lakes and guts which run in and out of them," he explained. "And it'll help you cover enough water to eventually pinpoint at least a few scattered schools of fish." (Which, I should add, is why it's sometimes not a bad idea to make a few exploratory drifts across a promising locale before determining the best location at which to hop out, rod in hand, and hoof it in a pair of waders.)

Given that speckled trout and redfish, like most other species of game, are sensitive creatures that don't hang around for long when things look or sound wrong to them, a reasonable degree of wind also assists the angler in covering his or her approach when conditions are pristine and waters are air-clear. Just like a leaf-rustling breeze helps mask the mistakes of a deer hunter stalking a hardwood riverbottom, a washboard ripple on the water surface does much to conceal the reflection of a drifting boat—or, to a lesser degree, mask the outline of an approaching wade fisherman.

"When you start seeing foam lines on the surface, you can pretty much write off the chances for good fishing action," Adams cautioned.

"Eighteen or 20 miles an hour is one thing; but once the foam starts ripping in the face of 25- to 30-mph winds, the water gets messed up to the point that the odds are *seriously* against you."

Another thing to remember, particularly when you're fishing the isolated tidal lagoons of the Texas and Louisiana coastlines: Extremely rough conditions will spook the fish. "They're not used to whitecaps in such shallow water," Adams emphasized. "Those that stay will get out in the middle of the lake and just hang there, waiting for things to settle down."

It's a natural reaction to key in on the leeward, protected side of the wind. But it can also be a real mistake. Unlikely as it seems, the wind gradually blows microscopic organisms and, in turn, baitfish species directly onto wind-exposed

banks. That concentration of forage, even in roiling water, can result in some surprising results if the fisherman only takes the time and effort to approach such an unlikely looking target area.

The aforementioned wind-blasted San Antonio Bay oyster reef will long stand in my mind as an excellent example of how conditions that look so distasteful—even downright butt-ugly—can harbor excellent opportunities for the select corps of determined saltwater fishermen who can force themselves

A howling 20-plus mph wind didn't keep Capt. Cody Adams of Port O Connor, Texas, from catching this 26-1/2-inch speckled trout.

to look beyond the discouraging facial appearance of off-colored water and a coarsely chopped surface.

I'd love to say we caught and released a dozen or more 27-inch specks after the initial surprise on Capt. Cody's badly-bowed line. Sadly, that wasn't the case.

That fish was, however, the biggest trout we took in three days of shooting video and still photos in the face of steamrolling winds that would've sent less hardened (more sensible?) anglers back to the ramp with their tails securely tucked in place. And we wouldn't have caught it if we had let the whims of the wind—depressing and defiant as they were—play a singular role in our decision as to whether or not to roll the dice and take a shot at fishing.

Our lines were in the water.

Chapter Five

Worth the Wade:
Wade Fishing Strategies and Gear

Why, I was recently asked, would a perfectly sane fisherman abandon the comfort of a perfectly good boat to get in the water and chase down fish? Because, I answered, you can only chase 'em so far in a boat.

These days, wade fishing is the rage. There's a good reason why. It's not because wading the flats is great exercise, even though it is. It's not because you get a much better fight out of a fish when battling it on a parallel plane as opposed to winching it upward from a boat, even though you do. And it's not because you're one-on-one with Mother Nature and the elements, even though you are.

It's because wade fishing is the single most potent method of catching inshore saltwater gamefish on a year-round basis for those who understand how, when and where to go about it and have invested in the specialized gear it takes to pull it off. Personally, I wouldn't trade wading and stalking the skinny-water flats with any sport in the world.

From the moment a fisherman's feet first make contact with the sandy bottom of a coastal bay, the task at hand changes dramatically. Being *in* the water as opposed to being on the water is a challenging and unique undertaking—and again, a very, very productive one for those who understand and get with the program.

Few places better exemplify the beauty—and the sheer potency—of wade fishing as well as Louisiana's Chandeleur Islands. Waters here re-define "clear."

Fortunately, I get to wade fish with a bunch of people who do.

Better yet, they don't mind talking about it while they're doing it. I, in the meantime, man a tape recorder and camera so that none of this collective angling wisdom goes by ungathered. After a long period of time and a whole bunch of note comparisons, it has all boiled down to a basic set of ground rules.

TEN COMMANDMENTS OF EFFECTIVE WADE FISHING

1. CHOOSE TIMES AND LOCATIONS CAREFULLY

Bass pro Rick Clunn taught me this one a long time ago. *The key to choosing a productive fishing location is to eliminate unproductive water.* Get the best available map of the area you're fishing, and study it like a military strategist on the eve of a major confrontation.

Carefully consider the weather and water conditions. Determine not where you should fish, but instead where you *shouldn't*. Apply basic fishing knowledge in regard to the habitat and conditions at hand, and couple that knowledge with educated hunches on what the fish should do and where they should go in relation to the available structure. Without too much agonizing, you can come to some basic conclusions as to where you need to concentrate your efforts.

To wit: Key in on protected shorelines and reefs, target sheltered areas that you know will likely hold at least reasonably clear water and—sorry for the repetition, but it's that important—*bypass spots that don't hold baitfish*. Time spent fishing—especially when you work so hard to get it—is a terrible thing to waste.

Wade fishing is an extremely targeted and precise process. At its best, it's meditative. You get to spend a lot of time out there, shuffling your feet and walking alongside the fish and the birds and the deer and the coyotes and everything else that owns a home in this life-filled environment.

Furthermore, you get a chance to exercise that doesn't require a drive to the local pool.

A few years ago, while working out at a Houston health club with my wife, Mary, I spied an elderly lady who had for quite some time been walking back and forth from one end of the swimming pool to the other. She noticed me watching her.

"I know it looks silly," she told me, "but walking in the water like this is a *great* form of exercise."

"Ma'am," I responded, "I do it all the time."

Unlike drift fishing, the goal of wading is not to cover a large amount of water in order to locate fish. It's to locate fish, get out and then hammer 'em one after another with a stealthy, cat-like approach that produces the absolute highest yield out of a relatively confined stretch of proven fishing territory.

Again, if possible, plan your trip to coincide with the new or full moon phases—preferably the new moon—and always take into account the degree of tidal movement as well as the wind direction and speed. If the latter is out of the

Luhr-Jensen tackle rep Ken Syphrett of Coldspring, Texas, landed this nice Rockport redfish while wade fishing on Aransas Bay. The Texas Coastal Bend provides some of the finest wade fishing action in the nation. From sand to shell bottom variety abounds.

west or southwest, mow the lawn instead.

Remember, too, that wind not only affects water clarity but also something else that's nearly as important—casting distance. Wade fishing into a strong oncoming wind is a tough assignment, so set up your approach to keep the breeze at your back whenever possible.

2. STAY COMFORTABLE

In order to pay attention to what you're doing while in the water, you first must be at least reasonably comfortable. And given the plethora of waders, quick-dry clothing, wade fishing belts, boots and accessories now on the market, there's no reason for today's wade fisherman to be uncomfortable. Tired, maybe, but not uncomfortable.

Wade fishing is really not all that grueling (except, of course, when you're walking on a soft mud bottom with the consistency of watery chocolate pudding). Fact is, the saltwater around you supports much of your weight and significantly reduces the strain on your legs.

You will at times, however, experience nasty muscle cramps between your shoulders—especially when wading in waist-deep water, where you naturally stand with your elbows raised above the surface.

You can't, however, blame it on the fishing. Stand in your living room for four hours or so with your shoulders hunched in the air and see how it feels. At least the casting—if not the catching—helps keeps the discomfort off your mind.

3. APPROACH QUIETLY

Shallow-water gamefish are super-skittish creatures. Make noise, and they're gone.

Worse yet, baitfish—specifically, mullet—are even spookier. An expedition we made to Baffin Bay with Capt. Jim Atkins of Corpus Christi on the ultra-shallow flats of the Upper Laguna Madre's isolated "Graveyard" comes immediately to mind.

Also known as the "Nine-Mile Hole," the Graveyard is classic sight-casting terrain. It's also so delicate, and already so scarred by four-bladed stainless props pushing tunnel-hulled flats boats at more than 50 mph across its vegetated expanse, that I almost hesitate

Edye Knighten of Houston shows off a healthy San Antonio Bay redfish taken on a 51MR slow-sinking MirrOlure. Note the Nu-Mark wade fishing belt utilized to hold stringer, pliers and lures.

to mention it by name. The Graveyard story, however, drives home a few significant points.

For one thing, it was here where I first realized just how bad mullet are about spooking shallow-water gamefish. At times I walked like I was barefooted on a loaded pincushion, and still the baitfish fled. Not always—but several times that

Capt. Pat Murray, now an assistant director for the Houston-based Coastal Conservation Association, shows that redfish will also take it to the top when it comes to hitting lures.

day—panicked pods of mullet spooked 26-inch-class reds that were—at least until then—in easy casting range of my weedless, pink-bucktailed quarterounce Johnson Sprite spoon.

For another thing, the Graveyard proved itself to be an excellent example of the controversial notion that we ought to set aside a few traffic-sensitive places that can only be approached by foot. Create a boat lane, and then let anglers wade out from there.

Modern flats boats are remarkable creations, and in the hands of an educated operator can open the door to some tremendous fishing opportunities. They can also, in the hands of those who either don't know better or simply don't give a damn, relentlessly mutilate vegetated nursery areas—delicate and priceless estuaries that are quite literally irreplaceable.

From both ethical and effectiveness standpoints, it's always best to—assuming the wind is in agreement with your plan—kill the outboard at least 100 yards out and drift your way in to your selected locale. If the wind is working against you, at this point an electric trolling

Rockport-based Capt. Tommy Ramzinsky can attest to the value of working shallow water. Stealthy waders often score big in below-the-knees oyster reefs and grassy sand flats.

motor really shows its worth.

Another critical point: Always ease the anchor over instead of tossing it. In very shallow water, a tossed anchor or even a dropped tackle box sounds like a seismic blast to nearby reds and trout.

Above all, when you finally do get out, work the area like you're stalking trophy deer. There's wade fishing, and then there's quiet wade fishing. The shallower the water becomes, the more imperative it is that the wader work as hard as possible to minimize noise.

Rest assured, it's very easy to spook fish when wading. Crunchy oyster shell bottoms only maximize the sound dilemma. Move into an area with the finesse of a drunken Frankenstein monster and you might as well throw bricks to let 'em know you're coming.

Some of the biggest speckled trout on the Western Gulf Coast, and even Florida, are partial to the skinniest of waters. I'm talking flats that might be a foot deep, water so thin that it doesn't cover the dorsal fins of the fish you're hunting. At this point wading becomes stalking. If you treat it otherwise, you might as well try walking up on a Boone & Crockett whitetail buck with a cranked-up boom box resting on your shoulder.

Capt. Bob Fuston, inventor of the original "Mansfield Mauler" clicker cork, eases back toward his shallow-running Shallow Sport tunnel hull "scooter." To fish in super-shallow waters, you need a skinny-water hull—and, the capacity to use it wisely when navigating fragile estuaries laced with marine grasses. It sometimes takes years for such marine vegetation to rejuvenate.

4. DON'T CROWD THE FISH

It's possible for a group of waders to fish together only if they work together.

Be meticulous. When you get a strike, stop in your tracks and thoroughly cover the immediate area. Have your companions do the same. Fish parallel to each other and perpendicular to the shoreline, reef or dropoff you're wading. In doing so, you'll not only avoid spooking the fish; in most cases, you'll also cover a wide range of potentially productive water depths. Practicing this basic but essential strategy, it becomes a relatively fast and simplistic assignment to locate the sought-after strike zone.

When you do peg a school of fish, move in quietly and honor your partners' turf. Stay on the outside edges of the school, and you can often work 'em over for an hour or more before losing contact with the fish.

5. WORK EACH AREA EFFICIENTLY

If wade fishing is anything, it's efficient. Match both your approach and your lure to the species you want to catch.

Take the flounder, for instance, a bottom-hugging and delectable coastal gamefish that's likely to concentrate in surprisingly large numbers within a small area (see Chapter 17). Closely pattern your casts in a circular sequence in order to cover as much bottom area as possible. For maximum efficiency, throw a bottom-bumping lure like a weedless spoon, grub or shrimptail or shadtail jig.

Work a wider area for redfish and trout; unlike flatfish, neither species minds chasing after a fishing lure. Spoons are great choices for covering a lot of water in a short amount of time.

I'm especially fond of the Rapala Weedless Minnow Spoon in green and gold. It's a perfect finger mullet imitation, casts like a rocket, is as snag- and grass-free as you can hope for and has an enticing, wobbling action that redfish can't resist. It's also a great bottom-bouncer for flounder that's especially effective when the flatfish are short-striking traditional soft plastics.

Topwater jerkbaits and jointed floater/diver plugs are finesse baits, and as such take considerably more time and effort to fish than either spoons or shrimp-tail jigs. The big mullet imitators are, however, superb choices for working the shallow, grass-laced areas so typical of the Texas and Louisiana coasts—particularly if you're after big speckled trout that are so partial to the live mullet that these floating artificials mimic.

6. READ THE WATER

This is a fishing writer's cliche' that goes back to the days of "Always Fish Structure," "Don't Horse Him, Charlie!" and "Match the Hatch." All four are still with us because they're absolutely true.

When wade fishing, look beyond what's immediately apparent. Constantly inspect both the surface and the bottom—a chore, again, that's virtually impossible without the aid of quality polarized sunglasses. For all-around water penetration and contrast, amber lenses are virtually impossible to beat. I don't leave the house without a pair of Hobies, Ocean Waves or Costa Del Mars tucked in the upper pocket of my Stearns vest. Without 'em, you might as well be wearing blinders; the advantage is that significant.

A quality pair of shades such as these will cost anywhere from $80 to as much as $150 or more, so take good care of 'em. Don't wipe them with paper towels unless you don't mind scratched lenses (remember, paper is made out of wood fibers). And *always* wear a retainer strap. Before I made it a habit to do so, I sacrificed two top-notch pairs of polarized shades to the Fish gods. On both occasions, the expensive and careless screw-up ruined an otherwise fine day of wade fishing.

Use your shades to their utmost. Be on the lookout as much for signals as for fish. Look for roving pods of mullet and shrimp, or the glittering flash of a school of glass minnows. Note any water color or bottom contour changes, no matter how subtle, and cast accordingly. In the Laguna Madre of Texas, key in on the sandy, grass-lined depressions called "potholes." Pay particular attention to shoreline points, coves and drop-offs.

Bottom line: Cast first, and ask questions later. For more details, refer back to Chapter One.

7. ESTABLISH A RETRIEVE PATTERN

Remain conscious of what you're doing with your rod tip and reel handle, and be prepared to immediately repeat the same exact process once a given retrieve pays off. What produced once will usually produce time and time again.

Unfortunately, this process sounds a heck of a lot easier than it actually is. Few fishermen are willing to invest the mental effort in staying attuned. In tournament situations, however, this simple angling concept has made the difference for more than a few victorious finishers.

The "adrenaline factor" also wreaks havoc on the fisherman who's doing his or her best to establish a pattern. You cast, time and time and time again, only to unexpectedly get a strike. Adrenaline kicks in, you get wrapped up in fighting the fish and often, by the time the deal is done, you have no specific recollection of what it was that you were doing with the lure that made it suddenly produce. If ever you've wanted to truly test your powers of concentration, here's the prime opportunity.

(A note from the "Laugh If You Will" department: If there's a tune in your head and you hit a fish while retrieving to the beat, remember that song. One Galveston-area pro with whom I spoke is especially fond of the snappy theme song to "Leave it to Beaver" when bay waters are warm and fish are aggressive.

"What the heck," he says; "If it works, do it." I couldn't agree more. (Don't tell anyone, but next winter I plan on trying the "Addams Family" and "Alfred Hitchcock" themes for sluggish cold-water specks.)

8. BALANCE YOUR TACKLE

Rod, reel, line and lure—each has a profound impact upon the others. Upset the balance, and you're making unnecessary trouble for yourself.

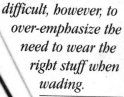

Carry two straight-handled rod/reel combos along with you for wade fishing purposes. Make one 7 feet long, light and almost whippy, for use with quarter- or eighth-ounce shrimptails and spoons and, on occasion, small topwaters and sinking plugs. The other should be a 6-1/2-footer with a medium or medium/light action and fast taper—the ultimate choice for "walking the dog" with an oversized topwater plug while hunting bigger fish.

Sometimes I feel like I'm better outfitted for a lunar expedition than a coastal wade fishing trip. It's difficult, however, to over-emphasize the need to wear the right stuff when wading.

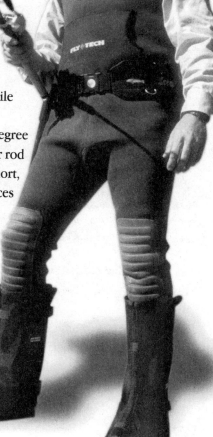

You'll be amazed at the extra degree of control you'll gain from using a shorter rod with topwaters and broken-backs. A short, fast-action blank also significantly reduces wrist fatigue.

If you need to stick with only one rod, make it a 7-foot medium-light. But pay special attention to the length of the rod handle, no matter what the action or length. A handle that's too long will stick you in the stomach or chest and make it much more difficult to effectively work a bait and handle a fighting fish. Ideally, a wade fishing handle shouldn't measure more than 7 or 7-1/2 inches.

As for reels, select a quality baitcaster with stainless steel ball bearings that'll hold at least 150 yards of 12-pound-test mono. And remember that even the best of reels will not hold up if not maintained. If you dunk it while wade fish-

Capt. George Knighten of Houston adheres to the "get there early; stay late" big trout ethic. Catch the sleep, though, and you'll likely lose the chance to nab a trophy speck.

ing, break it down and clean it. If you don't know how, take it to a tackle shop and have it done by someone who does. Or, prepare to buy a new reel every six months or so.

At the very least, spray your reel down on a regular basis. I'm a big fan of Blakemore's Reel & Line Magic. It softens the line, which minimizes backlashes, and it reduces line memory while it's at it—those nasty little curls that make your mono look like a Slinky. It also increases casting distance, prevents ultraviolet deterioration and does a great job of helping prevent corrosion on the reel and eyelet surfaces.

In conclusion, the best solution to rod and reel selection is to visit your local tackle store and see for yourself. There is a tremendous selection of high-quality gear out there, but like deer rifles, what one person loves and swears by another dislikes with a passion. Take your time and, above all, invest in the best tackle you can afford. The saltwater environment is horribly corrosive and unforgiving, so it pays to buy top-quality gear and then give it the attention it deserves with cleanings as needed and basic preventative maintenance.

For more info on choosing and using saltwater tackle, see Chapter 11.

9. DON'T RULE OUT LIVE BAIT

Artificial lures are certainly more exciting to fish than natural baits. They're also far less hassle, and they often catch just as many fish, if not more. And, you catch the gamefish you're after instead of losing expensive live shrimp to bait stealers like piggy perch, croakers and hardhead catfish.

But the fact remains, there are times when live bait rules. During spring and fall, when migrating speckled trout and redfish funnel through bay-to-Gulf passes, a small pinfish hooked through the lips and freelined or fished beneath a popping cork can be deadly. At the same time of year, live mud minnows fished on the bottom with "fish-finder" rigs are irresistible to flounder.

During the heat of summer, free-lined croakers are so effective that some people consider their usage to be downright unsportsmanlike. But when hot-water trout at the bases of gas wells, on the fringes of jetty rocks and along beachfront shorelines refuse everything else, croakers can be productive beyond belief.

Check out Chapter 14 for a complete wrap-up on natural baits and how to use 'em.

10. KEEP AN OPEN MIND

Anywhere you wade fish, the only bait, retrieve or strategy that absolutely will not work is one that is not given a fair chance. Experimenting is one of the great joys of fishing; just ask the buddy of mine who once caught and released a batch of skinny-water redfish with the aid of a chartreuse Strike King buzzbait. And to think they call it a "bass lure."

Suffice it to say that this is by no means everything you need to know about saltwater wade fishing. Far as I know, no one has ever gotten that far with sportfishing research of any kind. It is, however, more than enough to get you started. From here on out, the strategy and the pace is up to you.

Be forewarned, though. When it comes to wade fishing, it's real easy to go overboard.

WADE FISHING ACCESSORIES COME OF AGE

I'll never forget the first time I went wade fishing. I was dressed like everyone else. I had the same kind of tackle, was throwing the same lures and, as advised, was coated with a skin-thick layer of waterproof SPF 15 sunscreen. Nonetheless, there was a distinct difference between me and my companions.

They were all wearing wade fishing belts.

I wasn't.

That day, after a frustrating and Herculean aquatic hike across the seemingly endless expanse of fish-littered flats outside of Port O'Connor, I came to an absolute and unquestionable conclusion. *There is no better way to realize and appreciate the importance of proper wade fishing accessories than to go overboard without them.*

Until evolution takes over and wade fishermen sprout four arms (or preferably, six), that isn't going to change. And neither is the wader's need to carry more stuff than a mere two hands can hold.

Fortunately, an evolution of another kind has taken place. Wade fishing accessories have come of age, and at a period in time when more fishermen than ever are asking for them. Specialized gear abounds; here's a rundown of some of the items from which you can choose:

WADING BELTS

Houston-based TOKA/NuMark Manufacturing is a big player in the wade fishing accessory market, and some years back introduced a wading belt that can only be described as revolutionary. The NuMark Fish/Back Support Belt is designed not only to hold the typical assortment of belt-carried gear—rod holder, needle-nosed pliers, stringer, fillet knife and hook disgorger—but also to lessen the nagging misery of an aching back brought on by trudging literally miles at a time over sponge-soft bay bottoms.

With a 5-inch rear width, the Fish/Back Support Belt serves the same back-supporting function as a weightlifting belt—another product also marketed nationally by the company. Forward, the belt becomes thinner and latches securely via a corrosion-proof ABS plastic buckle.

Says NuMark Vice-President of Marketing Fred Epperson, "The belt, with its patented nylon construction and contoured design, provides flexible support that adjusts to the movement of the lumbar muscles."

Communication is invaluable when one wader is "on the fish" while others aren't. Here, Capt. George Knighten calls in on a hand-held Humminbird VHF.

None of us maintain perfect back posture, especially when we're in a rocking boat or wading in mud. This belt and others like it go a long way toward alleviating unnecessary discomfort and allowing the wader to concentrate on the task at hand as opposed to being distracted by nagging aches and pains. Offshore anglers should know that the Fish/Back Support Belt also converts to a custom stand-up harness via drop straps and an optional gimbal.

NuMark also manufactures a back support "Bass Belt" for bass fishermen, who through sheer necessity are forced to spend long hours standing at the bow of a bass boat while maneuvering a trolling motor or casting artificial baits. I have personally used all of these belts for the past five years or so, and like the venerable credit card, will now not leave home without 'em.

Houstonian Paul Perrin of Fish-N-Hunt Inc., also produces a top-notch wade fishing belt. As opposed to the buckle on the Nu-Mark belts, Perrin's back-support belt is secured with Velcro and sports Velcro-fastened rod holders. Like Nu-Mark's it's made to last many years.

Another high-quality wade fishing belt is produced by a relatively new company called Wade-Aid Enterprises. It, too, with its EVA closed-cell padding, does a great job of supporting your back. Though firm, it's softer than the other belts and as such is extremely comfortable. It also boasts not one, but two, offset rod holders as well as tackle pockets and a "quick-draw" stringer scabbard. Another aspect of the Wade-Aid belt is that although it's not Coast Guard approved as a personal flotation device, it will get you out of a bind should you step off into deep waters, acting as a "flotation device" of sorts.

Finally, the newest player on the market is Sabine Pass Outfitters. The company produces an inexpensive belt that is great for entry-level waders or those on a tight budget who all the same want a belt that'll do the job and last for ages. Sabine Pass Outfitters also produces a "Beverage Buddy" drink holder that attaches to almost any standard belt via a metal clip. It'll hold a cold drink inside of an insulated "Koozie," and on long, hot days is an accessory that any thirsty wade fisherman can truly appreciate.

LURE BOXES

Two miles away from an anchored boat is no place to discover that you should've brought along the same solid silver Storm Thunderstick that your buddy is using to terrorize the trout. The small lure box which attaches to your wade fishing belt will hold a surprisingly ample inventory of artificial baits, swivels, hooks and terminal gear.

Be selective, however. Carry enough lures to cover the most likely patterns, and then fish them with confidence. Almost invariably, you'll discover that—even when you bring along the triple-decker mongo monster tackle box—you rarely use more than a few select lures from the arsenal. Stick with what you know, and give each lure a fair chance before switching to something else.

Typically, I'll carry along several weedless spoons, two broken-back floater-divers, two non-jointed stickbaits (same as the broken-backs), a pair of top-water jerkbaits, a Corky or two and a section full of soft plastic bait tails and jigheads. Rare is the occasion when that Spartan assembly of lure offerings doesn't amply cover the necessary bases for successful fishing.

Just remember to take along swivels for the line-twisting spoons and Saltwater Assassins.

STRINGERS

Put this one in the bank. There is only one kind of stringer to use for saltwater wade fishing—a long, heavy-duty nylon cord with a large plastic foam float on one end and a straight metal pin on the other. Length is especially important because, although it doesn't happen often, sharks will on occasion relieve you of your catch—especially if one or more of your stringered fish are bleeding.

It's only happened to me once, while I was wading the deep-water channel ledge just off of Seawolf Park near Galveston Island in Spring of 1974 with my brother, Bill. But trust me; that one time was enough.

The float is there to keep the fish on the surface, not underwater, where you can't see it and it's apt to tangle around your legs. Again, the length aspect is critical to keeping your suspended "shark baits" a respectable distance from your body. Sunken, bleeding fish at knee level are as good as an open invitation to shark attack.

Most waders use stringers that measure from 15 to as long as 20 or 25 feet. In the Chandeleur Islands of Louisiana, where sharks are as common as South Texas ticks, no one hops in the water without at least a 20-foot stringer.

Perhaps most important of all, though, is the straight pin configuration. *Never* tie your stringer to your wade fishing belt. Shove the straight pin into the retainer on the belt, just as it's designed to be used, and if a 5-1/2-foot-long "Jaws" wannabe decides to dine on your catch all you have to do is pull the pin free and let the shark chow down while you quietly get the hell out of its dining room.

I reiterate; in well over 25 years of fanatically frequent coastal wade fishing I've had only one close encounter of the first kind with a stringer-seeking shark. I yanked the stringer pin free and eased my way back to shore, all the while wondering what it would've been like to slowly untie a stubborn knot instead of pulling free a single and unencumbered straight metal pin.

I still don't care to find out.

STINGRAY LEGGINGS

In 1984, Paul Perrin kicked off his company with the introduction of "Walk-N-Wade" stingray leggings. Using Velcro closures and enough layered ballistics cloth to stop a .38 hollow-point, the enterprising insurance man went from selling one kind of insurance to another.

To date, no one has visited Perrin's Southwest Houston shop to complain about the coverage.

It's not surprising that some of Paul Perrin's best customers are those who have been ankle-slashed by rays. The rest consist of those who don't care to be, and you can count me in that class.

I can, to a degree, understand the reluctance of many saltwater wading veterans to wear stingray leggings. They substantially increase the amount of resistance in the water, and call for a good bit more exertion. They can also be a real hassle when you're wading on soft, muddy bottoms.

In an embarrassing episode I'd just as soon forget

Stingrays pose an ever-present danger to wade fishermen who don't wear leggings. If you're unfortunate enough to get hit, first of all remember to leave the wound alone. Trying to remove the pieces of the barb will only make things worse. Put the injured foot in hot water (gathered from the outboard water pump); it'll help alleviate the pain. Then, get post-haste to the nearest emergency room. Infected ray wounds spell serious trouble.

but nonetheless feel compelled to relate, the bottom strap of my leggings once collected a big pile of Mesquite Bay mud and, when I tried to lift my right leg after standing in place for a while, offset my balance. I ended up with a bucketful of frigid saltwater sloshing about in my insulated waders—a nightmarishly uncomfortable scenario, but still nothing to compare with the piercing agony of a stingray wound.

If you get hit by a stingray just one time—excruciating pain aside—you'll discover that a trip to the emergency room is substantially more costly than a pair of stingray leggings.

Just ask my buddy Capt. Lowell Odom. To heck with sharks, he concurs; it's *stingrays* that pose a serious threat to unsuspecting wade fishermen. Thanks to a San Antonio Bay stingray that crossed paths with Odom in mid-1995, the veteran Rockport-based fishing guide lost the better part of his summer season while making numerous round trips to John Sealy Hospital in Galveston. It cost him a lot of money, and to hear him and others tell it, the indescribable agony of a stingray slash is apparently two steps up the pain ladder above a hot branding iron applied to bare ankle flesh.

Hassle or not, it just doesn't make sense to risk it.

Note: Even with leggings, it's wise to employ the old "bay-bottom shuffle." Drag your feet, and the bottom-hugging creatures will usually clear out of your path before you experience any close encounters of the worst kind.

Do *not* poke your rod tip at stingrays to "move them out of the way." I tried that particular defensive maneuver late one summer night while flounder gigging out of Port O'Connor with my uncle, Jim Bozka of Hallettsville, Texas, and the thoroughly irritated stingray launched a full frontal charge at me—all 2 pounds or so of him (don't laugh; even a baby stingray can hurt you *bad*). I was standing about 4 feet away from the floating Boston Whaler hull and made it back into the boat in a single leap.

It's amazing what a man can do when he thinks he's about to be shish-ke-bobbed by a ticked off ray.

WADE FISHING BOOTS AND "BOOTIES"

Booties look like diver's boots with heavy soles, and they're standard gear for a great many wade fishermen. Unfortunately, they tend to be less protective and ultimately, less comfortable than ankle-high wading boots.

Sand and mud somehow filter through the neoprene and end up beneath toenails, which often results in miserably sore feet at the end of the day. Doubling the dilemma is the fact that under the pressure of water, booties also compress tightly and tend to squeeze the toes. Lastly, they offer relatively little ankle support.

Canvas wading boots, in my estimation and experience, are a better choice. My favorites, not only because of their durability but also their affordability (around 30 bucks) are made by Fly-Tech. Altogether, they offer a good all-around solution to the discomfort factor associated with the less rigid neoprenes. They have a much more rugged sole, support the ankles, and are far less likely to be sliced open by sharp surfaces—mainly, upright oyster shells.

Though there are others like them out there, I'm also partial to Fort Worth-based Fly-Tech's insulated neoprene waders. There are three main reasons why—they fasten via Velcro shoulder straps, so you can adjust the strap length without messing with buckles; they have reinforced knees, in case you want to kneel down on a shoreline to work on tackle (or pray for fish); and again, they're affordable. A good pair of neoprene waders should sell for around 80 bucks and, properly cared for, last for many years.

FOR MORE INFORMATION:

Fish-N-Hunt Inc.
6727 Bissonnet St.
Houston, TX 77074-6129
Phone: 713-777-3285
Fax: 713-777-9884

Fly-Tech
c/o Stearns, Inc.
P.O. Box 1498
St. Cloud, MN 56302
Phone: 320-252-1642
Fax: 320-252-4425

Sabine Pass Outfitters
Eddie Bajalia
P.O. Box 1331
Porter, TX 77365-1331
Phone: 281-358-7040

TOKA/NuMark Manufacturing
802 E. Pasadena Freeway
Pasadena, TX 77506
Phone: 713-473-9100
Fax: 713-473-9199

Wade-Aid Enterprises
P.O. Box 17948
San Antonio, TX 78217
Phone: 1-888-WADE-AID

Chapter Six

Get the Drift:
Drift Fishing Strategies and Gear

Capt. Pat Murray cuts the grumbling Yamaha outboard, slides the flylon drift anchor over the port gunnel and slowly feeds out around 10 feet of rope. The lightweight sack of the Nu-Mark "Drifter" fills with light green saltwater, billowing like an aquatic parachute and slowing the drift of Murray's 23-foot Aquasport to a crawl. A few yards away, standing in my 18-foot Tracker Sport Jet with my wife, Mary, I do the same.

The Tracker jet boat is a super-specialized aluminum flats fishing machine, designed to hike its skirts and run high and dry in water that'll barely cover your calves. Murray's Aquasport, conversely, is a heavy fiberglass V-hull that slices through surging waves on open bay waters without missing a beat. No matter; the stretch of West Galveston Bay that we're drift fishing this morning is pool-table flat and averages 3 feet in depth. Both boats are right at home—ours for manning the camera equipment and Murray's for carrying a three-man party of paying fishermen out of Houston.

I have immense respect for Pat Murray, a 30-year-old saltwater pro who is wise and capable far beyond his years A full-time guide for over six years, he now works full-time as an assistant director for the Houston-based Coastal Conservation Association.

Capt. Pat Murray is one of the most knowledgeable drift fishermen I know. Drift fishing—just like wading—is an art form of sorts, and there is a bag full of tricks that the coastal drifter can utilize to greatly enhance his odds of locating and catching redfish and speckled trout. Often, after a drift fisherman has found the action in waist-deep or shallower water, he'll get out of the boat and meticulously probe the fish via wade fishing. Often, for every one you catch drifting, you'll catch two or three by wading. There is no substitute for stealth.

They couldn't have picked a better man.

Several years ago Murray moved his family to Tiki Island, a secluded waterfront community nestled on the northwest end of the Galveston Causeway. He firmly cemented his reputation as one of the Upper Texas Coast's premier fishing guides during the GCCA Upper Coast Guide's Cup Tournament held Sept. 30-Oct. 1, 1995. Despite intense competition from some of the biggest names in the area, Murray weighed in a two-day total of better than 46 pounds of redfish and trout and finished the event with a winning margin of almost 10 pounds.

I've watched him closely through the years, and if there is one thing this young man does that separates him from those who can't keep the pace it is to fish smart. Murray, like most other pros who pride themselves on selectively taking quality catches of speckled trout and redfish, is an inveterate wade fisherman.

Wading, however, is not always an option—if for no other reason than that fishermen who pay good money for a day on the water sometimes do not at all like the idea of getting out of the boat. At other times, drift fishing is a technique that's simply too productive—not to mention too fun and relaxing—to ignore.

Today is one of those days.

From spring through summer, Murray haunts the grassy shorelines and open reefs of East Galveston Bay in search of trout and reds. But with the first serious cold fronts of fall, the personable young pro sets his sights on West Bay. And it's there they remain until spring.

We are here on the tail end of one of those treasured premier cold fronts, a slight norther that pushed only a moderate amount of water out of the bay system and failed to cloud its continually clearing waters. On West Bay as elsewhere, the colder the weather, the clearer the water.

Super-shallow Jones and Greens Lakes, both just beyond spitting distance of the Galveston Causeway, become prime poling territory for taking

Capt. Terry Shaughnessy of Hackberry Rod & Gun Club prepares to apply the landing net to a Lake Calcasieu redfish. Carpeted with thick oyster shell, the Southwest Louisiana saltwater "lake" is perfect for drift fishing.

in the jet boat and following the trails of reef-running reds—thick-scaled brutes with stout amber dorsal fins that knife through a mere 10 inches of water or so.

North winds quickly push out the water, though, and when blustery cold fronts render shallow flats dry, Murray opts for the deeper climes of Carancahua Reef, Confederate Reef and, closer to the Causeway, Greens Cut and North and

Capt. Doug Bird, a true pioneer of modern-day fishing on Baffin Bay and the Upper Laguna Madre, used a "broken-back" Cordell RedFin plug to entice this keeper redfish from a shallow "pothole."

South Deer Islands. Where to go and how to make the approach, he contends, is purely a matter of fishing in sync with the fronts.

"For winter fishing, you simply can't pick a better spot than West Galveston Bay," Murray tells me. "In terms of habitat, it has all you need. There's everything from shell reefs to mud coves to flats with hard sand bottoms that are grooved with deep-water guts and channels. You can pattern the fish in almost any condition you encounter, outside of a 30-mph north wind on the leading edge of a cold front. As long as the weather stays consistent," he says, "the pattern stays consistent."

Anywhere you go, mullet are the keystone to the winter bayfishing equation. With shrimp virtually nonexistent in the bays, predator species make their moves in accordance with the baitfish. Key in on concentrations of finger mullet, and you can't be far from marauding specks and reds.

"The water gets so super-clear in the middle of winter," Murray notes, "that you can often get into real good action by drifting the open waters in front of Greens Cut, Confederate Reef and the flats around North Deer Island. The trick," he says, "is to look for color streaks or stretches of off-colored water. Color changes almost invariably translate into concentrations of baitfish."

So, with that in mind, we find ourselves drifting parallel to each other along the outside edge of Confederate Reef. Green Saltwater Assassins with split orange tails—the "fire tiger"—crawl and hop over scattered shell. One by one the wiggling offerings are attacked by keeper-class speckled trout. No wallhangers here, but every one a quality fish in the 20-inch range that bucks angrily and puts a respectable bend in the 7-foot All Star Shrimptail Special.

Murray's party, understandably, is plenty happy after some two hours later they have all the trout they want for the freezer and are playing catch-and-release with the greatest of ease. The pressure is off, and once again, Murray gives credit to the technique of drift fishing.

Back at Fat Boy's Marina (what a name), fish cleaned and fishermen headed home, Murray and I sit at the outside picnic table for a while to compare notes and reflect on trips gone by. The more we talk, the more I realize that despite our admitted rabid affinity for wade fishing, drifting the bays has pulled our fat out of the grease on many occasions and, to boot, has done so during virtually all times of the year. Like everything else he does, Murray takes this aspect of his fishing approach seriously.

He has it boiled down to a basic set of ground rules.

FUNDAMENTALS FOR EFFECTIVE DRIFT FISHING
USE YOUR EYES

"Reading the water is an important aspect of all types of fishing," Murray explains. "But some people tend to give it more emphasis when wade fishing as opposed to drift fishing, and that's a real mistake. A good pair of polarized glasses is in essence your eyes. Look for slicks, birds, mud boils, color changes or streaks and the general presence of baitfish."

"The best slick," says Murray, "is a fresh slick. The smaller the oily patch of water, the fresher the slick and the more likely it is to produce a good concentration of aggressively feeding fish. Moreso than just a single slick," he continues, "it's critical that you stay on the group of fish that is doing the 'slicking.' An old slick doesn't mean much, other than the fact that the fish were there at one point in time.

"You want to see *patterns* of slicks," he stresses, "and you want to note the direction in which they are moving and the speed at which they're doing it. Look

Judy Williams of Seabrook gets a helping hand from Capt. Bart Payne after landing a nice red taken while drift fishing the grassy flats south of Rockport. Reds often run in large schools.

for the freshest ones, and pay particular attention to where the next one or two pop up. Sooner or later you'll establish a migration pattern that you can use to drift your boat accordingly and stay in the action."

In the dead of winter, any baitfish is a noteworthy baitfish. It doesn't take but a few mullet to put cold-weather bay fishermen onto surprisingly good fishing.

Working flocks of seagulls are always likely to be spotted during the warm-weather months when large numbers of shrimp are present in the bays. As trout herd the panicked crustaceans to the surface, the big, raucous shorebirds dive-bomb from above and take advantage of the opportunity for an easy meal.

"Birds," says Murray, "are the 'billboards' of fish signs, by far the most obvious. You can glaringly see what direction they're moving in, and you can glaringly see what species of fish they're working over. Nine times out of 10, a big group of laughing gulls is going to be over fish.

"But," he cautions, "don't ignore the Forester terns. Even though they're generally referred to as 'liar birds,' they will nonetheless occasionally position themselves over some very worthwhile fishing territory. I've found some huge schools of redfish under liar birds, so don't ignore them altogether."

The trick, again, is to ascertain the pattern of movement and then follow.

"The current isn't always a reliable indicator of the schools' movements," Murray points out. "Sometimes the fish will go with the current; sometimes they'll run against it. Again, keep your eyes on the water and *never* stop looking."

The same thing, he explains, holds true for "mud boils," the muddy underwater clouds created by the sudden take-off of redfish, trout and flounder.

Houston Chronicle *outdoor writer and long-time friend and confidante Shannon Tompkins takes full advantage of what is perhaps the drifter's foremost tool—the electric trolling motor.*

"Indistinct mud boils only mean, again, that the fish were there at one time," Murray expounds.

"Use every sign the fish give you. Look for the little 'trademarks' that put you on the fish, and you'll find yourself tracking them just like you would a game animal. As for baitfish," he adds, "they can be so omnipresent that at times it's difficult to determine what truly 'nervous' baitfish is.

"During fall and especially winter it's easier, because the presence of almost any baitfish can be a great sign. Even a few mullet can put you on a lot of fish. During spring and summer, you're usually looking more for glass minnows, shad and shrimp. They'll be in tight groups," Murray continues, "little pods that will lead you directly to the aggressively feeding fish."

MARK YOUR WAY

"Use a drift marker or, if you have one, a GPS unit to mark your way," advises Murray. "It's vital to do so. People are so quick to drift a reef or flat, catch a fish here and there and then turn around and go back to being blind. Fish hold in groups by nature, and fishermen should use that tendency to their advantage.

"When you catch one fish," Murray says, "it's not explicitly going to be part of a group. But nine times out of 10, it is. If you catch a fish, toss over a marker—even if it's nothing more than an orange-painted plastic bottle or a foam float with a line and weight. Use about 12 feet of heavy nylon cord, and attach a heavy enough snapper weight—say, around 16 ounces or even heavier—to hold the marker in place.

"Heave it over the side," Murray instructs, "and you'll find it's unreal how much doing so can increase your catches. The proper use of a marker can turn a five-fish day into a 50-fish day. Locate one quality school of fish on a 'hard-bite day,' when the action is really tough, and the precise nature of that marker will keep you on top of quality fishing. If I end up dropping a few jugs in the same area I often anchor up, stay there a while and—more often than not—catch a bunch of fish before moving on to drift another area."

STICK IT OUT

"Get a PVC pole, and don't be ashamed to use it," Murray instructs. "A 10-foot-length of PVC pole can be used to poke around the bottom and determine what kind of bottom makeup you're fishing over. Ideally," he notes, "you're looking for shell.

"When you're wade fishing, you feel out the whole area with your feet. When you're drifting a section of bay that holds a variety of reef areas comprised of sand, mud, grass or whatever other structure, you have to essentially wade it without feet. And," says Murray, "the only way you can 'walk' and feel the bottom when there's 6 feet of water between it and the surface is to use a pole.

"You're not checking out the depth," he emphasizes, "you're looking for the structure. To do best, you need to know exactly where that reef tapers off. When the fish are feeding wide-open you can catch them all over the reef. But," he cautions, "there are times when they will lie on the edge between the mud and shell, sand and shell or whatever is down there. And that's when you're going to get your subtle 'finesse' bites. Stick that pole down there and notice there's a break in the shell, and you've just learned something that's going to help you out on your next drift."

USE YOUR TROLLING MOTOR

For working birds—and slicks, too, for that matter—Murray and I are both staunch advocates of the electric trolling motor as a stealth fishing tool. My transom-mounted trolling motor has become an imperative piece of equipment, and I use it as much to position my boat parallel to jetty rocks and quietly approach wade fishing areas as I do to patrol along with moving schools of gamefish under slicks or working gulls.

"You've gotta have it," Murray says. "You really need the quiet approach to move in on birds. When we started using trolling motors in saltwater our ability to catch trout under the gulls increased by quantum leaps. Now you can come to a flock and at times catch 20 trout from one beneath one group."

That's two Texas limits, you know—assuming, of course, that they're all 15-inch "keepers." When you're shooting lures at popping slicks, you never know for sure until your lure hits the water. Most—but not all—of the trout you catch from beneath working flocks of gulls will be schoolies.

It's that "but not all" part that keeps things interesting.

Chapter Seven

Action on the Rocks: Jetty Fishing Tactics and Gear

From an angler's-eye view, a jetty system is extremely hard to miss. The lumbering, piggy-backed veins of gargantuan stone blocks stretch and wind out into Gulf of Mexico waters as much as a mile or more, a parallel chain of mammoth boulders symmetrically stacked atop one another to form a sheer granite curtain that's impervious to the worst abuse Mother Nature has to offer. Jetties are, without question, bona fide engineering marvels.

What's truly marvelous, though, is that which we *cannot* see. Beneath the jagged, algae-coated blocks of quartz up top exists a thriving sub-surface ecosystem that's oblivious to the constantly pounding waves of the adjacent ship channel and rolling swells of the open sea. As supporters of the marine food chain, jetty systems are without equal.

They're built not for sport fishermen, but to safely accommodate a never-ending train of maritime vessels—crude oil-laden tankers longer than football fields, cargo-carrying freighters stacked high with containerized goods and imported sports cars, steel-hulled Gulf shrimp boats packed to the gills with iced-down catches of jumbo whites, diesel-powered oil field crewboats crammed with half-asleep chemical engineers and roughnecks and tug-pushed barges brimming with everything from bar gravel to benzene. A jetty exists to protect a channel or pass

61

Jetty granite magnetizes hungry speckled trout during the warm-water months. Given the abundance of forage held by the rocks, the presence of predators is only natural, but catching them calls for special rigging.

from the relentless hammering of continuous wave action and, more importantly, the threat of siltation and filling in. Like blue-water oil rigs near the Continental Shelf and gas production platforms planted in the sand of shallow-water bays, jetty systems exist for industry but serve an invaluable secondary function as major attractors of a myriad of fish species and tide-carried marine life of all descriptions.

A jetty might stand literally rock-solid, but the rest of the world swirls on around it in a near-constant state of flux. The dappled pink stone wall is innocently misleading from above, a fact that's miserably apparent to the multitude of rock-hoppers who periodically brave the moss-slickened and uneven surfaces of coastal jetties in search of sportfish. In the process they risk not only broken bones but also broken rods, broken lines and enough lost leaders, sinkers and other terminal gear to adequately stock the shelves of a wholesale tackle warehouse.

Fishing from the rocks is an athletic and often-frustrating form of fishing. Given the right gear, calm water conditions and a reasonable degree of tidal movement, the rock walker will score. Much more often, however, it's the boater who gets the most from plying jetty rocks. There's a simple reason why.

A jetty is roughly seven times wider at its base than at its peak, which means that a 10-foot-wide jetty rests on a 70-foot-wide foundation. Retrieving a lure or bait through a giant mound of sharp-edged rocks and getting it back is no easy task—particularly when it's firmly embedded in the bony jaw of a large and aggravated redfish, speckled trout, jack crevalle, Spanish mackerel, black drum or any of the other abundant rock-runners that patrol the stony edges when water temperatures are in the low 70s or higher.

In a cross section, a jetty is shaped like a pyramid. On one side is a dredged-out deep channel; on the other is an underwater sand dune that is naturally shallower. Snagging and losing terminal tackle is a much more prevalent problem on the channel side, where forceful tidal currents frequently sweep baits directly into the tight confines of granite crevasses. On the beach side, the currents tend to pile up sand against the rocks, making the water considerably shallower and bringing the smooth sand bottom much closer to the fisherman.

Though the sand is stopped by the jetty, the current is not. Actually, jetties are quite porous. Water flows through the cracks from one side to the other, carrying with it the multitude of microscopic animal and plant matter that is the mainstay of small baitfish which, in turn, draws the attention of the bigger predator species. As such, a jetty is essentially a baited hole. For the "bait" to be effective, though, a moving tide is a must. There is no other saltwater fishing scenario in which the ebb and flow of the tides plays such a critical role.

My father was an avid jetty fisherman. He took me on my first trip to the Galveston jetties when I was only 5 years old. I loved jetty fishing then, and I still love it today. From a standpoint of consistent productivity, a coastal jetty system is as reliable a year-round bet as a saltwater angler can hope to find. Perhaps above all, it's a great place to fill out the redfish "trophy tag" on a Texan's fishing license.

Personal experience aside, over the years I've interviewed a great many guides about jetty fishing. And I've come to discover a general rule of thumb that has rarely failed me. All things being equal, it's probably better to fish the channel side of a jetty system on an outgoing tide and the beach side during a rising tide.

The theory, and it's a viable one, is that predator species like redfish and speckled trout tend to forage in the shallows as the water is rising. Conversely, when bait-rich water is funneling out of a bay or estuary, these gamefish and others congregate within the current to feed. In practice, most fishermen usually

Small black drum, commonly referred to by many as "puppy drum," are regular visitors to coastal jetty systems throughout the entire Western Gulf Coast.

choose the side that is cleaner and calmer. And quite often, that's the correct choice—particularly if sight-feeding mackerel or specks are the preferred targets.

Some spots tend to be repeatedly productive. Jetty veterans all have their own favorite holes that produce when conditions are favorable. When the tidal flow is gunning down the rocks at a freight train tempo, deep-water holes and bottom breaks on the channel side are invariably good choices. Mullet and other baitfish have a great deal of trouble maintaining position in more than a knot-and-a-half of current, and accordingly they seek refuge from a full-blown tide in such protected areas. Behind them, just as often as not, are hungry redfish, black drum and sometimes even speckled trout.

Whether you're on the relatively short stretch of the Mansfield, Matagorda or Sabine Pass jetties or the mind-bending expanse of the Galveston jetties (incidentally, the largest jetty system in the world), a boat will provide you a decided strategic advantage. Dedicated jetty fishermen aren't afraid to move and move often—especially if fishing comes to a sudden lull after a frenzy of activity. Jetty-running gamefish do a whole lot of moving around, and the jetty fisherman has to do the same to stay on top of the game.

It's much easier—because of the way that jetty granite "stair-steps" to the bottom—for jetty fishermen to fish from a boat. The amount of current dictates the amount of weight—in this case, a half-ounce egg sinker fitted onto a fish-finder rig baited with a fresh squid head and dabbled near the rocks within biting range of two common jetty species—sheepshead and gafftopsail catfish. Both make for quality table fare. (Illustration by Larry Bozka)

Bottom fishing with natural baits is standard operating procedure for many jetty regulars. Live bait is generally best, but dead or even peeled shrimp, cut mullet and even sand trout will work, especially in dingy water. Tackle and line lean toward the heavy side, mainly because it takes stout gear to counter both the

Capt. Rick Kersey of LaPorte, Texas,—a member of the Yamaha, Hewes and MotorGuide pro fishing teams—slowly works his way down the Gulf side of the North Galveston jetty with the assistance of a transom-mounted electric trolling motor. A trolling motor provides an invaluable assist when an angler wants to cast artificial lures while maintaining a parallel position in relation to the jetty rocks. Transom-mounted models are well suited to high-bowed boats.

current flow and the rocks. Rock-walkers use long, 8- to 10-foot rods in order to keep their baits free of the granite. But for the boater, a 5-1/2- to 6-foot boat rod with a medium-heavy action is the ticket.

Most folks prefer light tackle, and many would rather cast artificials than chunk live or dead bait. Here again, a boat provides an unequivocal edge. Ditto for a strong, saltwater-resistant electric trolling motor for slowly working parallel to the rock line. Spoons, jigs or soft plastic shrimptails and shadtails whipped into the rock breaks can be deadly for trout, mackerel and bluefish, as well as the occasional red.

From a boat, the fisherman can cast directly into swirling rock eddies and then allow the lure to fall as it is "stair-stepped" down the jetty ledge. A lure thrown toward the rocks, like a one-way pendulum, swings back toward the boat as it sinks, ideally following the pyramid contour of the submerged structure. If a bait does snag up, it's much, much easier to get free than it would be if being brought back toward the structure.

A popping cork will keep a bait out of the rocks, however, there's a drawback. Fishing is best when the tide is moving, and a moving tide will rapidly sweep the cork into the rocks. In the absence of current, either fish on the bottom or free-shrimp or free-line grunting piggy perch, finger mullet or small croakers parallel to the rocks.

As for locating fish, the standard Saltwater Strategies™ apply. Find baitfish, and you'll usually find the big guys. In the bays it's typically a visual process. Shallow-water anglers hunting out quality wade or drift fishing areas rarely turn on their depthfinders, relying instead upon their eyes and instincts. Not so on the jetties. Here, an LCR or paper graph recorder is as essential as an anchor.

A trip to the Galveston North Jetty a few summers ago really drove home the point. Gusting south winds had churned up East Galveston Bay, so on a hunch, my partner and I headed west down the Intracoastal Canal and made the choppy run out the Galveston Ship Channel in his 19-foot Skeeter Bay Pro. We slowed just past the North Jetty bend, turned on the Humminbird LCR and scanned the bottom until we encountered a bottom break that was literally laden with fish.

Allowing for the current, we moved up-tide and dropped the anchor. With a long anchor rope and a firm GPS fix on the spot, we positioned the boat immediately up-current of the small, but distinct, hole. The reds were suspended—a fact we ascertained from both the depthfinder readout and the lack of strikes on the bottom. So we rigged half-ounce egg sinkers on fish-finder rigs and allowed single-hooked live shrimp to sink about halfway down.

The current held the baits high, the fish came up to hit 'em and we ended up with two keeper reds and several more oversized fish that were photographed and released. Had it not been for the depthfinder, we would have never known they were there.

PRONGED ANCHORS, AND THE ART OF ANCHORING SAFELY

When I was a kid, I used to enjoy watching my father make "jetty anchors." In retrospect, I'm sure I enjoyed watching him a hell of a lot more than he enjoyed the work. To my dad, all it meant was that yet another steel-pronged home-built chain-laden rock hook had fallen prey to the gear-thieving crevasses of the Galveston jetty bases.

There is indeed a great deal of junk at the base of every jetty system, and this junk invariably has an insatiable appetite for anchors. Dad's carefully welded jetty anchors were little more than U-shaped concrete reinforcing rods welded onto a long cast-iron pipe with a stout eye ring at the top.

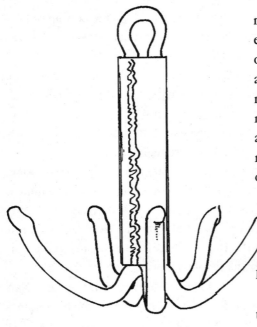

Trouble was, he tended to make anchors that were better suited to holding the *Queen Mary* than our battered old 16-foot Lone Star aluminum V-hull—a boat that my mother not-so-affectionately referred to as "The Scow." Overkill as it seemed, my father had great respect for the treacherous currents of the Galveston Ship Channel and their vicious habit of destroying fishing craft by pushing them lengthwise into unyielding walls of algae-covered Texas Hill Country granite.

Mom always made it plain that she preferred he bring my brothers and me home alive, and I suppose Dad figured that if we built our biceps by hauling his home-made metal monstrosities up off of the Ship Channel bottom then all the better. Still, were my father alive today, he would no doubt tip his hat to Louisiana entrepreneur Jep Turner.

Turner, in the true fashion of a successful inventor, has created a small jetty anchor that'll capably

Louisiana entrepreneur Jep Turner of Lake Charles designed the "Mighty Mite Space Saving Anchor," and it's an imperative accessory for jetty fishing regulars. Anglers who use double-fluked Danforth-style anchors adjacent to jetties often find that they're impossible to free from the rocks when they become too tightly wedged. The bases of most coastal jetties are virtually loaded with lost anchors that—when the water is clear enough and the tide is sufficiently slack—SCUBA divers retrieve by the boatload. (Illustration by Mark Mantell)

Brother Bill caught this hulking pair of 40-pound-class North Galveston Jetty black drum long before the current 5-fish, 14- to 30-inch Texas size restriction went into effect.

Jetty rocks are much more porous than most anglers imagine. It's the continuous exchange of water through and by algae-coated rocks that dictates the pace of the fishing action.

handle big jobs. Turner owns Ball Manufacturing in Lake Charles, and his "Mighty Mite Space Saving Anchor" is to jetty fishing what outriggers are to billfishing—not an option, but standard equipment. It's built along the lines of his former "Hang and Release" anchors, but is one-third the size. "It weighs a few pounds more," says Turner, "but it's a real space-saver."

The Mighty Mite sports five aluminum prongs, and will hold tightly to the aforementioned jetty bases. Difference is, unlike Danforth-style anchors with conventional flat metal flukes, the Mighty Mite and its predecessors will come loose if unexpectedly taken captive by a sunken metal cable, broken catwalk or jetty crag. The Mighty Mite weighs a mere 12 pounds, but will safely secure boats up to 24 feet in length. I carry along a Standard Danforth for anchoring up on hard mud bottoms, but when it's time to anchor up in the rocks, Turner's anchor comes out of the below-deck storage locker and goes in the water.

"I don't recommend using it in the open waters of the Gulf of Mexico, unless you're anchoring on a wreck or a rock bottom," cautions Turner, a retired Gulf charterboat skipper who years ago survived a mid-section ramming from an errant shrimp boat. "But in the bay systems and along jetty groins," he says, "it's all you need to stay in place. When you hang up, just use your outboard engine to pull it free; then retrieve the anchor and bend the prongs back in shape."

Filled with concrete, the Mighty Mite's aluminum shaft is front-loaded and the prongs are filled with grout material. In between, there's a 13-pound layer of lead. Even at that, it's best to attach a stout chain to the anchor's top ring in order to hold it securely on the bottom in the face of powerful bottom currents and to also provide protection from abrasive bottom junk. I've yet to find an anchor that will effectively hold on a channel bottom—especially one of densely compacted mud and dredged silt—that can handle the heat in the worst of scenarios without a length of chain at the leading edge. For optimal results, Turner recommends a ratio of 4 feet of rope (properly called "rode" within boating circles) per 1 foot of water depth.

OTHER ANCHOR STYLES

By the time we realized they were in trouble it was too late. Waters in the Ship Channel were clear, and a fast-moving tide had funneled some sizable schools of Spanish mackerel through the jetty mouth. The toothy, rocket-fast fish ate our spoons as soon as they hit the water, and with all the fun and commotion the last thing we were paying attention to were the boats around us.

We didn't see them. We *heard* them. The yelling wasn't the typical whooping and hollering of happy anglers knee-deep in fish; instead, the tone belied sheer, unbridled panic. By the time we looked over, their 17-foot fiberglass hull was bouncing on the granite, being mercilessly pounded up and down like a helpless rat in the jaws of a rabid pit bull.

We cranked up the outboard, pulled the anchor and raced to the scene, where three frightened fishermen clung gingerly to barnacle-laced rocks just above the waterline. We plucked them one-by-one from the jetty. Their hands and elbows were gashed and bleeding. As for their boat, it was totaled.

We ferried them back to the Galveston Yacht Basin, and they told us the grim story. Limited out on macs, they had decided to move to another hole across the channel. They pulled anchor, and then turned the ignition key only to realize that at this very critical moment the outboard had decided to get finicky. In less than a minute, the waves and tidal current had hurdled them into the rocks.

Their misfortune taught me a priceless lesson. *Start the motor first; then pull the anchor free.* It was only one of many such lessons I've learned in hundreds of coastal fishing trips, albeit one of the most important.

All too few individuals take boating safety courses before launching their fiberglass pride and joys. Unlike driving a vehicle, in many locales it's not a requirement. And so, like the aforementioned anglers, we tend to learn the hard way.

The process of selecting and using a boat anchor is one that gets little respect. Like a boat trailer, it usually doesn't get attention until it becomes a problem. And again, like a trailer, it's a simple matter of matching the equipment to the task at hand.

So many variables enter the picture. The size, type and weight of the boat. The depth of the water, nature of the bottom, strength of the current and intensity of the seas. All have to be taken into careful consideration. Fortunately, today we have options aplenty when making the decision.

For many years, the yachtsman's choice in

Capt. Cody Adams of Port O'Connor prepares to ease a Danforth-style anchor into the water. "Ease" is the key word here; an anchor thrown overboard sounds like a depth charge to nearby gamefish. The Danforth is an excellent all-purpose anchor, and is especially useful when you need the assistance of sharp-pointed flukes to dig into hard-packed bay and channel bottoms. Remember to affix a length of chain to the eye of this and other anchor styles as well; doing so will greatly improve the anchor's efficiency.

Doug Corry of Pasadena, my long-time friend and computer guru, proves that "red" comes in more colors than "redfish" when one is fishing the jetties. This small red snapper hit a live shrimp bottom-fished off the North Galveston Jetty. Jetty snapper are rare fish indeed.

anchors was narrowed down to relatively few types, most notably the sand anchor, the old triangular-fluked "kedge" with dull bills or a folding Navy anchor. But in the past several decades, radically new versions based on scientifically good design rather than mere mass have arrived on the scene.

Certainly, it's important to select an anchor heavy enough to hold under any conditions you might encounter. But there's no point in carrying and hoisting a 100-pound anchor when a 30-pounder of better design will provide equal or, in many cases, greater holding power. A thorough understanding of anchor styles and applications is a prerequisite to making a wise purchase.

We've already covered pronged anchors, my personal favorite for holding fast in the waters adjacent to coastal jetties—particularly when the wind is blowing away from the rocks and you are forced to drop the hook in the midst of the granite boulders.

Here's a rundown of the rest:

THE KEDGE

Kedge anchors are best identified by their roughly triangular flukes and dull "bills," the outside points of the bottom arm. Because of their dull bill edges, kedge anchors are at a real disadvantage when it comes time to bite into a hard bottom. For almost all typical sportfishing applications, the kedge anchor is a poor choice for anything but anchoring up on rocky bottoms. Even then, there are more modern designs (a.k.a. pronged anchors) that do a far superior job and simultaneously provide a considerably broader range of applications.

THE SAND ANCHOR

The trawl or sand anchor resembles the kedge, except that the fluke is small and the bill is sharp enough to enable the anchor to bite into hard sand bottoms. The proportions of sand anchor parts and arm shapes vary widely, so there can be considerable differences in the holding power of different patterns of equal weight.

Perhaps the best sand anchor design is the Bedell type. It bites readily into sand bottoms and, once in, develops considerable holding power even on a relatively short scope (the ratio of anchor line footage to water depth).

However, unless the boat being used is purely restricted to sand-bottomed areas, there are better (and much lighter) choices.

THE MUSHROOM ANCHOR

This anchor is exactly what the name implies, a mushroom-shaped (and usually plastic-coated) piece of lead. Though widely utilized by freshwater fishermen and canoeists, its coastal applications are virtually nil. If your new boat comes with one of these, use it for a doorstop.

THE DANFORTH

A classic design, the original Danforth anchor was the first anchor which lent itself to both large vessels and small boats. If I'm not using a pronged anchor, I'm using a Danforth—and always carry one of each, if for no other reason than to have a spare anchor on board. The Danforth is especially effective when the hard-packed mud bottoms of deep channels prevent a pronged anchor from digging in and gaining a firm and adequate bite.

Tens of thousands of Danforths were used on scores of different types of war boats, from small harbor craft up to huge, ocean-going ships. The flukes of the original design were long and sharp, engineered so that heavy strains would completely bury the anchor. In the Navy version, the flukes folded for easy and space-efficient storage.

The holding power of the original Danforth was rated at anywhere from 10 to 20 times that of many of the older anchor designs. Accordingly, the Danforth eventually became the most widely-used anchor on the market.

When the newer "Hi-Tensile" and "Standard" Danforth anchors were introduced, the popularity was only further intensified. Nowadays, the Standard Danforth is standard equipment on a large percentage of fishing boats as well as sailing vessels.

Original testing of the Standard Danforth showed that a 5-pound model would hold a 40-foot cruising sloop in all bottoms, including 6-foot-deep soft mud, in winds up to 25 mph. Over the years, the design of the Standard Danforth has remained virtually unchanged.

Today's Danforth anchors are easily recognizable through their sharp, triangular flukes. Depending on conditions, this anchor will hold up to 200 times its weight.

ANCHORING TIPS

A point worth reiterating at risk of boring repetition: With the Mighty-Mite, Danforth and—when it comes right down to it—all other anchor designs, it's advisable to attach around 3 feet of chain to the top ring. The chain serves two primary purposes.

As noted, it prevents the anchor rope from being severed by sharp-edged bottom structure. And again, the weight of the chain keeps the tie ring at the top of the anchor shank pointed downward toward the bottom. With the upper end of the anchor shank weighted down, the flukes or prongs are much more likely to gain a fast set.

Furthermore, when wave action is significant, the rope pulls upward on the anchor. The bulk of the chain prevents the rise and fall of the hull from inhibiting the anchor's ability to dig into the bottom and remain fixed in place.

Turner's 4-to-1 scope recommendation for the Mighty Mite calls for a lot of rope. However, I recommend it for any style of anchor on the market. Quality anchor rope isn't cheap; but then again, compared to the price of the boat it's protecting, the cost is a pittance. The more gradual the slope of the anchor rope, the more effective the grasp of the anchor. From a safety standpoint, this is crucial.

As for rope, enter the old adage of "You get what you pay for." Nylon is the cheapest and, as you'd expect from that fact, the least desirable option. Admittedly, it resists rot, decay and mildew. Its propensity to stretch allows it to absorb sudden strains and cuts the boat cleat or bow ring much-needed slack. But unfortunately, nylon rope is extremely tough on the hands. It also retains knots to the extent that they are often irreversible with anything shy of a hatchet.

Manila or cotton rope is more costly and more likely to wear out or deteriorate if not properly maintained. Difference is, it's extremely hassle-free to work with. It ties and unties easily. And it can be comfortably handled without gloves, if necessary.

Choose what you will; just make sure that you have more rope on the boat than you think you'll need.

Because sooner or later, you'll need it.

Lastly, be sure that the knot you tie to attach the rope to the chain is one that will hold, even when countered by the immense pulling force of an in-gear outboard engine. There are two virtually break-free rope-to-anchor knots—the anchor bend and the anchor bowline (pronounced BO-lin, see knot illustration on Page 149). Pick the one you like the best, and then use it. Incidentally, these knots will work just as well for attaching the fore end of the anchor rope to the boat's bow ring.

Boaters have more than enough chances to screw up when on the water, but few incidents are more embarrassing than dropping an anchor overboard only to realize that the rope is not tied to the boat.

Chapter Eight

Working the Wells:
Summer Fishing is a Gas

Fishing action on Gulf Coast bays can get tougher than dried squid when Mother Nature turns the thermostat to full-blown high. Happily, however, summer's notorious "dog days" are the sweltering pinnacle of fishing the wells.

There's no secret about the severity of the typical Texas summer. Featherweight cotton shirts and long-billed bonefishing caps help a bit, but any way you cut it, near-triple-digit days are the stuff heat strokes are made of. It's a blessing, therefore, that trout fishing on the wells can be no less hot for fishermen in the know.

Man-made structures—oil wells and gas production platforms— are the catalysts that hold the key.

"Fishing the wells" is about as sure a thing as a speck fisherman can find during the blistering days of summer. In the same manner that offshore oil rigs attract concentrations of red snapper, king mackerel, cobia and a plethora of others, the mid-bay structures virtually magnetize entire schools of speckled trout. Provided weather conditions are favorable, limits of 2- to 3-pound specks are at times remarkably easy to come by.

It's not, however, the platform that does it. It's what's below.

Beneath each well a dense pad of oyster shell serves to support the struc-

Houston attorney and long-time friend E.W. "Jack" Newman caught this healthy speckled trout from a Corpus Christi Bay production platform in August of '95. Note the live croaker dangling from the wide-gap single hook.

ture. In essence, it's a man-made reef. The thick layer of shell provides a contour break in the bay bottom, first drawing forage fish like mullet and piggy perch and, later, roving speckled trout.

Hot weather drives specks deep, and bay production platforms are usually situated in relatively deep water. The combination of cooler water down below and bait-holding structure makes a shell pad the ultimate destination for both summertime trout and the fishermen who pursue them.

You can expect company. The concept of well fishing is no secret, and those who have fished the wells in the past are quick to point out that cooperation and courtesy between boaters is arguably the most critical element of all.

Specks, as I've already repeatedly noted, are spooky fish. Even in the depths of an open bay, the chugging resonance of an outboard engine is an all-out alarm signal. For that reason, it's standard procedure to cut the outboard while 80 yards or so up-current, or upwind, of the well and then allow your boat to slowly and silently drift within casting range.

As the boat nears the target area, fishermen toss baits on each side of the structure. By doing so, they can determine the exact position of the school. One side of the shell pad may hold fish while the other remains barren, so it's wise to make at least a couple of exploratory drifts.

Once the strikes begin, the anchor is quietly slipped overboard. If that's not possible, drift well beyond the shell pad, crank up the engine, run upwind and repeat the process.

Be sure to *ease* the anchor over prior to reaching the strike zone. Drop it as far away as your anchor line will let you, and feed out rope until you reach the productive side. And above all, don't tie off to the rig or bump into it with your boat.

Mark Nichols, president and creator of D.O.A. Lures in Palm City, Fla., is a true renaissance man among contemporary lure makers. Though I tease him about his "Terror-Eyz" shad-imitating soft plastic baits being funky-looking, one of 'em caught this 16-pound snook from the St. Lucie inlet. The red-eyed lure is also a prime choice for reds' trout and flounder.

The "Redfish Wars" were interesting times indeed. During the late '70s hundreds of miles of illegal monofilament gill nets were confiscated and burned by Texas game wardens. The problem finally ended on May 19, 1981, when then-Gov. Bill Clements signed HB1000 into law.

The bow rail of Capt. George Knighten's 23-foot Kenner frames the sun as it rises over the eastern shoreline of Trinity Bay. If you're serious about catching fish—especially trophy speckled trout—it's a real good idea to arrive at your spot as early as possible.

The gradual comeback of the once-endangered brown pelican has been a real joy to witness. The Western Gulf Coast is blessed with a plethora of shorebirds, and their presence adds a wonderful dimension to being out on the water. Now and then, they'll also help you find a gamefish or two.

Pound-for-pound, no fish anywhere out-fights the brutally persistent jack crevalle. Mary Bozka caught this one while tarpon fishing with Capt. Jim Leavelle of Galveston in summer of '96. The 25-pound jack and 100-degree heat resulted in her suffering a mild heat stroke.

A lone seagull hunts for prey while a young pair of anglers outside of Redfish Lodge on Copano Bay prepare to do a little night fishing. When speckled trout get thick and active under the glare of the lights, the fishing is quite often nothing shy of incredible.

Sometimes it's hard to come to grips with the fact that it's time to go inside and eat dinner. And it's not made any easier by the tendency of speckled trout and redfish to provide some of the best fishing action of the day just as the sun is sinking below the horizon. That's one of the nuances of angling that only a fisherman can truly understand—you don't want to quit for one of two reasons: Either the fish are hitting and you're not willing to walk away from a productive situation, or they're not, but you suspect that "just one last cast" will turn the tables and somehow make things go your way. Perhaps moreso than anything else, persistence is the mark of the successful angler. Like my father, the late Bill Bozka Sr. always used to say, "If your line isn't in the water, I can pretty much guarantee you that you're not going to catch anything."

This early-model Shallow Sport "Scooter" was a harbinger of things to come. Shallow-water boat designs have made tremendous strides in recent years, but that progress comes at a price. Conscientious flats fishermen should take care to avoid destroying the precious vegetation that plays such a crucial role in the survival and health of our coastal bays and estuaries.

Capt. Tony Casarez of Friendswood, Texas, is not only one of the most talented professional lure-chunkers I've ever met; he's also as personable a fellow as you'd ever hope to meet. Personality and professionalism rank hand-in-hand in the making of a first-rate fishing guide. Don't be afraid to ask questions before booking a trip.

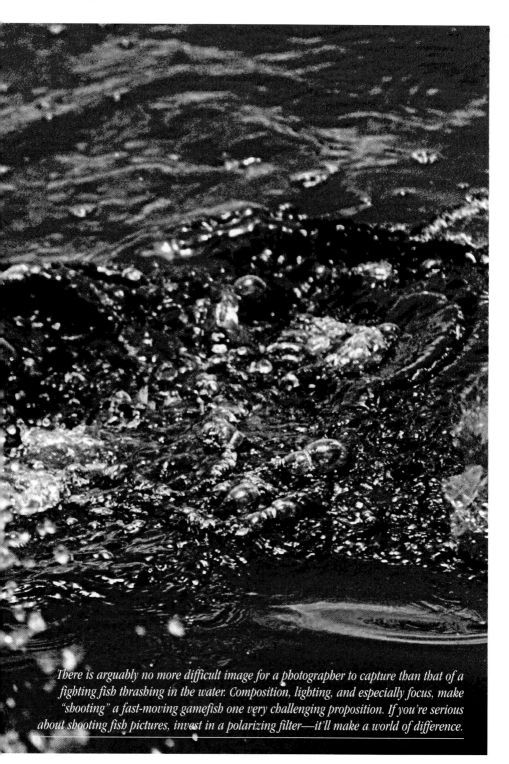

There is arguably no more difficult image for a photographer to capture than that of a fighting fish thrashing in the water. Composition, lighting, and especially focus, make "shooting" a fast-moving gamefish one very challenging proposition. If you're serious about shooting fish pictures, invest in a polarizing filter—it'll make a world of difference.

Capt. Gil Reyna of Houston caught this keeper flounder while wade fishing the shallow south-eastern shoreline of West Galveston Bay in November of 1997. The boat is a Blue Wave 220 Classic—a first-class flats fishing craft designed for the serious saltwater angler.

Capt. Cody Adams of Port O'Connor, Texas, and son Colt share a special bond that is unique to fathers and sons —or fathers and daughters—who make it a point to spend time together on the water. One thing I've learned is that you never have the time, you <u>make</u> the time.

It's easy to understand how a single inconsiderate or uneducated boater can ruin the fishing for everyone in such a situation. That's why veteran well-hoppers rely on abandoned well pads when everything else fails.

Though the rig or platform may be gone, the supportive shell pad remains. These "ghost" rigs are just as effective at holding well fish as their visible counterparts, but for obvious reasons don't receive near the fishing pressure.

Some bay maps reveal the locations of abandoned production platforms, but it takes a GPS unit and the

Trout holding on mid-bay rigs and shell pads usually tend to favor a certain position at the structure's base. Use your depthfinder to locate it before anchoring up.

knowledge to use it for a map to be of much use. Those without such amenities instead resort to the rudimentary but effective technique of stabbing the bay bottom with a long PVC or calcutta pole (in the same basic fashion profiled by Pat Murray in Chapter 6). When the soft mud or sand turns into crunching shell, slip the anchor over and begin casting.

A good depthfinder, of course, provides a major assist in both locating the shell pad and pinpointing the fish. Today's LCRs are as effective and user-friendly as they are inexpensive, and if you plan on doing much of this style of fishing I strongly suggest you make the investment.

Used to be, live shrimp was the hands-down favorite choice of well fishing regulars. Nowadays, although shrimp will still produce, the No. 1 gas well offering is a live croaker fished on the bottom.

The ragged layer of oyster shell at the base of a production platform dictates the use of a 12- to 18-inch monofilament leader testing at least 20 pounds. If there's an appreciable current an egg sinker should be slid above the leader's barrel swivel, its weight determined by the intensity of the flow.

Though they usually won't rival the potency of live shrimp, soft plastic shrimp or shad imitations are good second choices when the real thing isn't available. My favorites? Berkley's Saltwater Power Baits, specifically the Power Pogy. These are threaded onto the hook of a lead-headed jig and hopped across the bottom much like a freshwater bass fisherman works a jig and eel.

As for colors, it's awfully tough to beat strawberry, strawberry/white firetail, purple, purple/white firetail or root beer. In very clear water, try chartreuse or clear metalflake "firecracker" patterns. For the off-colored stuff, straight white (or "pearl") is a proven choice. Because of the nature of hot-water trout, it's best to slow down the retrieve a bit in order to allow the heat-stricken specks a chance to get at the bait.

Don't think for a moment that high water temperatures don't have the same nullifying impact on a trout's feeding tendencies as seriously frigid wintertime temps. I've watched surf trout turn away from or just outright ignore free-lined shrimp under the lights in mid- to late summer, when beachfront temperatures can reach a sizzling 90 degrees.

There are dozens of shell pads sprinkled throughout Texas and Louisiana bay complexes. But for reasons known only to the trout, not every well in a given bay area is going to hold a feeding school. Give each well several thorough drifts, but don't overdo it. If the fish are there, you'll know it; if not, move on to new and untried territory. Be persistent, and you just might find that you're really not in as big a hurry to say good-bye to the stifling heat of summertime as you thought you were.

Chapter Nine

Take it to the Bank:
Surf Fishing Strategies and Gear

Late spring and summer. If there is indeed a period in which one can best attempt to predict the weather of the Western Gulf Coast, it has to be right now.

Tomorrow's forecast, barring a stray hurricane, is as reliable as gridlock in Houston drive-time traffic. Highs in the low 90s. Later on in the summer, hotter, maybe even triple-digit hot. Winds are primarily out of the south and southeast along the entire coastal curvature, and we can expect widely-scattered afternoon thundershowers.

The Weather Channel ought to start running repeats.

Still, don't take it for granted. This period of relative atmospheric stability should be humbly enjoyed, one tide change at a time.

Proper timing is *everything* to the inveterate surf wader. His is a mystical world of swirling tides, migrating predators, shifting winds, subtle color changes and unexpected squall lines—fast-moving walls of billowing black clouds that sheath ragged shards of lightning and torrential downpours. The beachfront invader believes nothing but the radar screen and what he sees through the glare-kicking lenses of polarized sunglasses.

He anticipates what the beachfront water conditions are doing even as he is barreling down the freeway at 70 mph with a steaming cup of hot black coffee in one hand and the steering wheel firmly nestled in the other. Like a great many other fishermen who have found their niche, the devoted surf fishing strategist could aptly be described as "obsessed."

In his defense, he has to be. The suds are often cruel. They'll turn on you in a flash, like a frothing, watery version of Jekyll and Hyde. The death kiss of an unanticipated west wind rapidly turns vodka-clear beachwater

The remote and desolate waters of Fifth Pass, Mexico, beckon to beachfront enthusiasts everywhere. Even here, however, anglers are at the fickle whims of the ever-changing weather.

into truck stop coffee brown foam. The only certainty is that nothing is certain. Turn your face on the spring and summer surf and she'll slap you upside the head with a crashing 6-foot swell.

Trust not the weatherman, but your instincts. They will serve you well, especially if you also have a faithful beachfront informant who can look out the window of his or her beach house, surf shop or pier concession and provide a current (and, with all due respect to pier concessionaires, much more reliable) lowdown on water conditions. A trusted surf spy is an indispensable ally, a truly special person who you should always remember with extreme generosity on your Christmas and birthday lists.

In the absence of reliable beachfront informants, one is gravely disadvantaged. If you don't have friends on the water, make some. Even at that there are no guarantees—even when everything looks perfect. Over the years I have come to recognize surf fishing for what it is—a ridiculously unpredictable mix of the best and the worst that saltwater angling has to offer. I have also learned to rejoice at the arrival of June, July and August.

Mid-day temperatures are hellish. Therefore, dawn and dusk invariably

The old foam helmet does more than shield the sun's punishing rays; it's an overhead tackle box. But remember not to grab it when the wind blows it off. Personally, I prefer wade belt lure boxes.

hold the most promise, particularly the former. By the time carloads of bikini-clad beach bunnies start spreading out beach towels on the sand and applying the sunscreen, the trout—as well as the serious trout fishermen—have usually come and gone.

Like a huge and heavy sponge, the beachfront air is saturated with water. Cotton candy layers of cumulus clouds pile up like mattress stuffing on the hazy Gulf horizon. Afternoon thunderstorms come and go, but calm waters prevail, gently caressed by the mere whisper of a southeast breeze. The horizon gradually mingles and becomes one with the water while the ebb and flow of the tide courses over the nearshore sandbars and—with unimaginable force—herds skittish pods of finger mullet, menhaden and shrimp through the meandering guts in between.

Behind, carried in tandem with the coursing currents, predator species ultimately follow. The morning menu is a limitless smorgasbord of strikes waiting to happen. Speckled trout are the intended prize for most surf waders, but it's a proven fact that one does not always hook exactly what one expects after whipping an artificial lure to the dark green waters beyond the second sand bar.

Random schools of Spanish mackerel or bluefish, for example, are always there to cost you a lure or two (or do so, at least, until you make the change to steel leader). Then there are big jack crevalle; they'll take your lure *and* your line, thank you. Sometimes you get lucky, and connect with a hungry gathering of silver-sided pompano—powerful gamesters that share their cousin Jack's affinity for burning up reel drags—that when filleted, tossed on a grill and lightly buttered, suddenly come into a class of their own. It's this variety, this never-ending propensity to produce the unexpected, that to a great degree makes surf fishing so much fun.

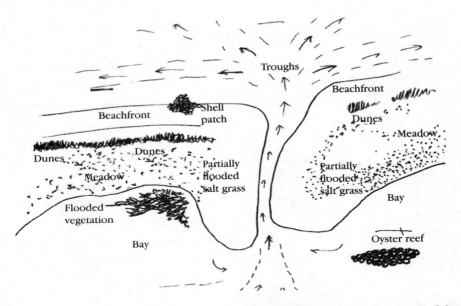

Coastal passes that link bay systems with the Gulf are the ultimate locales for saltwater fishermen—particularly during spring and fall, when gamefish like flounder and reds tend to move through them en masse. When fishing the outside beachfront, key in on areas that hold heavy concentrations of shell and sand bar "cuts" that allow both forage species and predators to cross over between the bars. Inside the passes, look for grassy coves holding baitfish, and probe them with topwater plugs or shallow-running "broken-backs." During moving tides, flooded saltgrass edges are prime targets for wade fishermen; the predator fish hold on the fringes, waiting for falling tides to "wash out" prime forage like shrimp, shad and mud minnows. (Illustration by Larry Bozka)

You want action? Key in on passes.

My money for summertime specks—particularly, big summertime specks—goes on surf or flats waters adjacent to major Gulf passes. Here, in the thick shroud of pre-dawn darkness, the surf fisherman steps out of his truck, surges, rod in hand, into night-cooled breakers, heaves his hardware to the sea and solidly hooks a 5-pound or heavier speckled trout on the first turn of his reel handle. At least, that's the way I always imagine it to be.

If only it were.

Even on the desolate stretch of sand below Brownsville called Third Pass, Mexico, where outfitter Ray Fiveash has long maintained a beachfront fishing lodge that caters to the world's most hard-core redfish and trout addicts, the odds of surf fishing success are no better than 50/50. *Period.* Take it or leave it. If you want bet-

The wind-blown dunes of the Matagorda beachfront serve as a backstop for some of my all-time favorite surf fishing waters—especially for fall bull reds and late-spring speckled trout.

ter than 50 percent odds, try bottom-fishing dead shrimp for whiting or chunk fresh strips of squid at gafftop catfish congregated off of pier T-heads.

He who cannot cope with the humiliation of being skunked should leave surf fishing to those battered salts who over the years have come to expect the good with the bad, the worst with the best. The ground rules for success are deceptively simple, and have been chronicled so many times in so many magazine stories that they now verge on cliché'. These rules are indispensable, and bear a bit of repetition.

First and most important: *Call your source and verify the water clarity.* When, at home, it's deader outside than a day-old mackerel, the beachfront—a scant 50 miles away—can instead be a frothing, sandy mess.

Second, *check the tide chart*. A four-tide day is invariably the best, especially for the fisher who targets the incoming flow. Just as important as the frequency of the tide is its degree of rise or fall. When the water moves a foot or more in only four or five hours, you can bet your favorite popping rod that sooner or later it will push the fish into your turf.

Note: Never forget to make the appropriate time correction for the specific location you intend to fish, and get there an hour or so before the water is predicted to start moving.

As soon as you arrive, *focus on the signs, and fish like you mean it*. Both forage and game species run directly down the guts between the sand bars, parallel to the beach, Do Not Pass Go. Present a lure often enough, with an eye on the critical "strike zones" of "nervous baitfish", color changes and other usual signs of activity, and ultimately it'll garner the attention of a passing predator.

Use appropriate artificials. Casting distance is critical. The lure should be capable of countering a strong incoming wind. You'll be hard-pressed to outdo a 5/8- or 3/4-ounce treble-hooked Tony Accetta, Rapala Minnow Spoon, Johnson Sprite or Luhr-Jensen Krocodile tied onto a 2-foot length of 25-pound-test shock leader and a small black barrel swivel—black, because small chrome swivels tend to draw unwanted strikes from surf-run fish, a great many of which sport line-cutter dental work.

In any spoon fishing situation, a barrel swivel offers an advantage in substantially reduced line twist. But in the surf, where currents are fierce and casts are long, line twist poses an even more pressing threat. It can be avoided easily enough with a quality ball bearing swivel.

Some contend that surf spoon finishes mean more to the fisherman than

Pier Fishing Principles

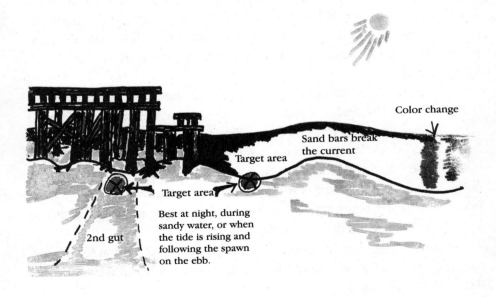

Color change

Sand bars break the current

Target area

Target area

2nd gut

Best at night, during sandy water, or when the tide is rising and following the spawn on the ebb.

Many pier anglers don't realize it, but heading straight for the outside "T-Head" can often be a major mistake—especially during high tide phases, when gamefish tend to move in close to the waterline. The bottoms of the guts between the bars are always potential "strike zones." Pier fishing is an affordable, and often productive, option for the boatless fisherman.

the fish. Throw whatever color feels good, whether it's silver, copper, gold or even one of the new multi-colored patterns. Arguably more significant is the addition of some sort of teaser to the hook ring. A flickering yellow bucktail or a tiny red plastic "teaser" tab almost invariably makes a world of difference in the effectiveness of a spoon.

See a Portuguese Man O' War, go the other way. The purple nitrogen bubble floats an immense and often lengthy trail of stinging "nematocysts" that'll burn you big-time.

Mullet imitators like the 7MR, 51MR and 52MR MirrOlures, Rebel Jumpin' Minnow, Producer Ghost, Heddon Excalibur "Super Spook," Rapala Husky Jerk, Luhr-Jensen Woodwalker and Storm Thunderstick or Big Bug are also good big-fish choices when winds are forgiving. For sheer numbers of fish it's often nigh-impossible to beat soft plastic shrimptails or shadtails rigged on 1/4- or even 1/2-ounce jigheads. The wind is the determining factor in the weight of the leadhead. What works in the bay will work in the surf, provided you can cast it far enough and, again, time your trip to coincide with prime conditions.

The latter, unfortunately, is considerably more difficult than the former. Do all your homework and hit it right just once, though, and you'll quickly come to understand why so many fishermen don't mind taking their chances in the late-summer suds.

A final and very important note regarding safety in the surf. The same surging tides that generate quality beachfront fishing also occasionally drown people who shun life jackets—especially in the vicinity of coastal passes, where massive amounts of saltwater are funneled through narrow cuts into and out of the Gulf of Mexico. I know; the surf has already cost me one good friend.

Mae West-type C02 cartridge rip cord vests are among the best, mainly because they won't lift you off the bottom when boosted by an incoming roller. For those who don't want (or are too "cool") to wear an over-the-shoulders vest, there are waist belts that provide unrestricted freedom of movement and are not inflated until the user pulls the lanyard to activate the enclosed CO2 cartridge and vest.

The Coast Guard approved Type III Stearns Inflata-Belt is one of the best on the market; another quality "belt vest" is made by SOSspenders.

At the very least, wear a ski belt. Undertow is an omnipotent natural force, not one to be challenged.

Being a good swimmer is a wonderful asset when you fall overboard in a Texas bay. In the surf, though, it doesn't matter if you swim like Mark Spitz. My son, Jimmy, when he was a toddler, used to worry about being eaten by the "under-toads" when Mary and I took him to the beach.

I didn't tell him otherwise for a long, long time.

Chapter Ten

Night Life: Night Fishing Strategies and Gear

There was a time, not too long ago in fact, when saltwater night fishing was a downright obnoxious proposition. Gasoline and diesel generators chugged loudly, coughed up noxious fumes and shattered the evening silence while pumping megapower to incandescent "railroad" lights that make your truck's high beams look like pocket flashlights. Amidst the glare and rumble, night fishermen pursued their sport with one basic concept in mind—"the brighter, the better."

But much has changed in the recreational fishing arena in the past decade. After-dark angling is no exception. The impetus today rests not on brute force but instead on effective finesse. The post-sunset saltwater scenario of the new millennium is serene, even tranquil.

But not for long.

It usually—not always, but usually—takes no more than 15 minutes for things to start hopping, specifically the rod tips of nocturnal fishermen who pitch live baits and lures to the shadowy fringes of coastal hotspots that are illuminated by the soft but penetrating glow of fluorescent lights powered by deep-cycle batteries. Magnetized by the eerie greenish hue, the marine food chain sometimes ignites like a prairie grass fire.

It begins with zooplankton, the tiniest links in the predatory connection,

Capt. George Knighten caught this keeper speckled trout while night fishing with the aid of Glenn Gentry's "Gone Green" fluorescent 12-volt light off the end of the North Galveston Jetty in August of '97. Fish the jetties after dark during the summer, and you'll see a line of green lights that seemingly extends for miles.

and rapidly advances up the living ladder to the marauding gamefish species that ultimately appear within easy casting distance.

The plankton attract small fish like glass minnows, menhaden and saucer-eyed shiners, and even shrimp and squid, which during the process of feasting on their microscopic brethren become easy meals themselves.

Night fishing under portable fluorescent lights is one of the most effective ways to fish for speckled trout and redfish that's ever been developed. Like every other aspect of angling, though, it is not foolproof. At the wrong time in the wrong place with the wrong conditions—lights or no lights—you're going to strike out.

I got serious about night fishing around five years ago. Since then I've enjoyed some outright incredible fishing while bathed in the lime-green glow. I've also weathered a few nights that—due to a sudden and forceful westerly shift in the wind—turned from hopeful to hellish. One trip in particular comes to mind. Capt. George Knighten, wife Mary, *Texas Fish & Game* Publisher Roy Neves, his wife, *TF&G* Ad Director Ardia Neves, two of their friends and I made a nighttime run on Trinity Bay in June '97 that I'll never forget. We'd no sooner anchored up on the Galveston Ship Channel spoil banks than the trout started eating. The fishing, in a word, was wonderful.

It lasted about 20 minutes.

The action didn't slow down, mind you; the weather cranked up. It was hard to leave, what with keeper specks hitting on literally every cast. But when the wind suddenly gained 15 knots and simultaneously shed about 20 degrees, Knighten hollered at me to pull up the anchor. Five minutes later, we were knifing full-blast between a huge and dangerous thunderstorm sandwich that was churning out enough electricity every few minutes to power the Astrodome for a year.

It was the first—and hopefully, last—time I had ever run a boat at such high speed in the dark. Fortunately, Knighten knows the Galveston Bay System, and knows it very well.

I followed behind him, the Blue Wave's 150 Evinrude cranked to the max while tracking close in the wake of Knighten's 23-foot Kenner. We made it back to Eagle Point Marina after a harrowing 20-minute boat ride. At that point I gave thanks to the Good Lord, congratulated Knighten on leading us back safely and vowed—once again—to never underestimate the life-threatening potential of lightning bolts dancing on the horizon.

Knighten and I have enjoyed many days of great fishing in the past few years, along with a fair number of outstanding nights. Bear in mind, I'm fishing here with one of the Texas Coast's top pros. The man reads the water like a symphony conductor reads music. All that aside, though, we get burned by bad conditions as much as everybody else.

Fluorescent light does not compensate for lack of tidal movement, poor water clarity, bad location or any other factor—like the aforementioned thunderstorm—that has the capacity to ruin a fishing trip. It will, however, take a good night of fishing and turn it into a great one.

When the simmering rays of summer get unbearably hot and the weekend crowds become almost unbearable at the coast's more popular fishing locales, a quiet, but determined, armada of in-the-know anglers patiently waits for the reddened horizon of sunset.

Night fishermen. They are a secretive lot, despite the fact that the "secret" of fishing with the aid of what are now commonly known as "green lights" is anything but a secret. Still, it takes a unique breed to become an inveterate night stalker.

While the sunburned and frazzled fishing fraternity of open daylight heads back to port to swap tales and wind down at the dock with the aid of a cold beer or two, these guys are pulling charger connections off of deep-cycle batteries and packing coolers with ice, sandwiches and drinks. A calm, cool night of fishing awaits, with no need to hold bowed-up trout rods low to the water for fear of being invaded and overtaken by inconsiderate opportunists who find their action only through the successful efforts of others.

I know this largely because I have an affinity and enthusiasm for the Galveston Jetty System that's matched only by my sheer aversion to the carnival atmosphere that prevails in this area while the summer sun shines over the island. The place becomes a zoo. If you think the cove-crashing water skiers on Lake Conroe are something else, then you really should check out the North Galveston Jetty on a Saturday afternoon in mid-July. Weekend jetty fishing is almost as much fun as taking a #4 treble hook in the earlobe. Destruction derbies and thrill shows are more laid back.

As one who's been there one too many times, I can resolutely assure you that it's not *nearly* so enjoyable as probing those same waters at night. Both fish and fishermen fare much better in water that's unmolested by the continuous roar and wake of 200-hp outboard engines.

Capt. Joe Mauro was one of the first innovators in the development of portable fluorescent 12-volt night fishing systems. Many have since followed, and more will no doubt come.

That the manipulation of light can be used to trick fish into breeding is no secret. Should you doubt it, inspect your nearest redfish hatchery. Gene McCarty (now TPWD Chief of Staff) and cohorts at the Texas Parks and Wildlife Department's coastal fisheries crew have been confusing big redfish for years by utilizing a "photoperiod" process which in essence—through the manipulation of lit and darkened periods—compresses time. The fish can't believe how fast another year has gone by, and next thing you know they're breeding.

The haunting green hue of a fluorescent night fishing light, on the other hand, tricks gamefish into *feeding*. To a certain degree, it's like you're presenting your own personal version of moonlight.

The power longevity of these systems is impressive. On the average, today's portable fluorescent fishing lights draw within a few decimal points of 2.5 amps. Which means that with the pair of fully-charged Exide Nautilus Dual Purpose Marine batteries that I keep on the deck for my VHF radio, depthfinder and trolling motor, I can also run a pair of green lights from dusk to dawn without going back to the charger. Even on only one battery, two lights will run strong for better than eight hours.

There is, again, a great deal more to night fishing success than simply affixing alligator clamps to a deep-cycle battery and casting a bait into lighted water. Foremost—obvious as this may seem—you have to be positioned in a proven spot. The favored locales that regularly produce quality catches during daytime hours are the same ones frequented by successful night fishermen. Bay reefs, jetty rocks, grassy coves and even production platforms all hold promise.

The magnitude of tidal flow is critical. Obviously, some degree of flow is essential, just as it is during the day. But the tempo of the current mustn't be so intense as to wash the baitfish past your boat or shoreline location. In order to attract gamefish, the forage species must be able to maintain a fixed position. A tidal flow in excess of 1.2 knots is marginal for everything except finger mullet and large menhaden.

If you're positioned over a reef on a moving tide, work the edge with your boat anchored on the down-current side. Cast up to the reef and let the bait come back with the flow in natural tide-driven fashion. Or, hit an area of shallow flats with a nearby ledge. When working salt grass stands in marshes, get as close to the grass as possible.

Though most green lights don't readily attract bugs it's nonetheless wise to take along insect repellent—unless, that is, you don't mind getting numerous bites of a much less pleasurable variety. Marsh mosquitoes tend to attack with all the subtlety of half-starved, rabid junkyard guard dogs.

As a rule, give your chosen spot no more than a half-hour to produce. If it doesn't, move on to another area that's pre-selected with both the current intensity and wind direction in mind. If all else fails, don't hesitate to try drift fishing— especially if you're in an area that holds abundant bottom shell or is close to a dropoff. Keep the anchor ready when drifting; if you locate an aggressive pocket of fish, slide it over quietly and cash in on the opportunity.

And, should you be a "purist" who's repulsed by the thought of chunking live bait, take your first shots with lead-headed shadtail jigs in "Night Glo" colors. Phosphorous is a natural element of the marine environment (watch your prop-wash for that eerie, propeller-churned green glow; kids of all ages usually find it fascinating). Accordingly, it adds considerable potency to a fluttering soft plastic. Charge the artificial with a dose of light from the fluorescent bulbs, make the cast and hang on.

As for using the real thing, the bait-drawing aspect of green light fishing is especially relevant. In this expensive day and age a quart of live shrimp usually sells for around 10 to 12 bucks. Most green light systems retail for $150 to $250. You don't have to do that much fishing, therefore, to eventually catch sufficient bait beneath your boat to break even on the investment—bait, in this case, which you couldn't buy at the bait stand even if you wanted to.

They are commonly known as "glass minnows," and are especially susceptible to the soft green glow. Good thing, too. As potent speckled trout baits go, a wiggling 4-inch glass minnow is one of the best offerings you'll ever cast. It is, after all, the same forage upon which the post-sunset specks and reds are feeding. With a small net it's no big deal to catch enough of the transparent baitfish to stock a fair-sized livewell.

There's a relatively new net on the market which is the absolute ultimate when it comes time to capture these and other hyperactive baitfish in both fresh and salt waters. Called the "Clear Catch Bait Net" and marketed by Clear Concepts, the revolutionary clear-rimmed net virtually disappears when immersed in water thanks to a unique "water flow" design. Its stealth can be attributed to not only the transparent rim but also a 1/8-inch mesh, 2-foot-deep, clear polypropylene net. The rim spans a 48-inch circumference, and a telescoping handle reaches out from 5 to 10 feet for maximum scope.

One look at this product and you'll understand why the Clear Catch Bait Net is going over in such

As "unique" fishing accessories go, the new "Clear Catch Bait Net" is a real headliner. Constructed out of sturdy but transparent Lexan, the Clear Catch sells for $49.95 and, in the space of two or three fishing trips, will literally pay for itself. Better yet, you'll be catching highly effective baitfish species—glass minnows and ballyhoo are two excellent examples—that are not available at coastal bait stands. The Clear Catch has also caught on big-time with freshwater fishermen—especially striped bass, catfish and white bass anglers, who for years have struggled with conventional castnets to capture live shad. For more information call Clear Catch at 1-800-801-6106, or check out their website at www.clearcatch.com.

a big way—especially if you've ever watched a pod of finger mullet scatter in all directions before your cotton or even monofilament castnet hits the water. I'd like to see the company someday introduce a landing net based on the same principle; seems to me it would go a long way toward reducing the "spook" factor of a big trout being brought to the mesh.

Rigging a glass minnow is an exercise in simplicity. With the minnow in hand, thread the barb from its bottom lip through the top and then free-line the baitfish on a wide-gapped single hook. Clamp a small split shot several inches above the hook eye, adding just enough weight to take the minnow down a few feet. Usually, the best action will occur on the outside edge of the illuminated area. Casting distance, as a result, isn't all that critical.

A quick piece of unsolicited opinion here: The use of treble hooks, in this and most other natural bait applications as well, is quite literally a case of overkill. Hook-up wise, today's high-grade single hooks boast at least an even ratio to their multi-barbed counterparts. And more importantly, wide-gapped singles are far less likely to injure a fish that you intend to release.

From glass minnows to Glo-jigs, bait preferences may vary. All the same, one fact stands firm. For warm-weather saltwater fishing action that can be as fast and furious as it is relaxing, there's no better time than the nighttime.

Turn on the lights. The party's a long way from over.

NIGHT LIGHT MANUFACTURERS

Portable fluorescent lighting systems have numerous applications that go beyond saltwater fishing. Striped bass and white bass fishermen on inland lakes love the effect they have on pods of shad, and crappie fishermen are coming to appreciate the appeal that such a light can give to a sunken brushpile.

Here's perhaps the most unique application of all: I haven't tried it yet, but some fairly reliable sources (they're fishermen, remember?) tell me that a well hidden green light is a feral hog hunter's dream come true. Hogs are primarily nocturnal feeders, see? And they *can't* see the green light. So, these guys tell me, you hide a battery and green light in the brush, aim the glow at the feeder, sit back in your blind and wait.

Sounds great to me. Matter of fact, it's on my "gotta try it" list and, thanks to some recent invites, may go on the experience roster before this book hits the shelves. Meanwhile, though, I'd advise anyone giving this proposition serious consideration to also think about calling the local game warden and letting him or her know that you may be doing some after-sunset shooting.

There's nothing like a quick volley of unannounced nighttime rifle rounds to liven up an otherwise quiet countryside.

With all of these applications, and more certainly on the way, it's not surprising that the number of small manufacturers getting into the "night light" business is slowly but steadily growing. However, the following leads should get you started toward the process of deciding which light system best meets your needs.

I am personally aware of five companies that manufacture first-rate portable fluorescent light systems. I have used all of these, and can attest to the fact that they are built to last.

Some systems hang over the gunnels and project light into the water; others are actually submersible. One, the "Gone Green Fishing Light" made by Glenn Gentry of Spring, Texas, literally rests in between. The Gone Green is unique in that it floats horizontally on the water and sports a reflective shield which concentrates and directs the light downward. It's also very well made, yet very reasonably priced. For info, call Gentry at 1-800-218-6199 (and while you're at it, ask him about those hogs).

In the pure submersible lineup, Bill Hawk of Pearland, Texas, manufactures the submersible "Fisherman's Green Light." As an angler, Hawk is one of the Texas Coast's best, an "amateur" who—judging from his tournament record—could turn pro guide tomorrow if he wanted to. Meanwhile, he'll tell you all about his Fisherman's Green Light if you call him at 1-800-388-1000.

A new and inexpensive player in the lineup is the "NiteStick," manufactured by Malcolm Hein of Bryan, Texas. It can be used in both floating horizontal (unweighted) and submerged vertical (weighted) fashion. For details, call Hein at 409-589-2760.

The newest—and arguably most slickly produced—fluorescent system is "The Green Magnet" from Gary Duge of Duge Enterprise in Corpus Christi, Texas. Duge has delved into the night light business in serious fashion. Aside from three lengths of Green Magnet lights—1-foot, 2-foot and 4-foot—Duge offers an extensive line of accessories—durable and attractive carrying cases, AC/DC power converters, mounting brackets and weights. The 1 - and 2-amp versions of The Green Magnet draw a mere 1 amp; the 4-footer draws 2 amps. For information, call Duge Enterprise at 1-800-252-3613.

Finally, the eldest of the still-in-business green light fraternity (which should tell you something): Houstonian John Beffano's "Star-Brite Night Light." The dual-bulbed fluorescent unit—which I first used in the late 80s—is contained within a durable and lightweight plastic housing that'll withstand a beating. (I know this because I've virtually beaten mine and they still work.) The above-the-water Star-Brite unit is designed to hang onto the gunnels of your boat and shine down into the water. It's also, because of its minimal weight and fiercely protective housing, the preferred choice for taking along as a camp light, or a beachfront fishing light when the bull reds are running after Labor Day.

Or, maybe even a feral hog "night hunting" light.

You can reach Beffano at 713-433-7700.

PLAY IT SAFE

A few brief notes from the post-sunset safety standpoint:

Unless you're: 1) back-of-the-hand familiar with your chosen boating territory or; 2) have a sequential series of carefully plotted coordinates to the fishing hole already logged onto your GPS; get set up before nightfall.

If you have doubts about your engine, fix it right or stay at home until it is. If your depthfinder has a bottom alarm, use it. Make sure your running lights are working before you leave home. And never rely on fluorescent light alone. I keep a high-intensity spotlight on my boat at all times, and make sure it's hooked up and functional before doing any controlled drift-fishing over bay reefs or anchoring up next to a jetty. And just to be extra-safe, carry along at least a couple of flashlights and some extra batteries.

Stow a spare anchor. If the motor conks out, you'll need it. Or, at the very least, take along a parachute-type drift anchor. There are several good ones on the market; again, I use a 42-inch diameter Nu-Mark "Drifter." It's an essential tool for the control of boat positioning and drift speed. It's also a life-saving accessory in the event the outboard croaks in rough water. Tied off the bow cleat, a drift anchor keeps the boat headed directly into oncoming waves and greatly reduces the all-too-real possibility of capsizing in heavy seas.

This one applies in the daytime as well, but is definitely even more critical after dark. If you have a VHF radio or a cellular phone, take it along. If not, let a friend or relative know where you're going and when you expect to return.

Ditto for a portable weather radio. For 20 bucks or so, you get one-push-of-the-button access to the most current NOAA weather report for your area (and, along with the tides and wave heights, immediate notification of storm and tornado warnings). Probably the easiest place to find one is Radio Shack. The little 9-volt unit I bought from one of the company's outlets in 1987 finally gave out in '97. The antenna mount broke, but the radio still works fine.

Think safety when night fishing, and then think more safety.

You may have been 9 years old the last time you remember being afraid of the dark. But then again, you were in bed with your teddy bear, not out on a boat frantically attempting to dodge oyster reefs, sunken pilings, channel markers, production platforms and rock groins. And that's, of course, assuming that you have no problems first with shrimp boats, barges, freighters and oil tankers—or, perish the thought, your outboard engine.

Personally, I think at least a tinge of the "fear of darkness" is a very healthy thing when you're running a boat on a lonely bay system in the middle of the night.

Chapter Eleven

In the Reel World:
Rod and Reel Selection

Every rod and reel combination for saltwater fishing has its own specific application, whether it's casting ultralight jigs beneath the shade and cover of mangrove leaves or dropping a pound or more of lead to the base of a Gulf of Mexico oil rig. Tackle selection is a matter of picking the right gear for the right scenario and the right range of baits. The catch is to buy the best you can budget, and to make sure that the rod you select is perfectly matched to properly balance with the chosen reel.

I take a bit of a tangential turn here, not in line of what to buy but instead *where to buy it.* I'm talking about boat, sport and fishing shows, and the reason for this somewhat unusual emphasis is that the two aforementioned considerations—appropriate gear selection at bargain prices—fall right into place at such an event. This contention is particularly true for the person who is either just getting into the sport of saltwater fishing or, on the other hand, knows his or her stuff and yet wants to get some hands-on experience and advice before dropping big money for a high-end rod or reel.

There are many consumer shows available to the Gulf Coast sportsman. The heavy concentration of boat shows falls in January and February, but that, of course, doesn't factor in the new swell of "summer boat shows."

Quite often, saltwater fishermen go after their quarry way over-gunned. Here, CCA TIDE *magazine editor Doug Pike puts "light touch" pressure on a 5-pound redfish that he nabbed on a 1/4-ounce spinnerbait from a small cove near Bay Tambour outside of Cocodrie, La. Surprisingly light spinning gear will wear down surprisingly large fish, provided that you're not fishing an area that's loaded with barnacle encrusted pilings, bottom junk and oyster shell. Even then, a 25-pound-test leader affixed with a Simplified Blood Knot will usually afford sufficient backbone to prevent cut-offs—especially if, as Pike is doing here—you hold the rod tip high and maintain as high an angle as possible in relation to the fighting fish. If you haven't yet tried light or even ultralight spinning gear on reds and trout, do it. It'll add an immensely enjoyable perspective to your angling experience.*

Though they occur year-round, the bigger fishing shows tend to be held in the early spring. The benchmark event for those of us in Southeast Texas has long been the Houston Fishing Show, conducted every spring by veteran tackle rep Dave Holder and his wife, Blanche. In better than 15 years of attending that show I've come to fully appreciate its value to the angling public.

The Houston Fishing Show, held at the George R. Brown Convention Center, usually runs for six days. Most metropolitan boat shows run from one to two weeks, and most these days have separate "fishing and hunting" sections. I have long used these shows as windows of opportunity in which to interview a whole bunch of angling professionals while they are all simultaneously gathered under a single roof. The tackle buyer can do the same.

As opposed to spending your day scanning advertised specials, getting price quotes over the phone or driving all over town, you can make one stop while enjoying immediate access to whatever info you want. Where else, after all, does such a wide spectrum of merchandise and know-how come together within the confines of the same location?

Fishing guides man their booths, booking trips and sharing tips. Many, throughout the course of the show, will conduct free seminars and instructional clinics.

Manufacturer's representatives show up in force, explaining the uses and merits of their respective product lines. They are, almost without exception, extremely knowledgeable and helpful.

Finally, the retailers who sell those products take the off-season opportunity to meet the public and gain valuable exposure. In doing so, they get the shopper's attention with remarkably low prices.

It's no secret that the typical Gulf Coast boat show is a buyer's bargain waiting to happen. What many don't realize, however, is that some of the best deals in the house apply not to boats and outboard engines but instead to fishing tackle and accessories.

Most saltwater fishermen tend to pretty well know what they want before they go shopping. The really smart ones, though, make it a point to consult the fishing guides and tackle reps before laying down their cash. And how much cash they have, of course, plays a *big* role in the selection process.

In the case of both rods and reels for inshore coastal fishing, the median price stands at around $100. A $200 rod and reel combo may sound steep to some; truth is, that's an upper-middle-class price range for top-notch gear. It is, I assure you, false economy to skimp.

Think $200, or even $300, is too much for a rod and reel combination that—assuming you take care of it—you can use for many years? Reflect for a second or two on how much that new deer rifle you want will set you back—and that's *before* you buy the scope, shells and accessories.

Those who can afford it often spend $150 and upwards on high-grade baitcasting reels, knowing that the investment will be rewarded in performance and longevity. When Shimano introduced the first Calcutta fishing reels, many felt that the company had erred—that despite the Calcutta's unprecedented quality the sportfishing consumer would never part with roughly $200 to own one.

The naysayers were wrong.

Today, serious saltwater fishermen have positioned Shimano's venerable Calcutta and Chronarch, along with other similarly priced reels from Abu-Garcia (most notably the new "Morrum"), Browning, Zebco, Pinnacle, Daiwa and others,

John Morlan of Johnson Worldwide Associates (JWA) caught this chunky 5-pound speckled trout on the company's "Fusion" superline while casting Excalibur Super Spook plugs on Lake Calcasieu, La., with guide Capt. Erik Rue. Superlines like JWA's Fusion and Berkley's Fireline are—unlike braided line—well suited to working topwater plugs.

in the category of necessary—not extravagant—coastal fishing gear.

Never forget that the horribly corrosive environment of saltwater and sand is pure anathema to low-end fishing tackle. Take, for example, ball bearing fishing reels as opposed to less expensive versions which offer graphite composite bushings.

"Everybody wants ball bearings for the smoothness," says long-time tackle dealer Joe Meyer. "Graphite composite bushings are smooth for a while, but they wear out much faster than stainless steel ball bearings. Ball bearing reels are the best by far," Meyer adds, "but they will be priced at least 25 percent higher."

Meyer's observations reinforce my major point: You don't get that kind of bottom-line advice just anywhere. And it's a primary reason why Joe and Danny Meyer have managed to keep Cut-Rate Fishing Tackle's two Houston-area locations in healthy business for around 20 years despite ever-increasing competition from large retail chains and mail-order entities.

Which brings me back to the point:

There isn't enough space in this book to evaluate the pros and cons of every rod and reel design and material available to the saltwater fisherman. And even if there was, you still would not be able to feel the rod grip in your hands, check out the wrappings and finish or crank the reel's handle. Furthermore, you'd be basing your decision purely on my experience and observations as opposed to the findings of a large group of experts.

As always, you get what you pay for. The situation with rods is much the same as it is with reels. However, I contend that it's a rare situation when an inshore coastal fishermen needs to spend more than $150 on a fishing rod. The quality of today's "medium-range" trout rods is far, far superior to the top-end graphites which were the hot new rage in the mid-'70s. What was considered "light" then now feels like a cinder block in comparison. Fishing rods have come a long, long way in the past two decades. Like calculators and computers, less money will now buy you a whole lot more.

Graphite composite rods are cheaper than high-graphite-content blanks, because they employ a mixture of graphite fibers and fiberglass. Fiberglass, naturally, is a lot less costly than graphite—which, depending upon its grade (1M6, 1M7, or the newer and more exotic materials marketed under a variety of names) also varies greatly in price.

The graphite/fiberglass combination makes the rod a little more flexible. As a result, composite blanks are much less likely to break than their almost-pure-graphite-content super-dense counterparts. Fiberglass sticks are all but bulletproof. But, of course, the high-grade graphite rod is much more sensitive and lightweight than glass.

As for one-piece vs. two-piece, Meyer contends it's no contest. "Fishermen prefer one-piece rods by around a 95 percent margin," he notes. "It's not that they think the ferrule is going to break; they don't like the fact that it sometimes allows the rod to twist and turn." Conversely, although I, too, admittedly prefer one-piece blanks, I own a small quiver of two-piece rods that have no substitutes when it comes time to hop aboard a small, gear-laden airplane in search of fish. It all depends, again, upon your specific needs.

Some fishermen maintain that the ferrule connection of a two-piece blank stiffens the action of the rod, a philosophy which at least partially stems from the days of rigid metal ferrules. "I have to at least partially disagree with that," Meyer comments, "because quality rods with well-made ferrules do have extremely good actions."

One other important note regarding rods: *pay special attention to the length of the handle*. The cork handles (and you always want cork) on my favorite All Star topwater rods measure 7-1/4 to 7-3/4 inches long. Why so short? Because when I'm throwing topwaters I'm wade fishing, and I need a handle that short in order to effectively keep the rod close to my chest and work the lure.

I also use shorter, fast-action blanks, from 6 to 6-1/2 feet long, for throwing surface lures. By doing so I get a rod that'll "walk" even a big MirrOlure Top Dog to death without wearing out my wrists. The added leverage and lure con-

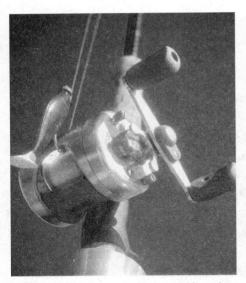

Modern baitcasting reels are incredibly sophisticated devices. As a rule, it's wise to buy the best you can and then take very good care of it. Stainless steel ball bearings are a plus.

trol—not to mention lack of fatigue—is absolutely invaluable.

Brett Crawford, president of All Star Rods in Houston, has been kind enough over the past few years to allow me to test several of the company's prototype rods before they were put on the market. Most recently, I played with a fast-taper 6-footer that by the time this hits print should be one of the first introductions to All Star's "Excalibur" rod series (so named because they are specially designed to go hand-in-hand with PRADCO's Excalibur lure series— in this case, the highly popular Excalibur "Super Spook" topwater, an up-sized, saltwater-specific evolution of the venerable Heddon Zara Spook).

The Super Spook prototype rod seemed alarmingly different at first glance, with its short handle, short length and anything-but-whippy tip.

For quarter-ounce spoons and shrimptails it's all but useless—too little length, too much "beef" on the front end. But when coupled with a heavyweight surface plug it becomes a sterling example of functionality and practicality in action.

I was amazed at how, using this stubby blank, it suddenly became no-brainer easy to "walk the dog" with the Super Spook, the Top Dog and other over-sized topwaters. Even more appealing, given my somewhat arthritic hands, was the way this rod literally took the pain out of incessantly "walking" a big plug for hours on end. It's a specialty rod, no doubt. But for its particular application, it's the kind of rod that will sway you forever once you've had a chance to give it a real workout.

Again, the point here is that you not only need to match the proper balance of rod and reel; you need to select the rod to match the specific size and style of artificial lure you intend to throw.

The proof of any rod and reel combo is in the testing, and some of the larger boat shows provide casting tanks exclusively for that purpose. A side-by-side comparison of several rods and reels rigged with identical casting weights or hook-

The wide-mouthed Frabill landing net—a heavy-duty net that'll handle virtually everything up to 50-pound redfish—claims another victory for outdoor writer and CCA TIDE *magazine editor Doug Pike and Cocodrie, La., guide Capt. Gerald Bryant. An important tip: always lead the fish head-first into the mouth of the net. Touch its tail, and it will bolt like a scared jackrabbit.*

less plugs will quickly erase any doubts about which one best suits a fisherman's personal tastes.

Nonetheless, to gain any benefit you have to be willing to ask questions. Reduced prices are certainly an incentive to attend a consumer boat or fishing show, but the information you can gather from the top experts in the field is literally priceless. Furthermore, their recommendations will save you a lot of cash that in the long run might otherwise have gone toward unnecessary or inappropriate purchases.

I contend that it's much better to drop your whole budget on two top-rate rod and reel combinations than it is to buy four of lesser quality. For most bayfishing applications, after all, two rigs are all you need.

If you intend to wade fish, buy rods with the above-mentioned short handles. If you're into two-handed casting from a boat, go with longer handles in the 9- to 10-inch range that are endemic to "popping rods." Anything over 10 inches, and you're talking either a long boat rod or a surfcasting rod.

And again, select the rod length and action with specific lure weights in mind—which is where the "two basic rod" concept comes into play. You need one that will handle lures from 1/4- to 3/8-oz.—preferably, a 7-footer with—based upon your own preference—a light to medium-light action. This, by popular description, is your "shrimptail rod."

The other, in my estimation, should be a 6- to 6-1/2-footer in a medium action with a fast tip—the "topwater rod" that's the perfect ticket for heaving half-ounce plugs halfway to the horizon. This rod will also pull double-duty as a tool for working live shrimp beneath popping corks, although some fishermen prefer a 7-footer with the same basic characteristics in order to gain more casting distance.

"Prefer." There's that word again. And it's the essence of gear selection.

You know what you enjoy the most: stalking redfish on shallow sand flats; drift fishing around oyster reefs; anchoring up adjacent to jetties or sitting in a lawn chair on the beach and waiting for an errant shark, red or jack to double over your surf rod.

The ideal of scoping out sports shows is fun for everyone, but it's really most important to the novice tackle buyer. Everyone likes a good deal, and there are certainly plenty of them to be had at large retail sporting goods stores like Oshman's, Academy, Bass Pro Shops retail outlets and others. (More and more of these stores, it should be noted, are offering free in-store "clinics" that, like boat and fishing shows, are virtually invaluable to the research-oriented tackle buyer.) With the passage of time, the inventory of quality (and appropriate) saltwater rods and reels—not to mention lures and accessories—is growing by the proverbial leaps and bounds in most of the major outlets.

Fishing tackle, just like the method in which you use it, is all a matter of preference. Do your homework. Once you know the essentials, you'll be ready to hit the road and shop any store in town for the best prices. But until you do, the lowest price in town won't make up for purchasing inappropriate gear.

Chapter Twelve

Faking It:
Artificial Lures, From Top to
Bottom

In the ever-changing world of saltwater fishing, one thing remains certain. *The more things change, the more they stay the same.*

Used to be, coastal fishermen could walk into a tackle store and find virtually every saltwater-specific artificial lure on the market in a narrowly sequestered 6-foot section of shelf space. Meanwhile, across the aisle, the local bass anglers had their pick of enough crankbaits, topwaters, spinnerbaits, buzzbaits, worms and jigs to fill every double-decker tackle box in town. Bass fishing, in particular tournament fishing, was on a roll.

That was the early '70s. And today, bass fishing remains a favorite pastime of many Texas and Louisiana fishermen. Difference is, coastal fishing is now on a major roll of its own, and the proof is on the shelves of the state's tackle stores. The saltwater lure industry is alive and well in a way that it has never before witnessed—which, given my self-professed and shamelessly admitted fanaticism for the sport, tickles me pinker than a fluorescent MirrOlure.

Ironically, freshwater lure manufacturers deserve most of the credit for the change. Bass-related research and development not only furthered technology; it afforded a generous dose of that knowledge and innovation to the makers of saltwater lures. It also greatly broadened the horizons of many a company which once manufactured solely sweetwater baits, but nowadays makes a full line of coastal offerings.

No wonder, then, that most of today's larger lure companies manufacture both freshwater and saltwater baits. When you get right down to it, the two are often close to identical. As just a few examples, consider the saltwater Heddon Zara Spooks or Storm Thundersticks, or perhaps the saltwater line of Bill Lewis Lure Co. Rat-L-Traps.

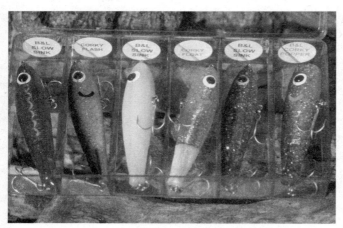

How 'bout the Bass Assassin? Given that name, who'd have ever thought that there would today be a "Saltwater Assassin" series—an increasingly popular line of lures that is now off-shooting its own series of saltwater jig heads? Examples like these go on and on.

Paul Brown's B&L Corky—the lure responsible for Houston angler Jim Wallace's capture of the 13-pound, 11-ounce Texas state record speckled trout from Baffin Bay on February 6, 1996—now comes in a wide and colorful variety of configurations. Wallace caught his behemoth fish on a chartreuse version of the "slow-sinking" model while sight-casting in shallow water to large, solitary specks.

Similar to freshwater originals or otherwise, there are now more baits than ever from which to choose. And that's welcome news to veteran saltwater lure fishermen. It can be, however, more than a bit intimidating for beginners.

It shouldn't be.

There are four basic types of saltwater fishing lures—lead-headed shrimp-tails, shadtails and grubs (bait tails), soft plastic slugs, plugs and spoons. To regularly use any or all of these with success, the fisherman has to first do some pre-trip homework.

The assignment—here we go again—is to understand and then capitalize upon quality fishing conditions. With experience, the coastal angler anticipates and recognizes the necessary blend of light wind, moving tide, reasonably clear water and abundant baitfish.

All that assumed, even the best spot on the bay won't produce fish without the right lure and the proper technique. As always, the fisherman's decision hinges upon several variables, not the least of which is the size of the fish desired.

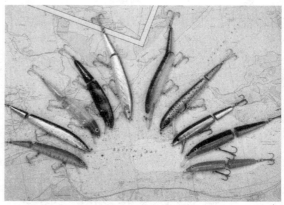

In recent years, floater-diver plugs like the Cordell RedFin, Bomber Long A, Storm Thunderstick, Rapala Minnow and others of their kind have been somewhat overshadowed by "dog-walking" topwaters like the MirrOlure Top Dog, Heddon Super Spook, Excalibur Spittin' Image, Rebel Jumpin' Minnow and Producer Ghost. Though trends change, these baits and other "old-timers" as well will continue to work for anglers who know the drill and fish them with confidence.

BAIT TAILS

LEAD-HEADED SHRIMPTAILS, SHADTAILS AND GRUBS

If there's a gamefish on the globe that won't hit a lead-headed soft plastic shrimptail, shadtail or grub, it hasn't yet been discovered. A fish goes after a soft plastic bait because it looks natural. But when the predator strikes the lure, the rod-induced deception goes one deadly step further.

The soft-bodied artificial *feels* natural.

Striking fish tend to hold on to soft bait for an extra second or two. As a result, the fisherman gets more time to react. This delay has cost many an unsuspecting gamefish a sudden and forceful trip to the landing net.

The jig head normally weighs between 1/4- and 1/2-ounce—enough to carry the airborne lure through all but the stiffest winds. Also because of the lead head, the bait tail sinks quickly. (An interesting note: Just because a jig head is labeled "1/4-ounce" doesn't mean it is. Jig head manufacturers sometimes take lib-

Eric Bachnik, sales manager for MirrOlure/L&S Bait Co. out of Largo, Fla., caught this nice stringer of chunky speckled trout and redfish from a shallow cove on Mesquite Bay north of Rockport, Texas, while throwing the company's "Top Dog" topwater during the "Four Amigos Rockfest" tournament in early May '98. He used a short-handled 6-1/2-foot medium-action All Star rod to make the catch. Relatively short, fast-action sticks of this genre afford the topwater fisherman a real advantage in terms of both lure control and reducing wrist fatigue. (Photo by Capt. George Knighten)

erties when it comes to assessing weights; for example, some don't factor in the weight of the hook. I've seen "1/16-ounce" jigheads that actually weighed a full eighth-ounce.)

Beneath working flocks of seagulls, where larger fish tend to suspend deeper than their surface-thrashing, schoolie-sized counterparts, shrimptail or shadtail jigs and grubs are the ultimate choices. Still, these catch-all fishing lures are not restricted solely to deep-water applications.

Fishermen on the Upper Texas and Louisiana coasts often rig shrimptail jigs below popping corks, sometimes in tandem with live shrimp. On the skinny-water flats of the Laguna Madre, lead-headed shrimptails were solely responsible for the creation of special "rattling" floats, most notably guide Capt. Bob Fuston's "Mansfield Mauler" clicker cork and, some time thereafter, the rattling Alameda cork. Shaped much like a conventional popping cork, but constructed of hollow plastic, the latter is now gaining growing acceptance on the upper half of the Texas coastal curvature as well.

The Storm Chug Bug—a concave-faced, water-spitting "bass fishing topwater" if ever there was one—is now available in saltwater models with corrosion-resistant hardware. The development and modification of bass lures like the Chug Bug and Big Bug, Heddon Zara Spook, Excalibur Spittin' Image, Rapala Husky Jerk (available in a suspending version) and others has had an incredible overflow impact on the evolution of saltwater baits.

The fluorescent orange Mauler is actually a modified crappie fishing cork. Threaded onto a stiff wire center, the unique specialty float is fitted with red plastic beads and small barrel swivels on each end. The lure is tied onto a short mono leader, just long enough to keep the bait above the bottom and out of the grass. When the float is popped with a light twitch of the rod tip, the lure mimics not just the movement, but also the sound of a tail-snapping shrimp.

Speaking of shrimp, one of my favorite lures to tie beneath a clicker cork is the D.O.A. Shrimp. In the water, the D.O.A. (meaning "Deadly on Anything," says Florida-based lure designer Mark Nichols) Shrimp looks amazingly like the real thing. I've used it for years, even one-on-one against other fishermen who were casting live shrimp, and have on occasion caught not only just as many trout as my companions but also fish that were on the average noticeably bigger.

Nichols' baits literally defy description. They merit this mention because, in essence, they can't be "categorized" with other styles of artificials. Mark Nichols' home-bred fishing lures are as unique as his personality. He's a renaissance man among lure designers, a seasoned saltwater fisherman with a quick, dry wit and captivating sense of humor who lives in one of the neatest Jimmy Buffett-style cabana hideaways I've ever seen.

He's also a real kick to fish with.

I've watched his soft plastic "Baitbuster" mullet imitations seduce whopper trout in the bays from Galveston to Lake Calcasieu, and I've seen 'em dupe many a big cobia offshore. His shad-imitating "TerrorEyz" plastics must also be used to be appreciated. I've caught scads of trout and redfish on 'em.

Shallow-water redfish and mullet-imitating topwater plugs make for a wonderfully explosive combination. With their low-slung mouths, reds have to virtually pounce on a surface plug in order to "kill" it. This one fell for a 97MR808 MirrOlure ("97M" denotes the body style, "R" stands for "rattling," and "808" is the catalog color pattern—in this case, a black back, fluorescent orange belly and gold scale sides). Listen to MirrOlure regulars start talking baits and you'll swear they're speaking in some sort of top-secret, ultra-clandestine military code.

Trust me. They look weird. *Really* weird. But they catch fish.

In June of '97, immediately prior to the Outdoor Writers Association of America (OWAA) annual convention in Orlando, Fla., Mary and I spent two incredible days fishing with Nichols on his home waters near Stuart, Fla. Casting the TerrorEyz, we caught and released tarpon on the North St. Lucie River in a way that I never imagined possible. Not big fish, mind you, but hordes of 5- to 15-pound *sabalo* that aimlessly rolled about on the surface like thousands of care-free puppies sunning their ivory bellies.

Using an ultralight Penn spinning rig, Mary brought in a 15-pound fish on 6-pound line. I, as usual, caught one *almost* that big—this one on an ultralight Shakespeare spinning combo. I've never seen gamefish in such numbers.

On day two we fished for snook—a magnificent sportfish species that is currently undergoing some experimentation from the coastal fisheries personnel at the Texas Parks and Wildlife Department. Until you get as far south as Port Mansfield, Texas, waters on the whole are a bit too cool for snook. (I do, however, know a fisherman who a few years ago caught a snook in East Matagorda Bay. Around Port Isabel-specifically in tiny South Bay—a fragile but viable population exists.) Where the fish *can* survive, I hope they're boosted as much as possible.

You've got to catch a snook—or a tarpon, redfish, trout or any other worthy gamefish—before you can truly appreciate it. We caught and released several fish up to 16 pounds, including one estimated 20-pounder that Mary hooked and lost due to an unfortunate and unfixable line tangle. I was the line tangler, and I still haven't been forgiven.

Can't say as I blame her. That was a hell of a fish.

Whether you're fishing for snook or specks, soft plastic baits of any sort—lead-headed shrimptails and shadtails alike—will cost you considerably less than plugs and spoons. However, they don't last nearly as long. Soft plastic is, of course, much more vulnerable to fish teeth than hard plastic or metal. But it's also, by no means, all the same when it comes to fishing lures. Take, for example, Berkley's "Power Bait" series.

The term "Power Worm" has become synonymous with worming on the South's top bass impoundments. And despite the strongly provincial nature of the coastal fisheries of the Lone Star and Bayou States, Berkley's Saltwater Power Bait series has also established a presence of its own along the Gulf Coast.

No matter who makes 'em, I don't fish baits that don't get results. These do, and in a very impressive and consistent fashion. Like the old American Express card, I don't leave home without them.

The Power Pogy (their spelling on the "Pogey" part), the Power Mullet and other lures in the line-up have, after more than a few years of research and development, reached maturity. The only drawbacks to these (literally) secret-formula soft plastic bait tails are: 1) They are not as durable as some of the other soft plastic offerings on the market; and 2) They cost more—in some cases, *considerably* more.

Neither aspect, however, is enough to give pause to experienced anglers. Even "expensive" soft plastics are cheap when compared to high-grade hardware. Personally, I'd much rather be catching fish and replacing bait tails than gloating over how splendidly my discount store worm bar soft plastic is holding up in the absence of strikes.

In the summer of 1997 Berkley debuted the new series of Saltwater Power Baits—lures that I had the opportunity to test several months earlier. Fishing with John Prochnow, the fellow who pioneered the Power Bait formula (and one of only two individuals on the planet who is privy to all of the formula's components), I spent two days casting for speckled trout out of Wild Horse Lodge on Baffin Bay with Jan and Capt. Calvin Canamore.

We made the trip in February. February is, after all, perhaps the most likely month in which to snag a Baffin Bay monster trout. It's also the most likely month in which to get blown out by inclement weather—a fact which, upon arriving at the Riviera (that's pronounced *Riv-EER-a*), Texas fishing lodge and encountering 30-mph winds we were not at all surprised to verify.

I started out with a Super Spook topwater in the hopes of snagging a wall-hanger fish for the cover of *Texas Fish & Game*. No such luck. Aided by such a powerful back-wind I was able to throw the stout, mullet-faking surface plug incredible distances. But with the retrieve taking place over foot-high whitecaps sporting blown-off tops, it soon proved to be a futile endeavor.

What better way, I wondered, to test out Berkley's New Power Pogy than to fish it in such outright lousy conditions? Prochnow—true to his mission and brimming with confidence—started out right away with the new shad-styled bait that he had so carefully formulated and designed.

Despite the howling north wind and subsequent coffee-brown water (only made worse by the deep and penetrating stain of what was at the time a frustratingly persistent brown tide) he and his "research team" ended up catching and releasing better than two dozen 20- to 24-inch trout.

It was an impressive demonstration—one that was the basis for a "Sportsman's Notebook" column in *Texas Fish & Game*. Prochnow went home victorious; I went home amazed. Truth is—Power Baits or no Power Baits—I wouldn't have given us a 1-in-10 chance of catching fish with anything shy of a gill net.

These baits are the newest of their kind, but certainly not the last. Soft plastics throughout the Western Gulf Coast have over the past 20 years witnessed an interesting evolution.

The KelleyWiggler, produced and promoted by the late Pat Kelley of Pearland, was the high-profile shrimptail on the market in Texas during the late '70s and early '80s. Popular during the same era—especially on the coast from Corpus Christi down to Brownsville—was the Norton Shrimptail, designed by south coast pro Bob Norton.

The first shrimptail—at least, the first I know of—was actually produced by Boone Tackle Company Inc. The name of the lure—the "Tout"—has since become a generic reference to shrimptails in general. Classic Fishing Products Inc. (Culprit) has long made a quality line-up of saltwater soft plastics—most notably the "Riptide" series; ditto for Gambler Lure Co., which owes its biggest splash to the flat-tailed "Flappin' Shad."

Hogie Lure Co., Ted Sheridan's Tidewater Lure Co. (Mr. Wiffle), Kalin (maker of the "Dorky Mullet"), Mann's (who made the original "Stingray" Grub—still a killer for a wide variety of saltwater gamefish), Creme Lure Co. of Tyler, Texas, (maker of the first plastic worm, a radically different bait that, at the time, some overly concerned bass anglers predicted would result in the eventual collapse of the entire nation's largemouth fishery), the minnow-mimicking H&H Cocahoe Minnow, a Louisiana-bred soft plastic which is a huge favorite in both its home state and in Texas, the custom-poured "Fish Trap" shadtail, What's Bitin' Lure Co.'s "Flounder Pounder" and the Flex-Jig

MirrOlure's new "Top Dog" surface plug is arguably the simplest bait there is for "walking the dog." It's a heavy bait, and as such comes in real handy when you're forced to cast directly into strong oncoming winds while wade fishing. This one is in the "Texas Chicken" color pattern—a garish-looking, but often deadly color combination that has served me well on not only this lure but also the Cordell RedFin broken-back floater/diver and others. Again, always affix this lure and other topwaters with a Loop Knot (see Chapter 13) or, at the very least, a large split ring threaded onto the nose.

Tandem Rig, B&L Lure Co.'s specialized soft plastic arsenal (including not only the now-infamous "Corky" mullet imitation, but also the B&L Shrimptail, B&L Shad and the B&L Sea Slug, all designed by leading edge lure innovator Paul Brown) the list is immense.

And it is by no means completely covered herein.

The aforementioned soft plastics are not the only ones on the market. They are, rather, some of the better-known models marketed on the Western Gulf Coast. When saltwater gamefish are on an aggressive bite, I daresay every one of these will produce results out of the same feeding school of fish.

Nonetheless, there are times when trout, redfish and flounder become ultra-finicky. It's those times when the fisherman who carries along a broader-than-usual variety of soft plastic baits will find himself with a decided edge.

When weather and water conditions are less than ideal—even outright lousy—I turn to Berkley's Saltwater Power Bait series as my "confidence baits." No matter your preference, if you're casting an artificial lure that you have great confidence in you're much more likely to catch fish on that particular bait.

SOFT PLASTIC SALT-WATER "SLUGS"

Most recently, the ever-popular shrimp and shad imitations were joined by the family of soft plastics now generically referred to as "slugs."

The slug craze began with the intro of the Slug-Go—again, a lure which made its debut in the largemouth bass arena. Many manufacturers now produce slug-style plastics. These lures look just like the name implies. On the whole, they sport blunt heads, sharp tails and grooved bellies which allow for the insertion of weedless hooks.

Two of the better known slug baits are manufactured by Fort Smith, Ark.-based PRADCO (Plastics Research and Development Co.)—first, the Riverside "Big Gun" and, later, the "Slingshot." (The latter is a center-punched version of the Big Gun, which in essence employs the welding together of two Big Gun tail sections and is fished "Wacky-style," with the hook threaded dead through the center and middle of the lure. Among my lesser-known but nonetheless memorable accomplishments in the world of fishing lures was coming up with the name for that particular bait while on a Sam Rayburn Reservoir field testing mission with PRADCO bait designer Gary Hughes and country-western singer Tracy Byrd. Naming a lure is great. Now if I could just learn to *design* lures like Hughes, I'd really have it made.)

The Slingshot is designed specifically for catching largemouth bass close to cover, and does an outstanding job of it. The bait is thrown as close as possible to a stump, brushpile or weedline, allowed to slowly sink next to the structure and then—once it's a short distance away—is retrieved for another cast. It's a highly productive no-brainer lure for bass fishing, but doesn't lend itself well to the water-covering realm of coastal fishing.

The Big Gun, on the other hand, is a great choice when you need a weedless and slow-sinking offering that can be whipped into thick vegetation and then worked back over anything from potholes to oyster reefs. Ditto for Berkley's Power Slug, a bait that sports the same basic body design but also contains the company's Power Formula. The B&L Sea Slug differs in that it has a fatter belly and thinner tail. That aside, it fits within the same basic genre.

No soft plastic slug, however, has arrived on the saltwater scene with as much fanfare as the Saltwater Assassin. Again, truth be known, it's merely a Bass Assassin with saltwater packaging. Be that as it may, it doesn't matter. Bass lure or not, it's as productive a soft plastic lure as you'll ever find when casting to coastal gamefish.

The Assassin also has a pronounced and fat belly, along with grooves in the body which allow for weedless hook positioning. Perhaps more noteworthy is the lure's split-tailed configuration. I've watched the Assassin sit dead in the water, without the assistance of any retrieve whatsoever, and am still impressed with how much movement comes out of that doubled tail by virtue of nothing more than a slight modicum of current. Fish will pick this bait up off the bottom while you're picking out a backlash.

The Assassin can be rigged three primary ways: 1) with the standard configuration of a conventional lead jig head; 2) with nothing more than a wide-gapped single hook like you'd use when Texas-rigging a bass worm; and 3) with a new creation marketed by O. Mustad & Son Inc.

In perhaps the easiest, most user-friendly rigging process you've ever tried, this innovative hook design renders the Bass Assassin amazingly weedless. It's called the "Needle Power Lock Live Action System." It'll work on virtually any soft plastic worm, trailer or jerk bait, and—because of the split-tailed lure's deeply grooved belly—really shines when fitted on the Assassin.

Directions: 1) Insert the pronged wire clasp attached to the eye of the hook straight into the nose of the lure; 2) Slide the hook bend up into the Assassin's belly groove; 3) Gently push the needle barb about halfway through the skin of the lure's upper end. That's it.

Remember, though, to always use a swivel when fishing the Saltwater Assassin in order to prevent line twist. I've been fishing these baits hard for the past several years, and dozens of trout and redfish later, contend that they're one of the most effective saltwater soft plastics you'll ever throw.

On the inside track: Only a week before this book went to press, lure rep and long-time informant and confidante Mike Haring of Katy, Texas, called me to tell me about a new slug-style lure developed by Bass Assassin owner Robin Shiver. The clear-bodied soft plastic comes fitted with a reflective insert, and is—believe it or not—a real innovation in the realm of what are usually at best recycled designs. The one Haring sent me was rigged with a 5/0 Mustad Mega-Bite wide-gap hook—a hook that has been used by the bass angling fraternity for around three years but has now at long last found its way into the coastal universe.

It's not been named as of press time (I've put in my vote for the "Flashback") and it won't be put on the shelves until mid-summer '98. Be looking for it, though. In shallow-water scenarios, especially where there is a lot of grass, this lure is going to break some brand-new ground. And don't forget about that 5/0 Mega-Bite hook; it'll also serve you well on not only the Bass Assassin, but also just about any other slug-style soft plastic on the market. It has a long shank, and on short-striking fish—especially flounder—is a real secret weapon.

A final note: If the bottom is carpeted with gooey "scum grass," or if you're fishing super-shallow flats, try casting the lure (rigging suggestion No. 2) Texas-rigged without a weight on a standard wide-gap worm hook like the Mega-Bite. The Assassin (and most other slug-type soft plastics, for that matter) is dense and heavy enough to be easily casted *sans* weight on the typical light-action 7-foot trout rod and 12-pound-test line.

Mustad is continually developing new jig heads and hook configurations, and you can expect numerous other innovations in the future.

RIGGING LEAD-HEADED BAIT TAILS AND GRUBS

Be especially careful to properly thread a soft plastic bait tail onto a jig head's hook shank. It's critical that the tail be positioned straight and unbent, directly in parallel proportion to the line of the shank. A hump-backed soft plastic is the mark of a rookie, and furthermore, doesn't do the fisherman any favors.

I've experimented with this task, and have arrived at a simple procedure which eliminates the guesswork. Position the tail against the jig head, with the head of the lure butted up against the base of the jig head. Assuming you're right-handed, clamp your left-hand index finger and thumb together to mark the *exact* location at which the bend of the hook passes through the top of the lure. If the bait has markings or perhaps a dorsal appendage which helps mark this point, use it and remember it. If not, mark the point with your thumb and then "nick" the back of the lure with the hook barb to pin-point the exit spot of the barb.

Run the hook point dead-center into the front end of the bait tail and thread it *straight-on* until it reaches the previously noted point of intersection. At

this point, curve the barb upward through the marked spot on the bait tail and snug the head of the tail against the base of the jig head. With any luck at all, you'll have a lure that's rigged to run straight and will avoid the telltale camel's hump of an improperly gauged application.

Talk about "specialized." Say hello to Mustad's "Needle Power Lock Live Action System"—in this case, fitted to a pair of Saltwater Assassins. The combination makes for a vegetation resistant weapon that is also easy to cast directly into strong oncoming winds.

POINTS TO PON-DER ON SALTWATER SOFT PLASTICS

Theories regarding the "best" colors for saltwater soft plastics are a continuing source of debate, but coastwide, strawberry and red shad still win by fair margin—particularly in dingy water. As much as anything else, the trend toward red may well be because it is the most-often used color on the coast. Other leading contenders for the title include purple, root beer, smoke, fire tiger, chartreuse and white.

The latter is especially potent in clear-water scenarios. A pearl-bodied, chartreuse-tailed Saltwater Assassin is awfully tough to beat when bay water looks like it's fresh out of the tap. In wintertime, when water temperatures are chilled and phytoplankton densities are down, that description isn't too much of a stretch.

Again, use a color pattern that you're confident with and—usually—you can hardly go wrong. I generally contend that the manner in which you fish a lure has a lot more impact on your success—or lack thereof—than the color pattern of that given bait.

Furthermore, as we're about to discuss, you might give some thought to the size of the bait you're throwing in relation to the size of the fish you hope to catch.

SALTWATER PLUGS

Although plenty of trophy-class trout have been taken on shrimptails and grubs, most of the specks caught on these lures tend to be smaller than those nabbed on mullet-imitating plugs. Consider the feeding habits of speckled trout, and the reason why becomes obvious.

Small speckled trout eat lots of small bites; big trout eat very few large bites. Yearling "school trout" feed primarily upon shrimp and other small crustaceans, and do so until they reach four pounds or so. At that time, their dietary preference shifts to mullet and other baitfish.

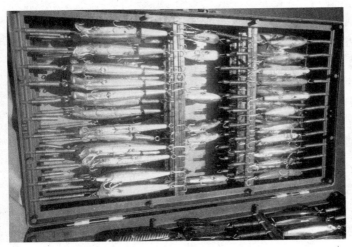

I'll never forget shooting this picture of Capt. Doug Bird's tackle box back in the early '80s. What really struck me was how many "freshwater" plugs he was using—especially at that relatively early stage of the saltwater bait boom—to pursue redfish and trout along the Upper Laguna Madre and the flats of Baffin Bay.

Accordingly, the lure of choice for big fish is—surprise!—a plug that looks (and acts) like a mullet.

Saltwater plugs come in a wide array of shapes, sizes and colors. Which model you choose depends upon where you fish—or perhaps more precisely, where exactly you want the bait to be positioned within the water column.

SINKING SALTWATER PLUGS

Naturally, sinking plugs are best suited to deep-water situations. They're a favorite of spring and fall surf waders as well as boaters who drift fish open-water oyster reefs.

On the Western Gulf Coast, and particularly in Texas, the term "sinking plug" is virtually synonymous with the MirrOlure 51MR and 52MR. Up front, it should be stressed that these are lures which demand some degree of skill from the angler.

The 51MR and 52MR, and their floating counterparts the 7MR and 97MR, are bona fide mullet imitators that lack diving lips, concave noses, inherently-designed wiggling body configurations or any other feature that makes the lure do something other than what it's directed to do via the rod tip and reel handle. Mirr-Olures do what you *make* 'em do. And in the right hands, they're lethal.

The primary difference between the 51MR and 52MR is the rate of speed at which they descend in the water. The 51MR is a slow-sinker; the 52MR, conversely, sinks about twice as fast. The eye ring on these baits also differs, with the ring on the 51MR positioned straight out the nose and the ring on the 52MR threaded into the head of the lure. The head placement of the eye ring on the 52MR allows the head of the lure to serve as an artificial "lip" of sorts, furthering its tendency to dive deep.

Says MirrOlure master and CCA honcho Capt. Pat Murray, "If you look real carefully, the 52MR is just a tad bit thinner than the 51MR, which reduces its water resistance and increases its sink rate. The 51MR, accordingly, not only sinks more slowly but also has an action that's not quite as 'tight.' Of the two," Murray explains, "the 51MR is more prone to shoot to one side and the other with a degree of twitch-and-stop motion on the rod tip."

Note, also, the "R" in the aforementioned MirrOlure model numbers. That particular consonant denotes these baits as rattlers. The importance of the noise-making element, no matter the style of any given plug, cannot be over-stressed. Fish react not only to sight, but also to sound. And that element of sound creation only becomes more critical with decreases in water clarity.

It is, by and large, a major reason that another former freshwater-only player has

Berkley's Saltwater Power Mullet in the making at the Outdoor Technologies Group's 300,000-plus-square-foot production facility located in Spirit Lake, Iowa.

made such an impact on coastal fishing in recent years—the Bill Lewis "Rat-L-Trap." Unlike the MirrOlure, the Rat-L-Trap is a bait that wobbles erratically—and as the name implies, very loudly—with every revolution of the reel spool and pull of the rod tip. Also unlike the MirrOlure, which again is a mullet imitator, the Rat-L-Trap mimics the body shape and flash of a shad.

There's also one other primary distinction between the two. The MirrOlure is more or less a "finesse" bait, designed to meticulously cover the water inch by inch. The Rat-L-Trap, on the other hand, is much like a spoon in that it covers lots of water in relatively little time. As such, the Rat-L-Trap is a great fish-finder.

It's not, in my experience, a specific "big-fish" bait like the MirrOlure. That only makes sense, seeing as how it is somewhat smaller and imitates small shad instead of finger mullet—the preferred menu item for 5-pound-plus speckled trout. That's not to say, of course, that a 1/4- or 3/8-ounce "Trap" won't occasionally account for trophy-caliber speckled trout. And there are even bigger versions, which I have yet to try on specks, which may work well as selective big-trout offerings.

By and large, however, the Rat-L-Trap is a "numbers" bait for speckled trout. It's perhaps at its best, though, when thrown into a school of feeding redfish. The Rat-L-Trap, as a selective redfish bait, ranks right at the top of the list. When worked near the bottom, it's also a great weapon for catching flounder—usually, bigger-than-average flounder.

Plugs are also desirable in that they can be cast long distances into oncoming breezes. That, as much as anything, is why I like to throw the Rat-L-Trap into the summertime surf. Rock-walkers who've tried it from coastal jetty systems love the "Trap" for the same reason.

One plug that, being a soft plastic with the body configuration of a hard bait is tough to categorize, is the B&L Corky. The sinking version of this lure, simply called the "Slow-Sink," (it also comes in a floater) brings meticulous retrieve techniques to a new level.

Pat Murray is one of the best I've seen at fishing this now-solidly-established big-trout creation, and in fact helped lure designer Paul Brown with the development of this and other B&L lures. "The sinking Corky is one of the most suspendible saltwater lures on the market," Murray comments. "Because of its wire core, the back fins on the lure are adjustable. The Corky is a crazy bait; it's about the only lure on the coastal market that you can 'walk' while it's beneath the surface."

The Cordell RedFin, a classic "floater-diver" plug, has a relatively long lip. Yet, it doesn't dive deep. Despite its deceptive nose job, the RedFin is a long-time favorite of flats casters who target visible redfish and speckled trout holding close to "potholes" and other skinny-water structure. The point here: You can't look at a lure in the package and inherently know what it will do once it's in the water. It's a good idea, in fact, to "test" your favorite baits in a swimming pool when the chance to do so arises. Check out, for example, the difference in the action of a jointed "broken-back" RedFin and non-jointed "straight-back" RedFin. The latter has a much tighter wobble. I have found that floater/divers are especially potent when waters are choppy.

Take it from me, though: Impatient reel-crankers need not apply for Corky fishing. Of all the lures I've thrown, none have demanded more patience and, when you get right down to it, outright skill, than both the floating and sinking Corkys. You'd think it would be easy to fish a lure so slow that you almost fall asleep in mid-retrieve.

It isn't.

There are, as always, exceptions to the rule. But if you want to score consistently while fishing with a Corky (or, the newer Kalin "Dorky Mullet"— what a name) you need to work it like you're on the leading edge of a coma. If it's cranking and winding you enjoy, you're much better off casting a broken-back floater-diver.

FLOATER-DIVER SALTWATER PLUGS

The jointed minnow, or "broken-back" plug is among the top-ranking topwaters in Texas. Technically speaking, however, it falls between the topwater and sinking plug categories.

Though it's classified as a topwater, this shallow-lipped plug is actually a floater-diver. Most often, attacking predator species will hit these lures on the stop, as they're returning to the surface. Matter of fact, just about every plug you throw is most likely to be hammered when it has just come to a halt.

These are mullet-imitating baits, whether designed in broken-back or straight-back configurations. Either will swim right to left on the retrieve. The straight-back "wounded minnow" (first introduced by Rapala) sports a tight, fast wiggle; the broken-back, a broader but—at least in my estimation—sexier and more appealing to-and-fro wobble.

With the advent of the newer and more in-vogue "pure" topwater plugs, the broken-back has been relegated toward the lower end of a great many coastal tackle boxes. It shouldn't be. There are times—especially when water conditions are a bit choppy—when a slowly-cranked, stop-and-go broken back will out-produce any other big-trout bait on the market.

Mullet-like topwaters—here, a Producer Ghost—are preferred for big trout. Still, you'll be surprised at times by the tenacity of "schoolies" that don't balk at striking big plugs.

Floater-divers offer another advantage: Unlike the pure topwater plug, which never leaves the surface, the floater-diver spends much of its time underwater. The "water backing" above the just-below-the-surface fishing lure does wonders to improve an angler's strike-to-hook-up ratio. The resistance of the water above holds the lure in place, and makes it much more likely that the attacking gamefish will end up with at least one hook barb embedded in its eager and open jaw.

As far as brands, the top players on the coastal floater-diver line-up are the Cordell RedFin, Storm Thunderstick, Bomber Long A and Rapala Minnow. The shallowest-diving of the lot is the RedFin, which is why it's such a favorite among skinny-water flats specialists.

There's a new twist in the floater-diver ranks, yet another borrowed from the shelves of bass fishermen—the suspending floater-diver. Of these, the one gaining the most steam seems to be Normark's Suspending Husky Jerk, now available in a brand-new saltwater-specific version introduced in spring '98. Take it down a foot or so and it'll stay there for a while. It ought to be a real beast in the surf and deeper bay waters; just be sure to use that suspending characteristic to its utmost. My guess is you'll get a lot of strikes when this lure is in the couch potato mode, just hanging there in the water column like a finger mullet begging to become a menu item.

Or, go with a traditional floater-diver like the Thunderstick and add a few of Storm's "SuspenDots" to achieve the same basic effect. The self-adhesive lead stick-ons are easy to apply and, with a bit of imagination, can expand the scope of almost any conventional floater-diver.

I'm still experimenting with the suspended bait concept in saltwater, but at this point it appears to offer a lot of potential—especially when working either surf or bay waters in excess of three feet or so. In the calf-deep stuff, it's best to stick with floater-divers that will dig down and then, like a rising mini-submarine, return to the surface.

Or, you can go to the top and stay there.

SALTWATER SURFACE PLUGS

Fact: As all-around producers of large speckled trout, topwater plugs have no equals. The "down" side, as just mentioned, is that they often result in an outright lousy strike-to-hook-up ratio. It's not unusual for the ratio of "blow-ups" vs. hook-ups to score no better than 50-50.

Aside from their propensity to seduce bigger-than-average trout, what is most appealing about a topwater plug is its visual nature. You see the strike. In fact, you often get to see the fish approaching the lure before it makes the hit. Watch a 28-inch redfish hump up the water in the wake of a topwater plug and you're in for an adrenaline rush that rivals the excitement of flushing a 15-bird covey of quail.

Used to be, anglers considered topwater plugs to be baits relegated only to shallow-water scenarios. Not anymore. I've caught too many respectable topwater trout from 6-foot-deep surf guts and bay reefs to believe that trout, or even redfish, won't come up a considerable distance to get a kill shot at a surface plug.

That said, topwaters are the natural choice for casting in calf-deep flats. From East Matagorda Bay and Port O'Connor south to the Lower Laguna Madre of Texas, you're in what for the most part is topwater territory. Ditto for much of the "inside" terrain of Louisiana's Chandeleur Islands as well as the shallow marsh shorelines out of Cocodrie, La., and Lake Calcasieu. Fact is, there is no place on the

Plugs are great "finesse" baits, but when it comes time to cover lots of water in an attempt to locate feeding fish as efficiently as possible, you just can't beat a spoon. This 5/8-ounce Tony Accetta is custom-made for defying the gusting wind and rolling breakers of the incoming surf; just be sure to add a brightly colored bucktail—and a swivel—to the lure before making your first cast. Beware: dry, first-cast line is very prone to backlashing.

Gulf Coast where surface plugs will not produce, given the right scenario.

Big speckled trout and redfish are partial to very shallow water. This is especially true during the early spring and late fall, when the warmth of the shallows offers temperature-sensitive baitfish a reprieve from the cold. Large, surfaced pods of mullet congregate in water less than 2 feet deep. Concentrated and relatively confined, the vulnerable baitfish are soon followed by hungry redfish and trout. These are by no means easy fish to catch. Nor are topwater plugs especially easy lures to fish.

Topwaters are finesse baits, and are much more difficult to master than either lead-headed jigs or spoons. Use a 6- to 6-1/2-foot fast-taper rod, though, and you'll find the task to be much easier (see Chapter 11).

I hate to admit it, but I'm still just a little shy of pitiful when it comes to working the MirrOlure 7MR topwater plug. I'm not sure exactly why—perhaps it's simply because I don't throw it that often (back to that "confidence" factor again)—but the 7MR has been, in my experience, one very tough lure to master. Then again, all fishermen are different. You may try it, catch fish on it your first cast and never want to throw anything else. I certainly hope so.

"The 7MR sits flat on the water," says Murray, who has a knack for working these plugs that I hope to someday obtain at least half of. "I call it a 'twitch bait,' and," he explains, "I think it's perhaps the truest of the twitch baits because it's at its best when the rod action is imparted with a whole lot of subtlety. Subtlety is the key to mastering this plug.

"You almost have to make it go just a bit sub-surface," Murray says, "so it can grab some water and can get the flash and wiggle that makes it produce. It'll turn over on its side and, given some slack, slow-float back up to the top. Since it's a smaller topwater compared to what we normally throw, it's deadly effective on 15- to 18-inch trout. But," he adds, "it's an exception to the 'big-bait/big-fish' rule. Lots of 8-pound-plus speckled trout have been—and will continue to be—caught on the MirrOlure 7MR."

I have to concur. Aside from Murray I've spoken with and, on occasion, watched a host of coastal guides—among the more notable, Capt. James Plaag, Capt. George Knighten, Capt. Jim Leavelle, Capt. Lowell Odom and Capt. Dwayne Lowery—flat-out terrorize big trout on this undeniably demanding topwater mullet plug.

Lowery, in particular, is a master of the 7MR. I've observed his style, and he works the lure with a unique technique that—at least when imparted via his young hands—is irresistible to big specks. After the lure hits the water, he lets it sit for a few seconds. Then, with a little bit of slack in his line, he points his rod trip straight toward the lure and shakes it vigorously. The vibrating rod tip transmits just enough motion to ignite the subtle action Murray pointedly refers to—another thing among many, I suppose, that I need to practice.

I've never made a fishing trip during which I didn't learn at least one new technique or strategy; that's a whole lot of the fun of fishing. Anyone who tells you that he or she knows it all is either a pathological liar or a television fishing show host.

Personally, I've found MirrOlure's newest topwater offering—the heavyweight "Top Dog"—far less challenging to work than the 7MR. The big surface plug is as easy to "walk" as anything I've ever seen. Given its weight, it'll also cast incredible distances. (In January of '99, the Top Dog will be introduced in a smaller version as well. I've experimented with the single prototype that was sent to me by MirrOlure's Eric Bachnik, and from what I can tell so far it's going to be every bit as hot as its bigger cousin.)

There are, again, a multitude of quality topwater plugs on the market. Rebel's "Jumpin' Minnow" was the first to gain big-time notoriety on the Texas Coast. It hit the Lone Star saltwater scene back in 1989.

The big surface bait rests with its tail down and head up, and is—like all other topwaters—a proven producer of not only speckled trout but also redfish.

Speaking of "Producers," next in line was the Producer Ghost, an inexpensive but deadly Heddon Zara Spook look-alike that has become a standard

PRADCO's Rebel Jumpin' Minnow, shown here in the company's colorful "G-finish," is one of my all-time favorite topwater plugs. On the Upper Texas Coast, it was the first topwater lure to gain serious notoriety and lend credence to the notion that surface plugs are just as effective on redfish and trout as they are on freshwater bass and stripers—even in the surf. Unlike the Excalibur Super Spook, Spittin' Image, Producer Ghost and others, the Jumpin' Minnow rests with its head on the surface and its tail partially submerged. The Jumpin' Minnow, like many other former freshwater favorites, now comes in a full line of saltwater color patterns fitted with corrosion-resistant hardware.

choice for fishermen coastwide. Then, there's the Zara Spook itself. It's been on the bass market for decades. Several years back, PRADCO introduced the venerable topwater plug in a saltwater version and, shortly thereafter, brought another Spook into the arena—the Excalibur "Super Spook." I've enjoyed some awesome trout and redfish action on this king-sized surface plug.

The Super Spook is a big bait and, as is the case with the others mentioned here, is designed to make noise. In the case of the Super Spook, though, you can hear the clacking, oversized surface lure rattling its heavy-duty ball bearing from a full 50 feet away. Now available with corrosion-resistant saltwater hardware, it cuts a large, mullet-like profile on the surface and likewise promises to maintain a high market profile on the coastal lure scene for many years to come.

The same goes for PRADCO's new topwater shad mimicker, the Excalibur "Spittin' Image," as well as its *brand-new* spin-off, the "Swim'n Image" crankbait. I first saw the shallow-lipped Excalibur Swim'n Image in early April '98, and have already talked to some field testers who have done very well with it—especially on redfish. PRADCO's Bruce Stanton, on his third cast over a shallow-water Louisiana flat, nailed a 12-pound red on this unorthodox saltwater fishing lure. I say "unorthodox" because crankbaits are still in the embryonic stage on the coastal fishing scene. I strongly suspect, however, that won't be the case for long.

A couple more new kids hit the block in '97; again, both are extensions of lures that made their initial splashes in the bass fishing arena—the Storm Saltwater Rattlin' Chug Bug and Saltwater Rattlin' Big Bug. A beefed-up and corrosion-resistant version of the bass-proven "Rattlin' Chug Bug" introduced by the Norman, Okla.-based lure company in 1993, the 4-1/2-inch-long, 7/8-ounce "SRCP" Big Bug is paying off for trout tournament big-fish specialists—especially when winds are high and waters are choppy.

The reason why? This bait, along with the smaller (3-1/2-inch-long, 3/8-ounce) "SRAP" Chug Bug, is unique in that it not only "walks" but also "spits," thanks to a cupped mouth that kicks up the extra commotion needed to attract gamefish in turbulent water conditions.

Fishing in May of '97 during our annual excursion to Capt. Tom Holliday's "Cocodrie Charters" fishing lodge in Cocodrie, La., *Houston Chronicle* outdoor writer Doug Pike and I nailed fast limits of bayou-running marsh reds on chartreuse/chrome SRAP Chug Bugs. It was sight-casting nirvana; just look for the gentle swirls of blue-tinged tails in the backwater pockets, fire a cast at the commotion and hold on. The fish climbed all over the lures.

Another thing that I really like about the Chug Bugs is that aside from the fact they are noise-making "rattlers," they also come fitted with pearl "FlashTails" that add a considerable degree of "breathing" action to the presentation. If a given surface plug comes without a mylar or plastic "trailer," you'd do well to add one. My buddy Capt. Mel Talasek of Matagorda adds small red tube jigs to the tail-end treble of his Super Spooks and swears by it. Given his consistent big-trout successes, I'm in no position to argue with him.

No doubt, there will more newcomers in the future that will gain just as much, if not more, notoriety than any and all of the aforementioned saltwater plugs. They all, however, will continue to produce fish—assuming that they are properly rigged and retrieved.

RIGGING SALTWATER PLUGS

Topwater plugs are designed to "walk the dog." in non-angler's terminology, that translates to "walking" the bait right and left in continuous but erratic fashion.

The way a surface plug is tied on makes a tremendous difference in a fisherman's ability to walk the dog. Imagine a lure with a basic knot like an Improved Clinch, Palomar or Trilene Knot snugged tight to the nose. The line, when pulled, literally pulls the lure. No slack, no "give," no ability to wander about. Just a straight pull.

Then imagine the same lure tied on with a either a Loop knot or a Surgeon's loop (for knot-rigging instructions, see Chapter 13). The free reign of a Loop knot—or, if you prefer, a split ring—allows the uninhibited lure to move freely to and fro. One way or another, *don't use a conventional knot when tying on a topwater plug*.

I've also in the past used Loop knots on soft plastic jigheads, and have found that the Loop has a very beneficial impact when the fish are being finicky. One day when you have nothing better to do and the water is clear, tie on a shrimp-

If you find yourself short on single hooks, you can tie a short leader to a treble-hooked spoon and attach it to a clear bobber. With the correct leader length, the spoon will suspend above the grass.

tail jig, let it sink and watch the fall. Then try the same process with a Loop knot. The difference in the flutter and wobble of the falling lure may well surprise you.

As for sinking plugs, your basic saltwater knots will perform just fine. Here, however, is a textbook example of a scenario which commands, in virtually all instances, the use of a heavy-duty monofilament leader. Sinking plugs go deep—all the way to the bottom, if you want—and that's where the oyster shell is. The rest of the equation doesn't require much explanation.

POINTS TO PONDER ON SALTWATER PLUGS

Whatever the body configuration, plugs of all sorts are available in a veritable rainbow of colors. Fortunately, there's no need to stock the entire spectrum.

Chrome, gold and black are all proven producers, preferably with a black back. In clear water, try clear, pink, chartreuse or blue-bodied versions. Orange, red and "fire tiger" patterns have gained a great deal of acceptance as all-around colors in recent years as well.

One other critical note regarding surface lures: If a fish "blows up" on a bait and misses, don't reel it in right away. Consider the perspective of the fish.

A plug and feather jig combo rig, a rarely used, but often effective means of enticing gamefish.

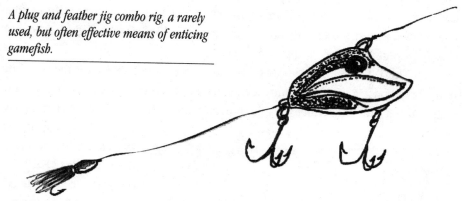

She's expended the energy to come to the top and smack the lure. She's wounded it. It's sitting there, stunned, and all that remains is another dead-on strike to account for another well-earned meal.

I can't tell you how many times I've caught both redfish and trout on the second go-around. If the fish doesn't go after the "wounded" lure again within five seconds or so, twitch it ever so gently. Or, shake the rod without reeling, to make the lure vibrate like a baitfish with the wind knocked out of it. The results are likely to make the inside of your waders as wet as the outside.

Again, saltwater plugs are not particularly easy lures to master. They demand concentration, exertion and a fair amount of expertise.

If it's simplicity and all-around user-friendliness you're after, try spoons instead.

SALTWATER SPOONS

These, it's safe to say, are the artificial lures you need most when abandoned on a deserted tropical island. They're made of metal and, barring corrosion or neglect, will last for ages. And that's how long they've been around.

When Capt. James Cook visited the Sandwich Islands (1771-1778), he noted in his journal that the natives fished with spoon-type lures fashioned out of seashells. The world has changed dramatically in the 200-plus years since Cook's travels, but the effectiveness of saltwater spoons has remained as constant as the ebb and flow of the tides—despite the fact that, with all of the new lure innova-

hulking jack crevalle, Spanish mackerel, bluefish and even pompano—is that it comes right out of the package with a quality barrel swivel.

Another top pick for probing the beachfront is the Rapala Minnow Spoon. This bait, like all of Normark's offerings, comes in a variety of color patterns that are not only effective but are also applied to the high-grade fishing lures like they're meant to stay there. My favorite is the mullet-like green-and-gold, followed closely by blue and silver and your basic gold.

The 1/2-ounce treble-hooked version is my lure of choice for the surf, but in the bays I have a decided affinity for the Rapala Weedless Minnow Spoon (could be because it's the lure which, despite horrendous southwest winds on Trinity Bay

Here's a different twist: Sinking plugs can be fished over grass-beds by rigging the plug beneath a float like an Alameda. "Pop" the cork as you would when fishing a live shrimp.

out of Baytown, Texas, in October '95, won me the "Biggest Redfish" division of the Texas Commerce Bank Saltwater Fishing Tournament and, thanks to its flounder appeal, played a major role in winning our team (guided by Capt. Cecil Howard) the "Heaviest Stringer" division as well. I've caught hundreds of redfish on this lure, not to mention enough fall flatfish to feed a small army. Strangely enough, I've caught very few trout on it, though.

Mann's "Loudmouth" is an unconventional spoon that you won't find in the angling arsenal of many coastal fishermen, but I'd advise you to pick up at least a couple (along with saltwater-resistant replacement trebles). The disadvantage of the "Loudmouth" is that it's made of plastic and, lacking the weight of its metal counterparts, won't cast nearly as far. That same hollow-bodied plastic design, however, allows for the inclusion of noise-making rattles. We've already discussed the importance of sound, and it's no less relevant to spoons than it is to plugs.

One other nice thing about the Loudmouth: it sinks much more slowly than a metal spoon. The advantages on shallow-water playing fields are obvious.

In both beachfront and bayfishing situations, spoons allow the fisherman to cover a great deal of water in a short period of time. Many coastal pluggers, in

tions in the world of coastal sportfishing, the spoon has become somewhat of a forgotten lure. Up until the 1980s, when shrimptails first went on the market with a great deal of fanfare, spoons were the mainstay of most old salts.

Regardless, they work every bit as well now as they ever did.

Spoons are without question the simplest of all artificial lures to fish. Ginger and Marianne—even Gilligan—could start catching fish on their first cast with a bucktailed spoon.

They're also among the most versatile of fishing lures, ranking in across-the-board effectiveness right up there with the soft plastic shrimp or shad imitators.

I've caught hundreds of surf-run trout on 5/8-ounce Luhr-Jensen Tony Accettas and Krocodiles, and would no sooner surge out into the suds today *sans* spoons than wade out to the third bar without my stringer.

Spoons are, however, even better suited to redfish. Why, I don't know, but a silver, gold or copper spoon is as good a weapon as you'll ever need for homing in on spot-tails. When bottom-bounced, they're also poison on spring and fall flounder.

Because of their con-cave shape, the solid metal lures wobble incessantly when

Capt. Lowell Odom of Rockport liberally applies the MirrOlure 51MR to the affected speckled trout.

retrieved. They also catch and reflect light like no other type of fishing lure, even in sandy or off-colored water. Better yet, spoons cast like ballistic wonders—a fact I always appreciate when surf winds are hitting me in the face at 15 mph out of the due south.

The 5/8-ounce "Tony A" is, again, along with the Krocodile, one of my absolutely favorite surf offerings. What I like about the Krocodile—aside from the fact that is has persistently produced not only beachfront reds and trout but also

A floating plug can be fished over weed and grass beds by attaching a ringed sinker 18 to 24 inches ahead of the plug. However, the sinker must be heavy enough to pull the plug beneath the water.

fact, use spoons to locate gamefish before switching to their favorite finesse bait, much like experienced bassers use spinnerbaits to pinpoint bedded largemouth bass before making the transition to soft plastic worms or lizards.

(Lizards for saltwater fishing applications. Hmm; there's another thought.)

RIGGING SALTWATER SPOONS

Because of its non-stop spin and flutter, a spoon must be fished on a snap swivel or, preferably, behind a barrel swivel and stout length of leader. No exceptions here. Skip the swivel, and the lure will promptly twist your fishing line into a hopelessly tangled mess that rivals the handiwork of nests constructed by mating pelicans.

Select an appropriate weight and design for the brand of fishing at hand. The same treble-hook-trailing 1/2-ounce spoon that serves you well in the surf will be a major-league hassle if you try to work it in shallow, grassy flats.

A "Mansfield Mauler" clicker cork, a short length of leader and a strawberry shrimptail jig is a killer combination for redfish and other gamefish in shallow, grassy flats.

A warning of special interest to surf and jetty casters: When line-cutting species like Spanish mackerel and bluefish cost you a lure or two, add a stretch of steel leader. Mackerel love spoons, and they'll keep 'em for good if you don't take the necessary precautions.

Furthermore, make sure that the leader used on a saltwater spoon is either smoke-colored or black. A flashy chrome leader, like a chrome barrel swivel, will often entice the striking fish to go after the leader or swivel instead of the lure.

That, I assure you, can become one extremely frustrating problem in very short order.

POINTS TO PONDER ON SALTWATER SPOONS

Assuming they aren't already fitted with one out of the package, always fit your saltwater spoons with either a yellow or orange "flipper tab" or, better yet, bucktail. The latter is preferable because it, unlike a flipper, will stay put despite the best efforts put forth by striking gamefish to dislodge and damage it.

A bucktail adds a great deal of sex appeal to a spoon; should you doubt it, try fishing a naked spoon while your companion works the same bait with the desired dressing. The color, not to mention the pulsation created by the bucktail, is an advantage you can't afford to do without in all but the rarest of scenarios.

HOW FRESH ARE SALTWATER LURES?

If I have ignored your favorite saltwater artificial, please forgive me. I agonized as to whether or not I should go into this much detail about specific lures, and then remembered that no one has yet to complain about getting too much information. Conducting the *Texas Fish & Game* Multi-Media Seminar Series taught me that rule in a hurry, and it's one that's stuck.

Nonetheless, the coastal lure market is growing faster than a 12-year-old country boy. There are—and will continue to be—new baits hitting the shelves every year. I added new ones to this ever-growing chapter until a mere week before press deadline. And it's a safe bet that when this book goes into its second edition, there will be even more brand-new hardware offerings contained herein. The innovation continues, and it's great fun to be a part of it.

It's assuring to know, however, that if there was never another lure designed or made for the specific purpose of catching saltwater fish, we almost certainly wouldn't suffer. No disrespect to the "new" baits hitting the market, mind you, but a nod of acknowledgment here to the primarily freshwater lure patterns that have been around for ages but only in recent years have become recognized as speckled trout and redfish catchers.

A lot of this "new lure" ground has already been covered. Who would have thought that a Heddon Zara Spook, perhaps the most revered topwater plug of the century for largemouth bass, would also be the undoing of so many trout and reds—

OTG research and development specialist Chris Pitsilos checks out a new "Frenzy" lure design in the company's computer connected "flow tank," part of a recently constructed million-dollar-plus research-and-development facility.

and, that it would eventually be produced with saltwater hardware for saltwater fishermen in saltwater color patterns including such notables as "pencil trout" and "redfish"?

I'm just glad to see saltwater fishing getting the attention it deserves.

I recall a trip I made in 1983 to Baffin Bay with trophy trout guru Doug Bird of Corpus Christi. Bird and I were drift-fishing the area around Yarborough Pass, and when he opened his double-decker Plano tackle box I was amazed to see a prodigious collection of freshwater bass lures resting in the racks. They wouldn't have been there, I assure you, had the personable and highly respected Lower Coast fishing guide not already proven them to be efficient fish-catchers.

Keep an open mind. And never underestimate the open-mindedness of the fish you're trying to catch. I'll never forget the evening a close friend called to tell me—with distinctly clandestine overtones—that he had slayed the shallow-water redfish of East Matagorda Bay on Strike King spinnerbaits. Strike King must have been listening; the company introduced a saltwater-specific spinnerbait to the market in late 1997 which has since blossomed into a new saltwater line of lures and jig heads.

Then there was the Day of the Huge Trout on the Freeport Jetties. My older brother and life-long fishing companion, Bill Bozka, Jr., hooked and, unfortunately, lost a *really* big speckled trout that fell for—get this—a purple Creme bass worm. The old kind, too, with the wire leader, beads and blades that made the front end look like a flashy in-line spinner while it carried a worm with two small single hooks rigged inside.

For some reason, perhaps a sudden impulse, Brother Bill became inspired by the combination of unorthodox lure and unusually clear water lapping the rocks. He pulled the brand-new "Wiggle Worm" from his amply-stocked tackle box, tied it on as if it belonged there and unceremoniously chunked it off the rocks.

I think Bill was as surprised as the fish was. It must've weighed at least 8 pounds. We watched it surface, like a rising purple submarine setting the crosshairs for a torpedo attack. Maybe it was the flashing blade on the nose; maybe it was the unusual length and exaggerated wiggle. Whatever the stimulus, the fish was hell-bent on killing that worm. The massive speck inhaled the bait, turned, and thrashed the water just long enough to let us know it was not at all happy with the situation.

The line popped like a firecracker. Then, the victorious trout slowly swam away. For a moment, I honestly thought Bill was going to dive in after it. A very quiet period of about 10 minutes ensued.

I caught a 9-even on the same late-spring day, though not through experimental means. It ate a big live shrimp free-lined in the crevasses of the granite immediately below. The 29-inch fish, taken in 1974, is my biggest speckled trout to date.

Hopefully, by the time you read this that will no longer be the case. At the time of the Day of the Huge Trout on the Freeport Jetties I barely had enough money to buy vegetable oil for cooking that fish much less mounting it. So, I'm still on the prowl for a taxidermy-worthy trout. If I get her in this lifetime, I suppose I'll dedicate my remaining energies to catching an even more taxidermy-worthy trout.

True Confessions? I'm getting impatient. The gaping hole on my office wall at *Texas Fish & Game* won't wait much longer, nor will my long-deprived ego. If it doesn't happen in the next few years I'm going to resort to an acrylic replica of the 9-pounder.

Back to using freshwater lures in the brine: As you'll soon discover, any lure with a package that doesn't specifically designate that bait as one with corrosion-resistant saltwater hooks will rust like a 20-year-old pickup truck parked up to its wheel wells in surf rollers. It's OK to use the factory-provided hooks on the first trip with a new bait of freshwater design. But after that, switch out.

There are scads of quality saltwater trebles on the market. One of my favorites, produced by Mustad, is called the "Triple Grip." These hooks borrow somewhat from the popular "circle hook" design, and though they won't increase your strike-to-hook-up ratio, they will certainly increase the odds of keeping a fish on the hook once it's there.

The only complaint I've heard, oddly enough, is that they're a bit difficult to remove after the fish is landed.

"So," I answer, *"your point is—?"*

SOME FINAL OBSERVATIONS

One way or another, and no matter how tired you are after the trip, give not only your tackle but also your lures a gentle freshwater bath before heading for the shower yourself. You'll be glad you did when you dive into your hardware the night prior to your next excursion and find baits that don't look like they've been marathon tested in Utah's Great Salt Lake.

Even with a topwater, always be aware of sub-surface structure (remember, many coastal gamefish—in particular, redfish—dive and run after they hit a floating plug). When it's really nasty underwater, add a length of heavy-duty leader material— at least 25-pound-test—to counter the razor-like impact of oyster shell, barnacles or other line-cutting nightmares. Use an Albright knot or similar connection to join the main line and leader (see Chapter 13).

Also, if you're working an area laced with steep oyster reefs that come close to the surface, remember to keep your rod tip high when fighting a fish. Where the reefs get really shallow, don't hesitate to hold the rod handle way above your head, with your arms fully extended, when doing battle. The higher rod tip creates a steeper tip-to-surface angle that just might keep you from losing a world-class trout or red.

The Most Critical Artificial Lure Rule of All?

If there's one practice which reigns supreme when chunking hardware, it's "establishing a pattern." Bass fishermen coined the term around 25 years ago, and it's every bit as important to trophy trout fishing as it is to casting for lunker largemouth bass.

Vary your retrieves, with an emphasis on stop-and-go. Watch the baitfish around you, and do as they do. Work the lure all the way back to you; it's not uncommon to get creamed when your bait is only 6 feet away from the rod tip. Execute each and every retrieve like it's the last one of the day, and assuming (heaven forbid) that your partner is catching fish and you're not, pay attention to the difference in your actions and adjust your technique likewise. Fish in accordance with the water temperature, the lower the slower.

Above all, remember exactly what you were doing with the lure when the fish struck, and then do it again. And again, and again and again.

Easier said than done?

No question about it.

Worth the effort?

Absolutely.

Chapter Thirteen

Ultimate Connections:
Knots to Know

The knot—or knots—you tie constitute the weakest connection between you and the fish you're fighting. Each knot has its own specific attributes, but on the whole, knowledge of just a few will get you through most any given angling scenario.

It's not only smart, but fun to know how to tie a "specialty knot" or two. The knots that follow include both—the basic, and the advanced. Next time you get a little free time on your hands, spend some of it learning the following connections.

At the very least, you'll impress your less-knowledgeable fishing buddies with your knot-tying wizardry. At best, you'll be prepared to create virtually any terminal rig imaginable that's of practical use to the inshore saltwater fisherman.

ARBOR KNOT

Time to come clean here. It was only a year or so ago that I learned to tie and started using the Arbor Knot. I bothered to look at the manual that came with a new Abu-Garcia baitcaster, and minutes later knew how to tie a very simple knot that every fisherman truly needs to know and utilize. Most anglers—myself included, until I learned better—use an Improved Clinch Knot to tie their line to their reel spools.

Bad idea.

For one thing, the Improved Clinch is inclined to slip through as you're cinching it down on the spool. That, after a time or two, can become very frustrating. Secondly, despite how tightly you cinch it down, the Improved Clinch is prone to cause "lumping" as the line is spooled onto the reel, since it leaves a vertical layer of sorts at the base. If the line is not distributed evenly across the spool, it will cause you some casting problems. Use the easy-to-tie Arbor Knot—in essence, two Overhand Knots atop one another—and your line spooling dilemmas will be forever solved.

An important note when applying line to reels: On baitcasters, apply the line in the same fashion as it is spooled on the mono spool. Reel it on with

1. Pass line around reel arbor.

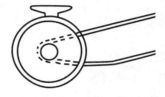

2. Tie an overhand knot around the standing line.

3. Tie a second overhand knot in the tag end.

4. Pull tight and snip off excess. Snug down first overhand knot on the reel arbor.

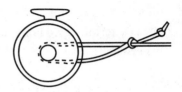

the same curl that's on the line spool. Fill the reel to with 1/8-inch of the rim; do not over-fill as an over-loaded reel spool is a backlash waiting to happen.

On a spinning reel, apply the line with the monofilament spool facing the reel spool, and again, apply it with the line curl wrapping exactly the same direction as the rotation of the pick-up bail. Line that's improperly applied to a spinning reel creates a mono-twisting nightmare that'll literally ruin your day. Remember too, when a fish is running or your lure or bait is hung on something, *do not* crank the reel handle. I can't explain exactly how or why, but doing so creates line twist that will come back and haunt you later in the day.

Used to be, I had someone—usually Mary—hold the line spool with a pencil stuck through the center and then cranked the line onto my baitcasting reels. That, however, was before I discovered the Berkley Portable Line Spooling Station Pro Kit. It comes with a metal arm that holds the line for you; the reel is affixed to the other end of the unit's base.

The Portable Line Spooling Station Pro Kit—introduced in 1997—includes a Portable Line Spooling Station with a line stripper. The line stripper is an incredibly useful tool; if you don't buy the kit, at least buy the line stripper. Powered by two "C" batteries, it'll strip 150 yards of monofilament off of a reel spool in less than a minute.

The kit also comes with 1,000 yards of Trilene XL 10-pound-test mono, a pair of fishing pliers/scissors and a carrying case. It's fully portable, and like the venerable Amex Card, I don't leave home without it. Used to be, I dreaded changing line in the field. Now it's a breeze.

Also, always wet your knots with a little spit before drawing them down. The knot wraps will slide more easily, and the knot will gain a bit more efficiency.

Finally, remember that dry nylon fishing line is the toughest to cast. Take it easy on your first shot; and don't start the macho spoon-slinging until your monofilament absorbs a little saltwater and softens somewhat. (And it does absorb water. Ever noticed how much easier mono is to cast after a half-hour or so of steady bait-chunking?)

If you're in a hurry, spray your reel spools with a line conditioner before you leave the dock. My personal favorite, and again, one I've used for several years, is Blakemore's Reel and Line Magic. At the very least, pour some fresh water on your spools and give it a few minutes to "soak in" before firing your first volley.

It's bad any time, but a backlash that explodes when the fish are biting is unmitigated torture.

IMPROVED CLINCH KNOT

This knot, I would guess, is used 90 percent of the time by 90 percent of the fishermen.

1. Pass line through the eye of the book, swivel or lure. Double back and make five turns around the

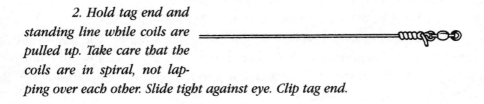

standing line. Hold coils in place; thread end of line through first loop above the eye, then through big loop as shown.

2. Hold tag end and standing line while coils are pulled up. Take care that the coils are in spiral, not lap-

ping over each other. Slide tight against eye. Clip tag end.

Lake Buchanan striped bass guide Joey Martin showed me this one back when I was hosting the *Texas Fisherman* television show on Home Sports Entertainment in 1991. I've used it extensively ever since, and it's never failed me.

Basically, it's an upside-down Improved Clinch Knot. What I really like about it is the way that the multiple overhand wraps slide down the main line

BAGLEY KNOT

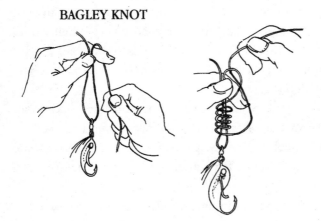

1. Run line through lure or book eye, then wrap over index finger. Make multiple wraps above book eye, run line through the loop at your fingers and cinch down tightly. (Illustration by Mark Mantell)

without—as is sometimes required on the Improved Clinch—pushing or forcing the wraps down the main line while having to hold the tag end in your teeth and maintain tension.

PALOMAR KNOT

The Ande Monofilament Book of Knots—from which Bill Monroe of Ande graciously allowed us to reproduce most of the drawings and instructions in this chapter—describes the Palomar Knot as "Easier to tie right, and consistently the strongest knot known to hold terminal tackle."

It requires running a doubled line through the hook or lure eye, however, and as such is not well-suited to hooks with tiny eyes.

It is, however, the knot of choice and No. 1 solution for tying superlines like SpiderWire, Fusion, Gorilla Braid, Fireline, Power Pro and others. There was much ado about knot slippage when superlines were introduced several years ago, and most manufacturers now agree that the most efficient and altogether reliable knot for tying superlines is the Palomar.

Big thing to remember: Superlines do not succumb to teeth and are clumsy to sever with a knife. There are several brands of small, saltwater-resis-

1. Double about 4 inches of line and pass loop through eye.

2. Let hook hang loose and tie overhand knot in doubled line. Avoid twisting the lines and don't tighten the knot.

3. Pull loop of line far enough to pass it over hook, swivel or lure. Make sure loop passes completely over this attachment.

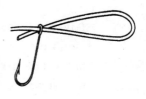

4. Pull both tag end and standing line to tighten. Clip about 1/8-inch.

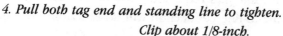

tant scissors on the market, and if you're fishing with superline they're an indispensable accessory.

TRILENE KNOT
The Trilene Knot, like the Improved Clinch and Palomar, is a time-tested and stress-proven standby for most connection requirements.

1. Run end of line through eye of book or lure and double back through the eye a second time.

2. Loop around standing part of line five or six times.

3. Thread tag end back between the eye a second time.

4. Pull up tight and trim tag end.

SIMPLIFIED BLOOD KNOT
I don't care if I'm fishing a bare sand flat without an oyster shell in sight for miles: I always affix a leader to my main line. The Simplified Blood Knot is the best way to get it done.

I love to fish light tackle, but I hate to lose fish. This knot allows me to spool 10-pound-test mono on a buggy-whip spinning rod but still rely on the insurance of a 20-pound-test leader.

Sure, you can use a small barrel swivel, but that's just one more weak link in the chain. Plus, you can affix 5 feet of leader to your main line and—unlike a barrel swivel—cast the connection through your guides without damaging your rod tip. Some lures—say, spoons or Saltwater Assassins rigged on jigheads—will twist your line and require the use of a barrel swivel. Most of the time, however, a line-to-line connection will do everything you need and more.

Remember, light line doesn't simply add more "sport" to the sport. It grants you a greater degree of casting distance, allows you to throw lighter lures, increases the amount of line at your disposal —which comes in real handy when an errant 20-pound jack crevalle beats your chosen surf trout to the bait—and in some scenarios, enhances the presentation of your offering. (As an example, diving plugs will dig deeper when pulled with thin-diameter line.)

Learn the Simplified Blood Knot, and use it. The day will come—probably when a 28-inch red is smoking your line over a beachfront sand bar—when you'll be very happy that you learned to tie this knot.

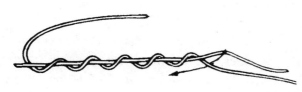

1. Take the two lines' ends and tie a simple overhand knot (which will be clipped off later). Then tighten to combine the two lines into one.

2. Form a loop where the two lines meet, with the overhand knot in the loop. Pull one side of the loop down and begin taking turns with it around the standing line. Keep point where turns are made open so turns gather equally on each side.

3. After eight to 10 turns, reach through center opening and pull remaining loop (and overhand knot) through. Keep finger in this loop so it will not spring back.

Hold loop with teeth and pull both ends of line, making turns gather on either side of loop.

4. Set knot by pulling lines tightly as possible. Tightening coils will make the loop stand out perpendicular to the line. Clip off the loop and overhand knot close to the newly

ALBRIGHT KNOT

Usually, the Albright Knot is used for joining monofilament lines of unequal diameters—for example, 12-pound mono linked to a 30-pound-test leader. It's also used for connecting monofilament to wire. Be prepared, though; this one takes a little practice.

1. Bend a loop in the tag end of the heavier mono and hold between thumb and forefinger of left hand. Insert the tag end of the lighter mono through the loop from the top.

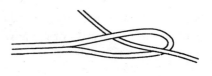

2. Slip the tag end of the lighter mono under your left thumb and pinch it tightly against the heavier strands of the loop. Wrap the first turn of the lighter mono over itself and continue wrapping toward the round

end of the loop. Take at least 12 turns with the lighter mono around all three strands.

3. Insert tag end of the lighter mono through the end of the loop from the bottom. It must enter and leave the loop on the same side.

4. With the thumb and forefinger of the left hand, slide the coils of the lighter mono toward the end of the loop, stop 1/8-inch from the end of the loop. Using pliers,

pull the tag end of the lighter mono tight to keep the coils from slipping off the loop.

5. With your left hand still holding the heavier mono, pull on the standing part of the lighter mono. Pull the tag end of the lighter mono and the standing part a second time.

6. Trim both tag ends.

SURGEON'S KNOT

As line-to-leader connections go, this one is a breeze.

1. Lay line and leader parallel, overlapping 6 to 8 inches.

2. Treating the two like a single line, tie an overhand knot, pulling the entire leader through the loop.

3. Leaving the loop of the overhand open, pull both tag end of line and leader through again.

4. Hold both lines and both ends to pull knot tight. Clip ends close to avoid foul-up in rod guides.

LOOP KNOT

Fishermen who hate tying knot after knot while changing surface lures rig the noses of their topwater plugs with split rings and leave it at that. And for many, that works just fine. My preference, however, is the Loop Knot. Call it superstition, but it's worked for me too many times over the years to go with anything else. Even on a split ring, I still tie a Loop Knot.

1. Tie overhand knot in line leaving extra length.

2. Run line through hook or lure eye and pass through overhand knot, make three loops.

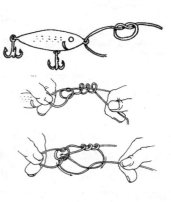

3. Run line back through overhand knot, thread through upper loop—just like an Improved Clinch—and then tighten and clip tag end.(Illustration by Mark Mantell)

I've used it for years without a failure; the only caution I'll give you is to be sure that you don't make the loop too long. If you do, it'll foul in the forward treble hook of your topwater plug as you're "walking the dog." The dog stops walking—it kind of "limps" instead— and I *hate* that when that happens.

KNOTS FOR FLY FISHING

My first encounter with the Nail Knot occurred in April of 1984, as I sat in a ceiling-fan-cooled cabana at Rio Colorado Lodge in Costa Rica with *Houston Chronicle* outdoor writer Joe Doggett and watched him work for hours to get one tied.

The next day, however, Doggett showed up at the dock with a freshly-lit cigar and a half-dollar-sized tarpon scale in his hand. It was his first nail knot, and his first fly-taken *sabalo*, and I suspect he's caught and tied dozens of each since then.

Which goes to prove, even big-time outdoor writers have to start somewhere.

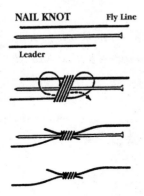

To tie the nail knot, lay fly line, nail (or a hollow tube) and leader butt as shown and hold all three with thumb and forefinger of left hand. Take leader but in right hand and wrap the leader toward the end of the fly line, making five snug turns. Run the free butt of the leader back through the loops. Holding the coils securely, pull on both ends of the leader and slowly withdraw the nail. With the nail out, pull tightly on all four strands of line. Trim ends.

To tie the "nail-less" nail knot, hold the line tip over the leader butt. Form a loop in the leader in front of the line. Pass the leader end through the loop and over the fly line five or six times. Pull on the leader end to snug up the wraps evenly and tighten the knot. Trim ends.

THE BOWLINE

"The fox through the hole, around the tree and back through the hole." Pronounced "*BO-lin*," this done-in-seconds knot is the boater's backbone in terms of overall rope handling. Use it to tie your anchor, moor your boat, attach a drift anchor—you name it. The Bowline is a must.

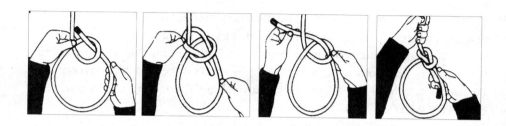

SOME FINAL KNOT KNOWLEDGE

I never really appreciated what went into the making of monofilament fishing line until I got my "Master of Monofilament Degree" at "Stren University" back in the early 80s. "Castability, Stretch, Abrasion Resistance, Tensile Strength, Memory, Water Absorption, Shock Resistance;" those were the names of the courses presented at Stren U.

After checking out of the historic Hotel DuPont in Wilmington, Delaware, I stopped taking it for granted when I looked at various spools of monofilament hanging on the local sporting goods stores' line racks.

Since then, I've attended two other major fishing line-oriented workshops. The first was at the Johnson Worldwide Associates (JWA) SpiderWire plant in Richmond, Virginia. There, JWA field rep Sam Heaton thoroughly briefed the first five outdoor writers in the nation allowed into the highly-secured facility on the attributes and applications of superlines—in this case, SpiderWire and Fusion.

After signing a confidentiality agreement, I watched them braid a few feet of SpiderWire. It is not a quick process; in fact, it's incredibly slow. And it's done with *extremely* expensive material—Spectra 2000—that is also used to make Boeing jet parts, Army tank lids, bulletproof vests and—believe it or not—kite strings for people who fly "stunt kites" in competitive events.

Most recently, in early May '98, Mary and I toured the Outdoor Technologies Group (OTG) plant in Spirit Lake, Iowa. (OTG collectively represents

Berkley, Abu-Garcia, Fenwick and the new economy-oriented Red Wolf line-up.) Again, the technology was mind-blowing—not only in terms of Trilene, Gorilla Braid and Fireline fishing line production but also the making of Berkley Power Baits and the company's incredibly-researched and brand-new line of "Frenzy" hard baits.

It was literally overwhelming. Over 2-1/2 days we covered over 300,000 square feet of factory and warehouse floor space. We attended in-depth workshops about everything from state-of-the-art computer software specifically designed to create and test new fishing lures to watching aquarium fish eat—or reject—various formulas made by Berkley and other companies that had been soaked into tiny cotton balls by Power Formula specialist John Prochnow. Prochnow recorded the fishes' every move; I got the feeling they knew each other very well.

We watched the utilization of an immense tank full of "test bass" that were released and allowed to chase (or not chase) various lure designs being pulled around the oval-shaped pool by a box-like mechanical robot. Each strike, each approach, was carefully recorded.

We watched super-thin layers of Aramid (again, ultra-expensive "bulletproof" material, this time made in Holland and called "MicroDyneema") being carefully rolled over pre-cut graphite templates and turned into $300 Fenwick Techna AV fishing rods. And, among other things, we watched Berkley Trilene become fishing line, from melted bricks of nylon poured out of what looked like cube feed sacks to precisely-extruded strands of exact diameters and predetermined break strengths.

I wish you could see this stuff, because you really have to see it in order to believe it—and, in order to fully appreciate it.

Many millions of dollars have been spent over the years creating and developing new types of fishing line. Not one of them is perfect. They all have strengths, and they all have weak points. Some are super-specialized, others will do just fine for everything from bass in the brush to bonefish in the Bahamas.

But I'll assure you of one thing. I've seen a couple of sub-par fishing lines introduced to the marketplace over the past two decades, and not one of them survived for long.

There's way too much high-quality line out there for a second-rate competitor to stay alive.

Chapter Fourteen

Ain't Nothin' Like the Real Thing:
Fishing with Natural Baits

THE TEXAS 'CROAKER CRAZE'

The water on the outside edge of Traylor Island beach washes olive-green onto a sandy, vegetated bank. An hour ago, Rockport fishing guide Capt. Bart Payne slowly nosed the 21-foot Skeeter Bay Pro to within 30 yards of the shoreline and then paid out close to 200 feet of anchor rope to eventually place the shallow-running, Mercury-powered rig just off the darker-colored second gut. Now, every half-dozen fish or so, he retrieves around 10 yards of rope and pulls the bobbing boat closer to shore and within casting range of fresh, unmolested trout terrain.

It has been exactly as Payne said it would be. A breeze. A relaxed and undemanding presentation of wiggling live croakers into surging saltwater that's virtually littered with big schools of keeper-class speckled trout. In essence, a gimme—the kind of slam-dunk fishing trip that keeps action-hungry anglers coming back to the Coastal Bend every summer in hot pursuit of broad-backed specks that react to free-lined croakers like buzzards to road kill.

I feel, quite honestly, somewhat guilty about this whole process. The majestic speckled trout, the elusive and lordly gamefish that year after year has forced me to struggle and stumble across quagmired bay bottoms while chunking scores of artificial lures in various patterns with carefully calculated retrieves for

Young Jimmy Bozka, back in the summer of '95, proudly shows off a speckled trout that he duped while free-lining live croakers with me along the outside beachfront of Traylor Island near Rock-port, Texas. My, how they grow (the kids, not the fish). Despite objections as to its efficacy, croaker fishing is a great way to get youngsters into the sport of coastal fishing. They want action, and more often than not, they get it with croakers.

hours on end, day after day, is now suddenly little different than a gullible channel cat homing in on a pungent pile of soured maize.

Fish that were once challengers are now chumps.

I have made a number of these trips in recent years—enough to know that all the seemingly overstated banter about the deadly efficacy of "croaker fishing" is indisputably valid. And I enjoyed those outings for what they were, opportunities to take home a few fresh trout fillets while allowing my teenage son Jimmy and his friends a rare chance to spend about as much time catching as they did fishing.

Croaker fishing, for those new to saltwater angling or who get precious few chances to do it, is a delightful experience. Along the coastline, especially throughout the Coastal Bend, it has become the hands-down standard technique for May-through-July speckled trout fishing. It's not, however, quite as simple as it sounds.

For one thing, procuring live croakers from coastal bait camps is like getting 50-yard-line bottom-level seats to the Super Bowl. Without connections, you're often out of luck. Even those who have cozy relationships with bait sellers must show up at 3:30 or 4:00 in the morning to make the buy. There are dealers who don't play favorites and sell the baitfish on a first-come, first-served basis, but they're the exception.

For another thing, croakers are expensive. The going rate for a dozen of the silvery, grunting little baitfish runs anywhere from $4 to $5. Trout want them fresh and frisky. A feeble croaker loses its potency, and in the off event that one goes untouched for two or, at the most, three casts, it's replaced with a new bait. In a good day of fishing, a three-man party can easily go through six to eight dozen croakers. Usually, however, the limits are filled by then—provided that the fragile baitfish don't go belly-up in the baitwell beforehand.

Livewell mortality is a real problem for croaker fishermen. The searing heat of summertime and subsequent lack of oxygen in the water only intensifies the dilemma. But it's not one that can't be countered.

At the least, regular croaker fishing enthusiasts treat their baitwell water with Sure-Life Labs' "Pogey-Saver." A 10-ounce bottle of Pogey-Saver goes for around $5.50, and given the fragile nature of the pricey live baits will pay for itself in a hurry. Pogey-Saver removes the toxic ammonia that's exuded through the fishes' respiratory systems and body functions. It also stimulates the protective slime coating on the croakers' scales and inhibits oxygen-eating foam on the baitwell surface.

The stuff works. (For information on Pogey-Saver, contact Sure-Life Labs President Tony Gergely at 210-372-2239.)

There is another remedy to the mortality quandary, albeit a much more costly solution. Aerate the baitwell with a feed of pure oxygen. Available from Oxygenation Systems of Texas, "The Oxygen Edge" system—an oxygen tank, regulator and air stone—sells for around $350. The OST system is incredibly effective for not only croakers but also live shrimp and other offerings. And when you consider that every dead croaker in your livewell is the equivalent of 40 cents tossed overboard, it doesn't take near as long as one might think to justify the expense. (For information on an oxygen system for your livewell, contact David Kinser of Oxygenation Systems of Texas at 409-267-6458.)

Lastly, remember that even the freshest of live croakers won't draw a response if fished in the wrong place. You have to be where the trout are, and during summertime that means the outside beachfronts and at the bases of bay production platforms.

In both scenarios, the baits are most often free-lined on wide-gapped "Kahle-style" single hooks. Run the barb immediately above the lateral line and behind the dorsal fin. Most of the trout taken on live croakers are keeper fish, and most are hooked in the edge of the jaw.

Perhaps the most difficult aspect of fishing live croakers for trout is resisting the urge to prematurely set the hook. The trout hits the bait to kill it first; afterward, she eats it. When the line begins moving, it's usually safe to strike back.

I recall fishing live croakers with my father along the rocks of the Galveston Jetties back in the early '70s. His fishing partner, Alvin native J. Hall, one summer yanked a 10-pound-plus speck off the "Coffin Hole" on the north jetty via a 4-inch-long croaker. With that precedent set, my brother Bill and I made it a point to use the baits every spring when fresh waters in Trinity Bay pushed the salt-sensitive specks out past the Bolivar Pocket and into the deeper waters of the Galveston Ship Channel.

It was, and still is, a downright deadly technique for trophy-caliber speckled trout. Matter of fact, my advice for anglers after a winning notch in the speckled trout divisions of CCA's annual S.T.A.R. Tournament is to head straight to the nearest jetty system and free-line a live croaker near the rocks.

Point is, croaker fishing is by no means a new technique. It has been around for years, but only in the past five or so has it become standard practice.

There are more hotspots for croaker fishing along the Texas Coast than space allows. Some of the more notable: the Sabine, Galveston, Freeport and Port Mansfield jetty systems all hold great potential. Ditto for the Land Cut from Baffin Bay south to Port Mansfield. From High Island south to Matagorda, Port O'Connor and all the way to the Lower Laguna Madre, surf waters caressed by light southeast winds are prime targets. Inside the Matagorda/St. Joseph Island barrier chain, Aransas and Redfish Bays are the central hub of mid-coastal summertime croaker fishing. And anywhere there are deep-water production platforms in the midst of Texas bays, where man-made structures are supported by man-made shell reefs, a once-in-a-while aficionado of hot-weather trout fishing can suddenly enjoy the success of a seasoned pro if only afforded a baitwell full of croakers and the wherewithal to correctly fish them.

For those accustomed to waterhauls, the sport of croaker fishing is a whole 'nuther deal. It can be a refreshing change to feel you have the advantage on your quarry. Sure, you can have croaker trips that are washouts.

But not often.

The consistent effectiveness of croaker fishing, however, may well preface its downfall. Too much of a good thing can come back to haunt us, and more than a few trout enthusiasts are afraid that if the popularity of croaker fishing continues to grow, the health of the speckled trout fishery may ultimately suffer in serious fashion. I'm one of them.

No one but us has the wherewithal to see to it that it doesn't happen.

TOO MUCH OF A GOOD THING?

There are those who asked that this not be written.

Already, the cry and hue for banishment of croaker fishing is rising like a surging spring tide. Too many people catching way too many trout, and having way too easy a time doing it. So, I asked Texas Parks and Wildlife Department Chief of Staff and former Coastal Fisheries Director Gene McCarty his take on the situation.

The consistent proficiency of the 500 or so fishing guides who ply Texas coastal waters, it appears, is at the front of the issue.

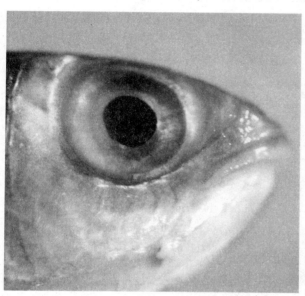

"For example, in 1994 and '95, fishing guides on Aransas Bay contributed about 12 percent of the year-round effort and harvested 36 percent of the fish," McCarty commented. "When you see that kind of efficiency, you've got to wonder what the growth of that industry and the growth of that efficiency could do in the long term." So far, several years later, the Texas trout fishery is still holding up. But it's interesting to note that Aransas Bay currently accounts for around 175 guides—a full one-third of the state's coastal guiding fraternity. The Upper Laguna Madre carries another 25 percent. And both areas are high-profile croaker fishing hotspots.

Finger mullet have been a mainstay of Western Gulf live bait anglers for many, many years. Procuring mullet, however, as well as fishing with them, is a whole 'nuther matter than using live croakers as baits. For one thing, though mullet will take trout as well, they're especially potent redfish baits. Croakers, on the other hand, are incredibly effective—and selective—speckled trout offerings.

So, I asked, are there plans to prohibit or in any way create specific regulations regarding the use of live croakers as speckled trout baits?

"I don't want to be in the business of telling anybody how to fish," responded McCarty. "I just want to tell people how many fish they can take and yet maintain a viable population. I would prefer not to regulate croakers or any other type of bait. We put bag limits and size limits into effect, and that's the way we prefer to regulate the fishery.

"What we see with the croaker is that it provides a real opportunity for the novice fisherman. But a really experienced fisherman who gets involved in fishing croakers is meat hunting instead of fishing," McCarty commented. "It's a very, very efficient means of catching spotted seatrout. As we continue to move into the next century and the next step in fisheries management, we're going to

have to start rethinking and talking about conservation and fishing ethics. If the current 'meat market mentality' grows, then we're going to have to start thinking about bag and possession limits."

Interpretation: No one wants to, or is likely to, regulate the use of croakers as live bait. However, if what McCarty so appropriately refers to as the "meat market mentality" continues in years to come, we can almost certainly expect to see a reduction in the number of fish we can legally take home from Texas waters.

I'm already convinced that the long-term use of croakers has had a profound impact on the number of 26-inch-plus speckled trout in Texas bay waters—particularly the waters of

The Texas speckled trout fishery is currently in great health. I'm concerned, however, about the long-term effects of so many fishermen using live croakers to catch—and keep—mid-range speckled trout in the 4- to 6-pound range. The sheer numbers of fish won't likely suffer, but the numbers of trophy fish can't help but experience some adverse impacts.

the Upper Laguna Madre and Baffin Bay, where dozens of fishing guides every summer are hosting hundreds of fishermen who think nothing of bringing home full-limit stringers of 4-, 5- and even 6-pound specks. Like I said, croakers are selective big-fish baits. Trout this size are not unlike basket-racked, 2-year-old 8-point whitetail bucks. Take them out of the population, and the odds of seeing truly big specimens go way, way down after a year or two. The croaker craze has already had far longer than that.

It's something to think about.

NATURE'S OTHER BAITS

LIVE SHRIMP

Given all the clamor centered around the croaker craze, you might well think that the little panfish are the only natural bait worth throwing.

Not so.

Brown and (the larger) white shrimp have long been the mainstay of coastal anglers who prefer live bait. The various applications of fishing live shrimp are exhaustively covered elsewhere in this book. Perhaps the most important thing to remember is that there are virtually no finfish in the bay system or beyond that won't readily hit one of these kicking and erratically tail-swimming crustaceans.

The down side?

Live shrimp are notorious for attracting bait-stealers like piggy perch, yellowtails and croakers. And when the hardhead catfish are thick during warm-water periods, they'll drive you nuts. If there's one thing to bear in mind when fishing live hoppers, here it is:

A live shrimp that's cut in half when a fish strikes means that the predator fish which made the hit is most often not one of the aforementioned "trash fish." On the other hand, if the legs or eyes are nibbled off, or if the body is surgically sucked away with only the head carapace or shell remaining, you might as well write off your chosen location.

Live shrimp can work wonders in the right place. An excellent example is a free-lined live shrimp drifted into the crevasses of jetty rocks when granite-hugging speckled trout are abundant (in the same way you would free-line a croaker or a pinfish). But in a locale that's overrun with swarms of small panfish, all you're going to do is waste a bunch of time and money messing with small and undesirable reef fish that you don't care to hook, much less catch.

Unless, of course, you wish to use those little fish as baits for heavyweight gamefish—which, in my estimation, is always a good idea. Next trip out, take along some tiny but long-shanked perch hooks (the long shank is very helpful when it comes time to remove the hook from a piggy or croaker that has taken it deep). All it takes is a minuscule chunk of dead shrimp on a tiny hook like this to set the scene for catching an eye-bending speckled trout.

GLASS MINNOWS

In my estimation, these transparent little baitfish (they might measure up to 5 inches or so, but average around 3) are every bit as potent as speckled trout baits as are live shrimp—especially at night, when they tend to come out and roam in numbers. For details on how to catch and rig them, see Chapter 10.

FINGER MULLET

Call me a "potlicker" all you want to. I almost never leave home without a 3- to 5-foot monofilament castnet securely stashed in my boat storage.

Any mullet over 6 inches or so is good for nothing but cut bait. And even I, with my professed open-mindedness and lack of willingness to be ranked among those closet-minded elitists who refer to themselves as "purists," would just as soon call it quits as fish a bleeding chunk of cut mullet—unless, that is, it's affixed to a circle hook intended for surf-cruising bull redfish.

Free-lined finger mullet, whether soaked near bay reefs or off of a coastal jetty system, are wonderful offerings for redfish of all sizes. A bit less often, they'll do a great job of enticing whopper speckled trout—and I do mean *whoppers*. In the surf, I'm likely to hook finger mullet much like live croaker, with a wide-gap single hook barb threaded beneath the aft end of the dorsal fin.

When freelining a mullet, however, I've found it's much better to run a smaller single hook through the lower lip and beyond the upper lip. Both ways, the hooked baitfish will emit the plaintive and critical distress signals of a wounded forage species that makes redfish, trout and other predators selectively seek it out over the hundreds of unencumbered and non-injured baitfish of the same species within the same given area.

Furthermore, when surf breakers are mellow, a lip-hooked finger mullet in the 3- to 4-inch range makes for an irresistible presentation to the beachfront's bigger predator species. The wiggling, suspended mullet will be passed up by the majority of finny passers-by, but when the cork finally slips beneath the foaming surface of the surf you can bet the fish doing the eating is one worthy of setting the hook on.

MUD MINNOWS

Properly called "Gulf killifish," these pot-bellied, round-tailed estuarine minnows are a flounder fisherman's delight. In recent years they have become much more readily available through commercial bait stands—largely in answer to the growing demand. If you insist on catching your own mud minnows, a castnet or small seine used adjacent to marshes or in shallow tidal ponds can sometimes produce an easy (and cost-free) batch of these highly effective flounder baits.

Yes, they will catch other species. I've taken both redfish and speckled trout on mud minnows, but those mud minnows were actually intended for flatfish. Rig the minnow on a fish-finder rig, hooked through both lips, and either work it on the bottom or rig it beneath a float so that it is suspended a few inches off the bottom.

BLUE CRABS

Blue crabs, unbeknownst to many, are the sirloin steaks of a redfish's diet. Redfish, like speckled trout (which incidentally are also members of the drum family) have stout crusher plates called "otoliths" situated at the rear ends of their throats which can promptly pulverize a crab or even a hard-shelled barnacle.

The mud minnow—properly known as the "Gulf killifish"—is the No. 1 natural bait preferred by flounder fishing regulars. Though carried by some bait stands, anglers often are forced to catch their own.

Should you doubt it, check out the stomach contents of the next keeper red you take to the cleaning table.

Rig a small blue crab on a wide-gapped "Kahle-style" single hook with the barb punctured through the sharp end point at either side of the crustacean's carapace, or shell. With larger crabs, remove the carapace and split the crab in half. Then, thread the hook barb through one of the animal's leg openings and out of the top of its body.

When big bull redfish are stoked up during the autumn spawning run, live or even dead crabs will usually outperform any other natural bait offering there is. They're also ultra-effective for the big black drum which frequent the state's major

fish, give a striking fish a few moments to take the bait before setting the hook.

FISH-FINDER RIG

This is perhaps the most oft-utilized terminal rig in existence. Extremely versatile and effective, the fish-finder rig is at home everywhere from Gulf of Mexico oil rigs to inland lakes and bays. It is also the near-exclusive choice of speck fishermen who throw live croakers in late spring and summer.

The No. 1 benefit of the fish-finder rig is sensitivity. The line is threaded

Capt. Bart Payne of Rockport applies a dose of "Pogey Saver" to the croaker-filled livewell of his Skeeter Bay Pro. Some fishermen even invest in costly oxygenation systems to help keep the pricey little baitfish alive. "Oxygenated" natural baits become unbelievably frisky.

through a barrel (egg) sinker and then tied to a swivel. An appropriate length of leader heavy enough to counter the given terrain is then tied to the swivel and fitted with a hook that corresponds with the type of natural bait being used.

Wide-gap single hooks are more than adequate in most situations. They'll gain a firm hookset in a fish's jaw and yet—assuming that the angler's hands are wet and that care is taken while removing the hook—greatly minimize the potential of injuring a fish which is to be released.

With the weight settled on the bottom, a frisky baitfish can swim free throughout the length of the leader. The sinker stays in place, but the line slides through when a gamefish strikes. That lack of resistance is what makes the fish-finder rig such a favorite. While biting the bait, the fish doesn't feel the unnatural pull and tension of the weight. At the same time, the fisherman feels every move

coastal passes during February and March. But for some reason, they're used as redfish baits by only a select fraternity of the redfishing public.

On an excursion many years ago to Chub Cay in the Bahamas, I discovered that small live crabs in the 2-inch range are literal poison for flats-cruising bonefish. I suspect the same is true for redfish holding in calf-deep shallows, though I've yet to test the theory. I have little doubt, however, that Florida-based D.O.A. Lure Co. as well as others in the lure manufacturing industry would not have introduced side-running soft plastic blue crab imitations were it not for the fact that the scuttling little creatures issue serious invitations to redfish strikes.

A worthwhile side note: If you're an avid offshore angler, you can do a lot worse than to dangle a wiggling crab off the side of your boat when an inquisitive ling (cobia) rises to the surface to find out what all the prop-produced commotion is about.

Sure, when artificial lures will do the job I'm not going to resort to natural baits of any kind. But when they won't, I'll be among the first to stab the dip net into the baitwell.

Natural Bait Rigging and Presentations

Considering the never-ending debates about the "right" ways to attach artificial lures to the receiving ends of fishing reels, it's a bit surprising that the same attention isn't given to natural baits. After all, a huge percentage of coastal anglers wouldn't think of hitting the water without first putting at least a pint of live shrimp in the baitwell.

Some consider it insurance, just in case that hot new plug, spoon or jig fails to work as well as it did on the midnight infomercial. I've watched many a "purist" grab for the finger mullet, mud minnows or shrimp in my livewell after conceding that catching fish is more fun than fruitlessly casting artificial lures in adverse conditions. But before making the cast, just as it is with artificials, it's important to match the rigging of natural baits to the task at hand.

Four basic rigs will suffice for most any kind of saltwater bait-fishing you can imagine. Learn them, and you'll be covered on just about everything from nearshore oil rigs to calf-deep flats.

FREE-LINE RIG

The free-line rig is the simplest of all terminal rigs. Most anglers tie the

The issue of incidental "bycatch" is one that is going to in all likelihood only gain more notoriety as heavy shrimping pressure on our bays continues.

line straight to a wide-gap single hook, but in areas laced with heavy shell many prefer to add a short length of stronger monofilament leader via a Simplified Blood Knot See Chapter 13). The Simplified Blood Knot is a line-to-line connection which eliminates the need for a swivel and can therefore be cast through the rod guides without damaging them. Some fishermen prefer an Albright Knot; either one will work. Others, myself included, often go ahead and use a small black barrel swivel (remember, chrome will flash and invite cut-offs from slashing ribbonfish, bluefish and Spanish mackerel). Just take care to reel the swivel to the tip of, but not inside, the rod guides. Otherwise, you stand a very good chance of cracking or breaking your guides and rod tip when you make the next cast.

Small, round "split shot" are clamped onto the line around 16 inches above the hook. Use just enough weight to counter the current and keep the bait several feet under water.

Again, the free-line rig is most often used while probing the craggy sides of coastal jetties for speckled trout and redfish. Live pinfish, finger mullet or croakers should be hooked just beneath and behind the dorsal fin. When fishing shrimp, take special care not to run the barb through the black spot which is the crustacean's brain. Thread it immediately beneath the saw-shaped horn on the shrimp's head. Be sure, too, whether the bait is a shrimp or a baitfish, that the hook barb protrudes completely through.

Cast the bait, and then feed out additional line with your hands. Engage the reel bail, set the drag fairly light and hold on. If the offering is a swimming bait-the striking fish makes.

The amount of weight used on this and all terminal rigs is dependent upon the size of the bait and the degree of current flow. Croaker fishermen after trout off the beaches often use 1/8- or even 1/16-ounce egg sinkers, switching to heavier leads only when the current necessitates doing so. Conversely, grouper fishermen in the Bahamas often run a literal stack of egg weights above the swivel of a fish-finder rig in order to reach extreme depths, a setup that has come to be known as the "Nassau" rig.

The versatility of the fish-finder rig really comes through when the need arises to get off the bottom and use a float. A standard popping cork with a slit side can be affixed above the swivel and then slid up and down to achieve the desired depth. Ditto for an Alameda float.

If you learn no other saltwater terminal rig for natural baits, learn the fish-finder rig.

SHOCK LEADER

A dressed-up version of the fish-finder rig, the shock leader is particularly suited to fishing the beachfront. Strong current flows through surf guts make it all but impossible to keep a bait in place beneath the breakers unless it's anchored with a wire-pronged "surf spider" weight. Though it's most often used by beachfront and pier longrodders, the shock leader will also perform admirably in other situations.

The main line is tied to

Main line to reel, at least 25-pound-test

Barrel swivel

Plastic bead

Snap swivel

"Surf Spider" sand weight

18-inch length of 40- or 50-pound-test mono leader

Barrel swivel

Plastic bead

24-inch-length of 40- or 50-pound-test mono leader

Wide-gap "Kable" style single book or— my favorite for conservation reasons—a 12/0 circle book

a barrel swivel, which is then tied to 18 inches of heavy monofilament leader. A plastic bead and then a snap swivel are threaded onto the line. The line is then run through another plastic bead and tied to another barrel swivel. A 24-inch length of heavy-test mono leader is then tied to the bottom swivel. At the tag end of the leader, tie on the hook.

If using a surf spider, be sure to bend the weight's wire prongs into "U" shapes before making the cast. Then, after the cast, hold the rod tip low and gently pull on the line to force the wire prongs into the sand and firmly anchor the bait in place.

The element of "shock" occurs on the strike. The fish picks up the bait and runs with it. The 18-inch mid-section leader slides through the snap swivel attached to the surf spider (the plastic beads are there to keep the sliding snap swivel eye from damaging the knots on the barrel swivels). When the upper bead hits the snap swivel and pulls on the dug-in sinker, the resistance of the weight and ensuing "shock" drives the hook barb into the fish's jaw.

If you're after bull reds in the surf, circle hooks are required terminal gear. Sometimes called "tuna hooks," circle hooks actually set themselves as the fish moves with the bait. Almost invariably, the fish is hooked in the jaw. And after a quick snapshot, it can be released unscathed along with its precious cargo of eggs.

THREE-WAY RIG

For fishing deep channels, especially areas laden with rocks or underwater junk, the three-way rig is an excellent choice. To be most effective, however, it's important to properly gauge the respective lengths of the dual leaders.

Tied on, the three-way swivel leaves (surprise) two free swivels at the bottom. One carries the weight, the other the hook and bait. The weight line should be at least 6 inches longer then the bait line. Most often, the three-way rig is used with either a bank sinker or a pyramid sinker. The latter, though effective on deep sand flats and reefs, is notorious for hanging up on rocks and bottom structure.

In areas conducive to hang-ups, it's a good idea to use a lighter pound-test monofilament leader on the longer line for the weight. Then, if the weight gets wedged to the point of no return, the leader will break and allow the angler to retrieve the remainder of the rig.

Chapter Fifteen

Head 'em Off at the Pass: How to Take a Trophy Red

Close to 20 years ago, while working as editor of the Coastal Conservation Association's *TIDE Magazine*, I was rudely confronted one summer day by a co-worker who, as he walked past my gear-laden 4-wheel-drive Blazer, took one look at the surf rods and wire-pronged spider weights in the cab and turned pale as a freshly laundered sheet. "I don't believe it," he gasped, staring at me through mistrusting and fearful eyes.

"You're a potlicker!"

Word quickly spread. Around the office I became an outcast, shunned by all. Had there been a leper colony nearby they might well have put me in it. I gathered my shattered pride and from then on sneaked out on selected Friday evenings to spend my weekends in exile, conducting covert beachfront operations at San Luis Pass with all my potlicking friends. I carefully stashed my terminal gear, and never again spoke about chunking cut mullet past the second sand bar unless I was in the trusted company of fellow potlickers.

I've run boats of various makes and sizes, all of which have seen more than their share of duty in summers past, from the wells of Aransas Bay to the swells of the Sabine Jetties. With the arrival of Labor Day weekend, though, the boat gets a break. Come September, try as I may, I still can't shake the urge to break

Shakespeare's main PR man Mark Davis unleashes a monofilament castnet on the Matagorda Island surf. There's no better bait for pursuing big, surf-run "bull" reds than the kind that you catch yourself, straight out of the breakers. Fish finger mullet alive; use bigger ones for cut bait.

out the surf rods. Too many memories to relive. Too many fish to catch—or, at least, *try* to catch.

Sometimes it seems like it's up to the stars. Cast your lot in the breakers and wait. And wait, and wait.

Surfrodders are an optimistic lot. Have to be, or they'd give it up after the third or fourth consecutive waterhaul. Being boatless, you can't just fire it up and head somewhere else if things turn sour. After a few years, you learn not to go unless winds and water conditions are favorable. It's either southeast 5 to 10—or at the least, a light September north breeze with a moving tide—or I stay home and clean fishing reels.

Worst part is, even with the *best* of conditions the likelihood of striking out remains frighteningly real. So why mess with it at all?

Because longrodding from the beach is elemental angling at its best. There's perhaps no other rush that beats the long-awaited thrill of snagging a heavy-weight redfish or other brine-cruising gamefish with your feet planted firmly on the sand. No elbow-to-elbow multitude of rod-swinging pier casters to contend with, no fee to hit the T-head. Hop out of the truck, stab the PVC rod holders deep in the sand, tie on the shock leaders, crank up the CD player and head offshore—afoot. Steam into oncoming suds, surge through the first gut and over the bar. Then, tide allowing, tippy-toe through the second gut as far as you can before slinging a tail-hooked live mullet or a chunk of a fresh cut dead one well beyond the third.

It's a romantic notion, this catching of huge fish from the beach. Having been disappointed far too many times, though, I now restrict my longrodding ventures to late summer and early fall. As beachfront surfcasting goes, no season beats the suds of September.

The advent of the trophy redfish tag on Sept. 1, 1994, did much to revitalize the sport of beachfront longrodding along the Texas coast. Even before then many of us never gave up the ritual, opting instead to use circle hooks and practice catch-and-release. Beach bumming gets in your blood.

Labor Day heralds the redfish run, and most of these brutes are well over the 28-inch Texas maximum. Bull reds are the glory fish, but there are others—burly jack crevalle, Atlantic sharpnose and blacktip sharks, hulking black drum and slimy but delectable gafftopsail catfish—that keep the longrodder guessing. Some, like stingrays the size of washtubs and toxic-finned hardhead catfish, you'd much rather do without.

Sorry, Bud. You have to take the bad with the good. Stay at it long enough, and you'll get plenty of both.

I got over the stigma of being a live-baiting "potlicker" a long, long time ago. As I've already no doubt overstated, I'd rather use artificials when I can. Most often, I do. But in this case you don't cast the bait to the fish; you cast the bait in the fishes' path and then wait them out.

My nose-in-the-air hardware-only critics need make only one of these Spartan all-night outings to realize that this ain't a sport for girly-men. Even with moderate waves pushed by light southerly breezes, we usually take an old-fashioned country butt-kicking before the night is over.

Live finger mullet don't just jump into castnets; you have to work for them, hours at a time. Lines have to be checked and re-baited at least every half-hour. In a 10-hour trip, that's 20 200-yard round trips to the third bar and back, fighting the seas and current every watery step of the way. Seaweed piles on strung-out lines like wet blankets and blows all the way up to the rod tips. Heavy mono severs waterlogged hands. Jellyfish and Portuguese Man O' Wars scald bare, tender flesh that's then scrubbed blood-raw by gritty beach sand and cauterized with sea salt.

When the action is slow—make that *nonexistent*—and clicker-buzzing redfish runs are merely the wild fantasies of wishful thinking, the vision of a warm bed, clean sheets and soft feather pillow will not disappear. Endurance is imperative; so is the biblical patience of Job. Without either, you're lost in the woods.

Trips begin a few hours before sunset, carefully timed to coincide with a tide change, and usually don't conclude until billowing, mountain-high thunderheads on the eastern horizon turn rose-pink above the Gulf. If the sunrise shines on green water we stay even longer, forsaking surf sticks for 7-foot trout rods and gold 5/8-ounce Tony Accetta silver spoons and 1/2-ounce Rapala Minnow Spoons or, maybe, 51MR MirrOlures. If it's really slick, we'll break out the topwaters. The dawn patrol never misses a fair shot at early-bird speckled trout. When you're on the surf and conditions jive, you take full advantage of every scenario possible.

It doesn't happen all that often. But when it does, it's magic.

This particular addiction began over 25 years ago in the form of post-Friday night high school football game beachfront all-nighters. By the fourth quarter we were watching what the wind was doing to the ballpark flag as much as the ball game itself. Today the excitement of hooking up is the same, but the tackle has changed a bit.

I've spent a lot of time in the past few years experimenting with braided line, specifically saltwater SpiderWire. Given its attributes, it's custom-made for beachfront longrodding. With no stretch, braided line like SpiderWire or Gorilla Braid will uproot a dug-in surf spider weight without a hitch. Zero stretch also means an immediate hookset. Furthermore, 50-pound braided has the diameter of 10-pound mono, which means you can spool enough line on a Penn Squidder, Ambassadeur 7000 or Shakespeare Intrepid to leave several hundred yards on the reel even after the bait is thrown well beyond the third bar and walked back to the beach.

For that reason and more, I've now gone to 150-pound-test braided line. It's still plenty thin, but allows just that much more power when wielding a 10- to 15-foot surf rod.

The big question? Castability.

Put this in the bank. There's no worse nightmare than a monster backlash on a moonless night, and braided line as such is a surfcaster's dream come true. Three-foot shock leaders make for unwieldy casting, but the braided stuff handles it well. Backlashes and tangles are scarce, assuming the caster has some semblance of grace and ability. Like swinging a golf club, casting a surf rod is more dependent upon momentum and follow-through than it is sheer power. And when the reel *does* over-run, picking the line free is remarkably easy compared to snarled monofilament.

An important note on braided line, though: It doesn't take the place of a heavy monofilament shock leader (for rigging specifics, see the shock leader diagram in Chapter 14).

Redfish can be a finicky lot. They often don't go for steel leaders—particularly when water conditions are exceptionally clear—and because of the visibility aspect they're usually not wild about the presentation of braided line, either. From experience, I'm convinced that the angler who ties the hook directly to braided line is at a disadvantage. And in this fickle, unpredictable and unforgiving game you need all the advantage you can muster.

One other note: Always spool a layer of monofilament "backing" beneath your braided line. Use monofilament that is equal in diameter to the braid. Doing so will relieve stress on the reel spool, as well as the potential for warpage than can occur when that line-to-spool stress becomes too intense. Again, this stuff does not stretch. *Period.*

I've taken a tip from the East Coast longrodding crowd who vie for saltwater stripers and bluefish and have done some extensive experimenting with heavyweight spinning gear. Came to find that for sheer simplicity it's impossible to beat. A Shakespeare BWS 1100 10-foot Ugly Stik two-piece rod fitted with a 2200 Series Sigma 080 or Intrepid (60) SS 3880 spinning reel now ranks among my favorite beachfront gear.

Not only are backlashes eliminated—and I assure you, that is a *major* consideration—there's

Rust-free PVC pipe makes the best rod holder there is for beachfront angling. It also keeps your rods and reels off the ground and out of the sand.

much to be gained in precious casting distance as well. And should you have fears about battling 50-pound sharks on spinning gear, consider the generous line capacity afforded by braided line.

Heck, let the fish run. Why not? In most scenarios, there's nothing out there to cut you off and the fight, after all, is why you're there.

Spinning gear of this magnum caliber will whip down just about anything out there shy of a 9-foot tiger shark or the Loch Ness Monster (according to a recent edition of *Weekly World News*, she's still out there somewhere, and she's not a happy camper). My newest addition to the beachfront spinning arsenal is a 15-foot-long Ugly Stik—again, a BWS 1100. With a medium-heavy action and the capability to handle anything from 12- to 40-pound-test monofilament this rod, to borrow a phrase from *Houston Chronicle* outdoor writer Joe Doggett, is a "rhino-chaser."

The corrosion-resistant Shakespeare Intrepid 3880 SS spinning reel is an affordable and effective medium for longrodders who don't want to deal with backlash-prone baitcasters. We caught some huge bull redfish from the Matagorda and Freeport beachfronts on these reels in fall of '97, and never once feared being over-powered.

The aforementioned Sigma 080 has ample capacity for 260 yards of 30-pound-test mono; the Intrepid SS 3880 will hold 230 (and that's monofilament, not the thin-diameter braided stuff). Don't know about you, but that's all the gun I need to handle anything I'm after. The more I longrod the surf, the more fond I become of spinning gear.

Be forewarned, though. When you retain this stuff with your right-hand index finger before swinging back and launching the leader, use a light, quick-release touch. Braided line is no less tough on human skin than it is on beach sand, and it'll play hell on your finger if you don't let the line fly free at the exact right moment. Just to be safe, wear a glove.

A critical gear-related note here: No matter how tired you are (and you *will* be tired), always rinse your gear with fresh water upon returning home. The beachfront environment is horribly caustic, and the corrosive and abrasive mix of salt and sand can destroy even the best fishing tackle made if precautions aren't taken.

Cut 1-inch diameter 5-foot lengths of PVC pipe for rod holders, and use them to hold rods that aren't being used as well as those which are. Reels laid on the sand, given enough time, are as good as ruined.

Time, when you get right down to it, is everything to surf casting. Gamefish use the guts between the bars as highways, but the traffic is seldom steady. It's a waiting game that'll challenge your stamina as well as your patience.

However, as always, perseverance tends to pay off. And when it does, you'll be glad you waited—dead tired or not.

Chapter Sixteen

Super Specks:
Surefire Strategies for Trophy Trout

Angling may be said to be so like the mathematics that it can never be fully learnt.

Izaak Walton

In his time, ol' Izaak was arguably the trout-fishingest fool to ever set foot in a pair of waders.

Granted, his brand of trout fishing was a tad different. He waded mountain streams, not knee-deep coastal flats, and he went after fish that, on the whole, are considerably smaller than the speckled variety we so ardently pursue on Gulf Coast bays. We're talking 12-inchers here not 12-pounders.

Those differences aside, however, Walton nonetheless left behind a timeless legacy of fishing philosophy. The above quotation is a good example.

Izaak was smart enough to realize two critical aspects of the sport: One, there is no way to know everything you need to know about fishing; and two, the ability to catch fish consistently hinges upon taking the fullest advantage of what you *do* know.

That premise applies to all types of angling, but when your target is a trophy speckled trout—say, an 8-pounder or better—it becomes the cardinal rule.

171

Note the plastic "teaser tube" rigged on the tail hook of this Excalibur Super Spook. From chang-ing hooks to custom painting, there are many ways to modify the appearance and performance of fishing lures. Experimentation with baits is a large part of the fun of coastal fishing.

With very few exceptions it's a calculated approach, not luck, that puts a wall-hanger speck on the receiving end of your line. And in order to calculate, you first need a formula. Thus, the purpose of this particular chapter.

I interviewed nine of the Texas coast's leading bay guides, and presented each with the following scenario:

It's mid- to late March. Fishing conditions are excellent.

A cold front passed through three days ago, and the weather and water have since settled down. Winds are light out of the southeast; the water is almost as clear as the sky. The tide is moving, and the sun-warmed shallows are draw-ing in pods of mullet like kids to cotton candy.

Given these conditions, what is your formula for a trophy trout?

The answers I received represented a collective total of more than a cen-tury of coastal fishing experience. Even more important, however, is the fact that when cross-referenced, they reveal a surprising number of concurring opinions and theories.

So, with the facts and philosophies combined, here are the basic elements of what it takes to fool the trout of a lifetime:

THE SUNRISE/SUNSET RULE: Go early or late

It's a widely held opinion that big trout are primarily nocturnal feeders, so this one should come as no surprise. Most pros prefer to leave the dock at least a half-hour before sunrise, and they like to make their first cast while the sun is still below the eastern horizon.

Night fishing is a less popular but equally effective option. Start an hour or so prior to sunset, and stay with it for at least two hours afterward.

Early-morning action is generally best on either side of the new moon; after-dark fishing shines brightest close to a full moon. In either situation, make sure you're familiar with the territory before striking out across the flats in the dark.

A bow-mounted flasher unit is invaluable for monitoring the water depth. Know your compass headings, and if you own a GPS unit, use it. Stay in channels and deeper areas for as long as possible. Reduce your running speed, and use a high-intensity spotlight to shine the way.

THE "BAY-BOTTOM SHUFFLE" RULE: Wade fish

You don't get out on the water to catch a trophy speckled trout; you get *in* it.

Drift fishing through oily bay slicks and beneath wheeling flocks of diving, shrimp-nabbing seagulls will never lose its following. Both are fun ways to fish, and both methods will produce an occasional head-turner. For the most part, though, these are numbers games. And for quantity, it's the best way to play.

For quality, though, you wade.

Silent, slow and nigh-invisible, the experienced and light-footed wade fisherman is the trophy trout's nemesis. Undetected, the wader flanks the shoreline, reef or island and strafes the water with a steady and premeditated series of casts.

Wade fishing is a specialized art, and to be enjoyed to its utmost requires a modest arsenal of equipment and accessories (see Chapter 5). It also ranks as the fastest-growing style of inshore saltwater fishing on the Western Gulf Coast.

A trend like that doesn't occur without a good reason.

THE "SKINNY WATER" RULE: Fish shallow

This one's unanimous.

Shallow water, naturally, warms up first and fastest. Mullet and other small baitfish move in, and are soon followed by oversized but somewhat lazy speckled trout.

The trout's favorite meal usually concentrates in the shallows, and is accordingly much easier for the lethargic early-spring whoppers to capture. At this time of year the water is still relatively cold, the spawn is under way and the big sows are full of eggs. (As evidence, consider the 13-pound, 11-ounce Texas state record taken Feb. 6, 1996, by angler Jim Wallace.)

Twelve-year-old Craig Freeman caught this 25-inch, 5-pound speck on a Saltwater Assassin while fishing with his mother Pat during a Texas Fish & Game *"Trophy Quest" with Matagorda Bay pro Capt. Bill Pustejovsky in November '97. Needless to say, it made his day. Though trophy specks are generally considered "plug fish," some serious wallhangers are also taken on soft plastics and sometimes even spoons.*

Given those factors, the larger trout tend to expend as little energy as possible. In addition, the warmth of shallow water steps up the metabolism of egg-laden spawners, allowing their roe to ripen at a faster clip.

Many beginning waders underestimate the potential of very shallow water. Three feet is about the max; 2- or even 1-foot-deep water is preferred. Often, you'll catch more fish when you're chest-deep, but the tradeoff comes in size.

Zig-zag the shoreline, walking an in-and-out pattern from 1 to 3 feet. When you connect, remember where and how it happened and stay there until it stops.

THE "CLIFF-HANG" RULE: Fish near a drop-off

During late winter and early spring, the weather is anything but predictable. The spring of '96 was an excellent example. Late-season cold fronts, like the one that blind-sided bay fishermen and dropped temperatures on the Upper Texas Coast to the mid-40s during the May '97, can pull down water temperatures with remarkable abruptness.

Gamefish are instinctively aware of this fact. Therefore, they hold close to escape routes as long as the threat of a freeze even remotely exists. If you want a big trout, do the same. Work a very shallow area that's adjacent to a drop-off.

Shakespeare's Mark Davis hoists a 42-inch "bull" redfish taken from the East Matagorda Island beachfront in early September '97. This fish, and three others of roughly equal dimensions, were caught on 11-foot Ugly Stik surf rods and Intrepid SS saltwater spinning reels rigged with shock leaders and 12/0 Eagle Claw circle hooks. Though many beachfront longrodders remain partial to conventional "squidding reels," the use of heavyweight spinning tackle is fast gaining momentum–largely because the constant threat of monster backlashes is virtually eliminated. The other three fish were caught and released that sultry night; this one was fitted with a "trophy tag" and forwarded to taxidermist Joe Lesh of Sportsman's Gallery in Spring, Texas.

The high-bowed, shallow-running El Pescador boats made by Davis Gordon of Port O'Connor are capable of doing everything from anchoring up in 4-foot surf breakers to venturing into calf-deep flats. Here, Gordon pulls a 24-footer up to the banks of the Intracoastal Canal in preparation for a late-evening photo shoot.

Split ring pliers like these made by Darrell Lehmann of Texas Tackle in Richardson, Texas, are handy tools when it comes time to change out hooks or—in this case—modify the rings and hooks on an Excalibur Super Spook. Lehmann's "Point Maker" hook sharpener is another unique speciality product that can provide the serious angler–pun intended–a serious edge. Be sure when changing hooks to use corrosion-resistant replacements of the same size.

Capt. Bill Pustejovsky of Gold Tip Guide Service in Matagorda, Texas, found this near-9-pound speckled trout floating dead on the surface with a 14-inch mullet lodged deep in its throat. The fish quite literally bit off more than it could swallow. It's not uncommon for big trout like this to attack incredibly large baitfish—which explains in essence why large, mullet-imitating plugs— particularly oversized topwaters—are such excellent choices as selective trophy trout baits.

Rockport-area fly fishing master Capt. Chuck Scates of Redfish Lodge on Copano Bay–who incidentally, on July 8, 1989, broke the IGFA 2-pound tippet speckled trout world record with an 8-pound, 11-ounce sow he took from the Lower Laguna Madre–dukes it out with a 6-pound redfish that was caught from an inland tidal pool on Matagorda Island and subsequently released, while Capt. Brian Holden mans the poling platform. Though small percentage-wise, fly fishing is the fastest-growing segment of saltwater angling throughout the entire Western Gulf Coast.

Capt. Tom Holliday, owner of Cocodrie Charters in Cocodrie, La., caught this hefty marsh red on a custom-rigged spinnerbait fitted with a No. 4 gold Colorado blade and a white, black-backed "tuxedo" Cocohoe Minnow shadtail. The use of spinnerbaits for reds, trout and even flounder has yet to catch on along the Texas Coast, but the shallow-running artificials are a mainstay of Bayou State coastal fishermen.

Thomas Newlin of NuMark Manufacturing in Pasadena, Texas–makers of the NuMark Fish/Back Support Belt and a host of other angling accessories–hand-lands an 8-pound speckled trout that hit a Saltwater Assassin worked over a shallow, sand-bottomed Carlos Bay cove near Rockport in May '98. A light-action, 7-foot All Star rod coupled with a Saltwater Assassin did the trick. A quality wade fishing belt is mandatory gear for the serious coastal angler.

A summer '97 Trophy Quest trip with Capt. Ethan Wells of Rockport, granted young Bradley Clark a beautiful redfish that he caught from a mere foot-and-a-half of water near San José Island. Shallow-water redfishing–especially when the bottom browsers are "tailing" and become targets for sight-casters during August and September–constitutes coastal fishing at its finest.

You get an enlightened view and totally different perspective of what a coastal estuary system is all about when you survey it from 2,500 feet out of the cockpit of a Cessna 172 Skyhawk. Pilot Mike Hyde of Cliff Hyde Flying Service in LaPorte, Texas, took us up last winter so we could shoot video footage and still photos of East Galveston Bay and Trinity Bay while the water levels were still low from a fresh norther. (Photo by Mary Bozka)

Beachfront vegetation–in this case, a colorful pasture of blooming sea oats on South Padre Island–is a vital link in the prevention of sand dune erosion. Tropical storms and hurricanes devastate the delicate dunes; in many areas, organizations now gather discarded Christmas trees and use them as "backstops" to gather sand and help resurrect the wave-beaten dunes. Such programs have been immensely successful.

Long-time Lake Calcasieu fishing guide Capt. Terry Shaughnessy, owner of Hackberry Rod & Gun Club, bottom-bounces a soft plastic shadtail on the ledge of a deep-water channel adjacent to the popular Southwest Louisiana hotspot. Since the elimination of illegal gill netting, Calcasieu fisherman have caught 8-pound-plus speckled trout in numbers that they never before considered possible.

"Drop-off," bear in mind, is a relative term. On the Upper Texas and Louisiana coasts, it might mean as much as 6 feet. On the Lower Texas Coast, it could be as little as 6 inches. North, south or central, it's a critical characteristic of your targeted area.

Where the bottom changes, the fishing often does the same.

THE "READING SIGN" RULE: Look for signals, not fish

Back to Chapter 1: Plain and simple, *read the water.* To do it right, quality polarized sunglasses are a must. Get good ones—Ocean Waves, Costa Del Mars or Hobies—and wear them religiously. (Keep 'em on a "rope," too. They ain't cheap.)

Pay attention to subtle surface details—the streaking wake of a fin, skittering splash of nervous baitfish or darker-colored hue that indicates a hole or ledge. Again, when in doubt, cast first and ask questions later.

Rockport veteran Capt. Lowell Odom pulled this 28-inch Mesquite Bay whopper trout with a MirrOlure 51MR slowly twitched through a color change.

THE "FLOATER" RULE: Throw topwater lures

"Big fish, big bait," they say. A bit of a cliché, but true all the same.

Pardon the repetition, but when trout are small, they eat a whole lot of little shrimp. When they get big, their culinary fancy turns to a very few big mullet.

No wonder, then, that topwater plugs are the coastwide favorites of trophy trout hunters in Texas and Louisiana. Surface plugs are mullet imitations, and they stay in the strike zone, right in the midst of a surfaced pod of the real thing.

Furthermore, topwaters are perfectly suited to the terrain. If it's too shallow for a topwater plug, you're not in the water.

THE "COLOR" RULE: Fish plugs with black backs

A few basic colors, it seems, fill the bill of most bayfishing pros.

At the top of the list are blue with black back, chrome with black back, gold with black back or, in low-light conditions, solid black. For off-colored water, try a bone-colored version; if the water is super-clear, stick with blue, clear or silver.

Why the black back? A twitched surface plug momentarily dips and dives. The dark back apparently gives the lure a brief but appealing flash that effectively mimics the real thing.

For whatever reason, it works.

THE TOPWATER "TORTOISE" RULE: Slow it down; then slow it down some more

Topwater plugs are finesse baits, and if there's anything a trophy-seeker needs, it's finesse. Like the shampoo commercial says, "Sometimes you need a little Finesse; sometimes you need a lot."

Capt. Rick Kersey, a master at working the B&L Corky, caught this 25-inch East Matagorda Bay speck on a chartreuse "Slow-Sinker." The Corky requires tremendous patience and concentration if you hope to use it effectively.

Never forget that the shallow-water monsters of March are terribly fickle creatures.

Most fishermen tend to over-work the bait—even those who think they're going slow. It's tough enough with a conventional topwater; for a really trying scenario, try working a floating Corky. It's not nearly as easy as it looks.

Twitch the plug with one or two light jerks; then let it stop. Not a quick stop, mind you, but a dead stop. Lower the rod tip a bit, allow just a bit of slack and watch the bait closely as it rests. That's when, experts say, you're most likely to see the surface explode.

It's enough to make you awfully nervous when a backlash interrupts that first crank of the reel handle, leaving the plug floating and vulnerable to a strike from what—given my luck—is likely to be the biggest fish of the day.

THE "GOOD HABITS" RULE:
Establish a pattern

Tournament bass fishermen first coined the phrase, but the concept applies to all varieties of angling that involve the use of artificial lures. For repeat success, establish a pattern.

Experiment with different retrieves and different lures. Try everything from stop-and-go to steady cranking, and if that doesn't work, try another color. Above all, pay attention. And again, always use a Loop Knot (See Chapter 13) or, at the very least, a split ring on topwater plugs. The difference it makes in the action of the lure is nothing short of critical.

When you hit on the correct combination of lure, color, retrieve and water depth, remember it. More often than not, it'll produce again.

And if all else fails, hold your tongue different.

THE "MISSED STRIKE" RULE:
Hit 'em with your best shots

Topwater fishing is as frustrating as it is exciting. Though the problem is a bit less evident with lipped floater-diver versions like the Storm Thunderstick, Bomber Long A and Cordell RedFin, true surface baits like the Producer Ghost, Super Spook, Big Bug, Spittin' Image and MirrOlure Top Dog lack the "water backing" afforded by their sub-surface counterparts. As a

In fall of '92, back when he still had his ponytail: Capt. Pat Murray hand-lands a big East Galveston Bay speckled trout. On the whole, veteran waders prefer to land fish by hand as opposed to using a landing net and snagging the plug in the webbing.

My close friend and fishing buddy, artist Mark Mantell of Friendswood, Texas, "topwatered" this hefty speck out of Lake Calcasieu—a Southwest Louisiana locale.

result, missed strikes, or "blow-ups," are maddeningly common.

Remember, just because a big fish strikes once doesn't mean it won't strike again. Many, many big trout have been taken only after repeated casts were made to the same exact spot.

If a whopper speck takes a shot at your plug and misses, try her again—and again, and again.

THE "GAME PLAN" RULE:
Stick with it

Lots of fishermen say they want to catch a trophy speckled trout. Very few, however, are willing to stick with it.

With good intentions and reasonably solid conviction, they book a reputable fishing guide and set out in quest of "One Big Fish." Often, usually after two or three tedious hours of grinding away to no avail, they begin to lose their resolve.

It's all too easy to do.

Catching a batch of school trout is fun. Catching a trophy-caliber speckled trout—that "One Big Fish"—is a commitment. A commitment, in fact, that can—and usually does—go on for many, many years.

Chapter Seventeen

Flat-Out Fun:
Fast Action for Flounder

Tickled by a light northerly breeze imported by the Upper Texas Coast's first real cold front of the season, Smith Point's olive-green shoreline flats shimmer brightly in the piercing glare of a fast-rising sun. Small flocks of bluewing teal buzz overhead like downsized fighter planes, laughing gulls cackle and fuss in the distance and, mere inches from waving strands of saltgrass on the gumbo-mud bank, tiny glass minnows erupt like sparklers from the mirrored surface.

The transparent baitfish aren't "nervous." They're terrified.

Trinity Bay pro Capt. Rick Kersey whips a white-and-chartreuse shadtail jig almost directly into the dense mat of shoreline vegetation and then gently drags it back into the water. The fluttering, paddle-tailed lure sends more minnows flying on its way through the pod, begins a slow, fluttering descent off of the ankle-deep ledge and is immediately hammered by a stoked-up fish that seconds later smashes the surface and sends delicate shards of salt spray flying as if someone had hit the water hard with the flat side of a garden shovel.

"*Flounder*," Kersey mutters. "*That's* what's been chasing the bait around here. Looks like there's a bunch of 'em too, judging from all the commotion."

The veteran guide's assessment is correct. In less than 30 minutes, we each string a half-dozen flatfish in the 2-1/2-pound class, all of which have fallen

TF&G Trophy Quest winner Debbie Dawson of Austin, Texas, inspects her first-ever flatfish. I somehow suspect it won't be her last.

prey to soft plastic shadtails threaded onto 1/8-ounce jigheads. No doubt about it; we can stay and limit out.

However, Kersey can't quite get the persistent image of shoreline-hugging sow trout out of his head. And honestly, I don't mind. Six keeper flounder will make just as many meals for me, wife Mary and son Jimmy. And these days, for this species, conservation really counts.

The southern flounder—*Paralichthys lethostigma*—has seen its better days along the Texas coast. In November of 1990, author A.C. Becker, Jr. of Galveston and I had just completed the last in a three-title series of saltwater fishing books, "A. C. Becker's Flounder: How, When & Where" (now out of print), and the ink had barely dried on the pages when I began to receive a steady stream of calls and letters from frustrated flatfishing regulars—long-time flounder fishers who were growing increasingly alarmed at the sudden scarcity of their favorite sportfish.

Their concern was all too justifiable.

There had been several consecutive years of poor recruitment, a period during which the flounder population was not producing a sufficient number of juvenile fish. Furthermore, the average size of the fish was also going downhill.

Altogether, my friend Gene McCarty of the Texas Parks and Wildlife Department tells me, those factors combined indicated "a pretty classic representation of an overfishing condition." That depressing scenario, McCarty says, was what prompted TPWD to make the first round of recommendations for increased regulatory management of the Texas flounder fishery.

Flounder regulations were indeed changed, effective by order of the Texas Parks and Wildlife Commission on Sept. 1, 1996. The minimum length limit was increased from 12 to 14 inches; bag and possession limits were decreased as well, from 20 in the bag to 10 in the bag and 40 in possession to 20 in possession. And, for the first time, commercial fishermen—who catch their fish almost exclusively via sharp-pronged "gigs"—were relegated a possession limit of 60 fish per day.

Now, in the summer of '98, we are already witnessing some degree of pay-back. Two fall spawning runs have passed since the regulation change. Thousands of foot-long flounder—fish that almost certainly would have been retained—have been released and allowed to venture into the Gulf of Mexico to spawn. As such, more and more of the highly-prized eating fish are returning to the bays with each passing year.

"Probably the bulk of the spawning population comes from the smaller-sized fish in the first year of spawning," McCarty notes. "A 14-inch flounder is a 2-year-old fish, one that's capable of producing lots and lots of offspring.

"All of the biology that we have on these fish tells us that the 14-inch length limit should work as well for flounder as the 15-inch length limit did for Texas' spotted seatrout ("speckled trout," to us non-biologist types). We're basically looking at the same biological characteristics," McCarty adds. "For example, the bulk of the female population becomes sexually mature at 14 inches.

"The added protection of increased length limits should dramatically improve recruitment," he continues. "I think we're going to see some real productive results, these regulations changes are going to have a very positive impact on fishing success. I can't say enough about what length limits do. Everybody kind of bemoaned the 15-inch length limit on spotted seatrout. Now," he concludes, "everybody just swears by it. The result is that speckled trout populations in the state are now as good as they've been since—*gosh, I can't count back that far.*"

Hopefully—and in all likelihood, given McCarty's impressive track record for accuracy on such matters—it won't be long before we can say the same about the Texas flounder fishery.

However, while sport (and now, at long last, commercial) flounder catchers are doing more to protect this valuable species, untold thousands of baby flatfish continue to be scooped up by the indiscriminate nets of the inshore shrimp fleet. The same "bycatch" dilemma that has continually plagued the Gulf red snapper fishery is likewise having no small impact on flounder populations within our bays and estuaries.

There are, simply put, *way* too many shrimp boats operating in the state's inshore waters. It's a typical quandary between ecology and economy. And with the socioeconomic equation being what it is, there's little likelihood that the nagging adverse effects of shrimp boat bycatch will lighten up any time in the foreseeable future.

So, we do what we can do. And that, just as in the case of the red snapper fishery, translates to regulating that which we can—namely, the sport and commercial harvest.

A fair solution? Certainly not. An inevitable result? Unfortunately, it is.

Our bays, and the fish species that reside within them, have historically been remarkably resilient. Personally, I have no problem with the tightened restrictions, and will support—if necessary—even further tightening of those regulations.

The bay shrimping fraternity has, over the past five years or so, begun to realize that—in the oft-quoted words of the cartoon character Pogo—*"We have met the enemy, and he is us."* For the shrimpers, the dilemma boils down to more and more boats catching smaller and smaller shrimp. The bycatch of flounder, crabs and other species is just another troubling element in the overall overharvesting equation. Somehow, legislatively or otherwise, the problem will be addressed.

Meanwhile, despite the fact that things could conceivably be much better, Texas flounder fishermen should revel in the fact that the positive, but somewhat painful, steps being taken are going to result in improved fishing throughout the coast.

Most of the flounder brought to net are the same kind taken by Kersey and me that cool November morning—incidental catches granted to fishermen who are primarily out to catch redfish and speckled trout. Indeed, flounder are prone to haunt many of the same locales as reds and trout, and to hit many of the same lures and baits.

All the same, there are plenty of fishermen who specifically target these strange-looking bay fish. Even in the face of greatly reduced populations, such specialists continued to take respectable catches of flounder by adhering to a reliable set of basic ground rules.

Foremost among them is understanding the nature of the quarry. The autumn season is to Texas coastal flounder fishing what January is to South Texas Brush Country antler rattling for rutting, wide-racked whitetail bucks—prime time, the best the calendar has to offer. It's the undeniable demand of Mother Nature to reproduce that puts both trophy deer and big "saddle blanket" flounder at somewhat of a disadvantage when the season finally dictates.

The fall flounder run is almost purely dictated by cold fronts. While unseasonably mild autumn temperatures can extend the action for everything from speckled trout to tarpon, they can keep the fall flatfish migration in near-neutral gear. Flatfish enthusiasts wait it out until a "real" cold front arrives and then assault the bays with premeditated strategies that year after year continue to produce results.

Flounder, fortunately for us, are delightfully predictable creatures. With the run finally engaged, they move from the deeper waters of bays and estuaries toward passes which connect with the open waters of the Gulf. The trick, therefore, is to set up at such a pass and intercept the fish as they work their way through.

From my perspective, there's no more effective—and certainly no more enjoyable—way to take fall flounder than to wade fish. Large numbers of flatfish tend to concentrate in surprisingly small areas. The angler who stands amongst them and "pattern casts" in a fan-like manner, placing each cast a few feet apart, can catch a limit in short order.

I can't over-stress the importance of pattern casting. It would be fascinating indeed if we could clearly see all of the fish resting on the bottom around us as we stand in the mouth of a shoreline cove or on the edge of a pass. I have stood in place and, by thoroughly covering the water around me, caught three or more flounder before moving on. Flounder don't tend to move very fast; fishermen who want to catch them should take the hint and do the same.

The smaller males are traditionally the first to migrate. Many will be undersized. The bigger flounder that follow are almost exclusively egg-laden females that are on their way out to the Gulf.

After months of lounging on bay bottoms, the thick-bodied females migrate offshore to water depths of 100 feet or more. Once there, they lay their eggs and in turn

Son James shows off a 16-inch West Galveston Bay flounder. The smile tells the story; I've never met a kid who—given the chance—didn't love to fish.

those eggs eventually wash back through the passes and into the estuaries in which they hatch and develop. Coastal passes are a critical element of the flounder's life cycle, and are as well the mainstay of fall flounder fishers.

Top spots along the Texas coast—to name only a few of the better-known—include Sabine Pass, Rollover Pass at East Galveston Bay, Seawolf Park above the Galveston Jetty channel, San Luis Pass at West Galveston Bay, the

This one's a bona fide "saddle blanket." Capt. Dennis Jochen of Crosby, Texas, caught it while wade fishing the south shoreline of East Galveston Bay in the spring of 1996. The spring flounder migration doesn't rival the intensity of the fall run, but it shouldn't be ignored.

Freeport Jetties, the "Locks" of the Intracoastal Canal and the "Diversionary Canal" at Matagorda, Pass Cavallo at Port O'Connor, the Lydia Ann Channel at Port Aransas and the Land Cut between Baffin Bay and Port Mansfield. All of these areas offer the water exchange that's so imperative to successful autumn flatfishing.

My trip to Trinity Bay with Kersey, however, drove home another important flounder-related factor—the presence of baitfish. No, flounder don't gather beneath shrimp pods, push them to the surface and draw working seagulls from miles around. The baitfish element here is much more subtle, but arguably just as important.

Specialized flounder fishing demands specialized baits. The most popular of the lot is the mud minnow (See Chapter 14). The pot-bellied forage fish can be bought at bait stands or captured with a castnet or seine. Hooked though the lips and fished either on the bottom with a fish-finder rig or suspended just above it with a float, mudfish are nigh-irresistible to hungry flatfish.

Live shrimp will also catch their fair share of flounder. However, unlike mud minnows, they also attract bait-stealers like piggy perch, croakers and—worst of all—hardhead catfish. For this reason, mud minnows get the nod. Small finger mullet can also be deadly flounder baits, especially if you're hoping to catch nothing but heavyweight fish.

Nonetheless, artificial lures hold a solid niche in the flounder fisher's arsenal. Though I've seen big flounder taken on everything from 52MR MirrOlures to floating Corkys, the undisputed favorites for flatfish action are either soft plastic shrimptails, shadtail jigs or weedless spoons.

The key to fishing either is to keep the lure in the strike zone, down near the bottom where the flounder lie in wait. The fish don't tend to chase baits very far; instead, they prefer to ambush their prey.

A bit of bet-your-buddy trivia: Flounder boast some unique, even bizarre characteristics. They enter the world swimming upright, just like almost every other fish. But by the age of two weeks, the Southern flounder's right eye "migrates"—yes, *migrates*—over to the left side of its head.

It's a trait that's characteristic of all flounder species. If the eyes end up on the fish's right side, it's referred to as "dextral." If, as in the case of the Southern flounder, the eyes come to rest on the fish's left side, the fish is "sinistral."

Perhaps the most intriguing trait of all, however, is the flounder's remarkable ability to "camouflage" itself, to match its upper body coloration (the lower body is snow-white) with the surrounding terrain. Flounder on plain mud bottoms appear—well, plain. Conversely, fish resting on grassy bottoms sport a mottled coloration.

The ability to blend in does much for the flounder's ability to ambush its prey. The fish lies on the bottom, waits until a baitfish or shrimp swims within striking distance and then, with jaws that can open to surprising proportions, surges up and grabs the hapless quarry.

Two basic elements of lure presentation hereby enter the picture: One, the bait must be presented as close to the fish as possible, in essence bounced along the bottom, and: Two, the fish must be allowed to hold the bait for a moment before the angler sets the hook.

The latter is especially pertinent to fishermen who use natural baits. The initial strike comes when the fish grabs the bait; the second throb of the rod tip signals time to drive home the barb.

With artificials, the "wait-to-set" rule is diminished somewhat. One reason I like spoons so much is because the fish, when grabbing the lure, also grabs the hook. An immediate hookset on a spoon isn't near so risky as it is when the fish hits a soft plastic. They tend to grab the latter by the tail. I can't tell you how many flounder I've brought in only to have the fish release its clamped jaws and send the lure sailing back at my face.

For that reason, I strongly recommend you use jigs that sport long-shanked hooks. The farther back the bend and barb is situated within the lure's soft plastic body, the more likely it is that the fish will take the hook instead of merely the plastic trailing behind it. (My personal favorite is the 5/0 Mustad Mega-Bite, though other similar styles will also perform admirably.)

If you're serious about landing a flounder, whether wade fishing or casting from a boat, use a landing net. And always remember to apply the net only when the fish is headed toward the mouth of the net. A flounder—or any other fish—will bolt like a bullet if approached from behind. Touch its tail, and unless it's very solidly hooked it will more than likely come unglued, throw the barb and make its escape.

A bit more flatfish-related trivia: There are more than 200 species of flounder in both the Atlantic and Pacific oceans. However, in waters west of the Mississippi River, the Southern flounder makes up around 95 percent of the sportfishing harvest.

The biggest flounder I ever caught weighed 6-1/2 pounds and hit—of all things—an oversized Cordell Hotspot plug thrown to the bank of the Land Cut below Corpus Christi. Any fish over 5 pounds ranks as a legitimate whopper.

In June of 1994, I made a trip to Southeast Alaska with outfitter Bill Bush of Katy, Texas. There was much about that excursion that I will never forget—100-foot-tall Sitka spruce

There are more than 200 species of flounder in both the Atlantic and Pacific oceans. Along the Western Gulf Coast, though, it's the southern flounder that rules.

trees with monstrous, moss-covered trunks, whales surfacing around our 15-foot inflatable boats, grizzly bear hairs embedded in the trunk of a tree only a few feet from my tent, where a big Alaskan brown had briefly paused to rub its itchy rear end in the middle of the four-hour-long Alaskan night.

It was the 100-plus-pound halibut I landed on the second day of our week-long adventure, however, that sticks most firmly in my mind. Two hundred feet down, the mega-flounder ate a pair of sardines for breakfast and treated me to a battle royale that I will never, ever forget. Even a "small" fish like that can hurt you bad if you don't handle it carefully (they reach weights in excess of 500 pounds). Mine was released after more than a bit of effort to free the hook.

Sometimes I wish halibut lived in Galveston Bay. We'd certainly never bring one to the landing net on conventional trout tackle, but I guarantee you they'd put a whole new light on the bycatch dilemma.

Chapter Eighteen

Learning the Longrod: Saltwater Fly Fishing

There are pinnacles every angler reaches throughout the course of his life, long-awaited and rare events which stick in the far recesses of the mind like grass-burrs to cotton socks. So it is with this 2-pound speckled trout dancing in the dark-ness just beyond the range of the zillion-megawatt spotlight mounted above the back porch of Redfish Lodge on Copano Bay.

At a mere 32 ounces he's by no means a wallhanger. Catch is, he's attached to the receiving end of an 8-weight Loomis GLX fly rod.

OK, so maybe I'm cheating a bit. School trout under lights are not exact-ly nature's most fickle creatures. But so what? He's fighting for his life, jumping, diving and cartwheeling like one of those mountain brookies you used to see in slow-motion on the yuppie beer commercials. Standing in waist-deep water, oil-slick fly line singing through my trembling fingers, I feel his every move in a way that compares with nothing I have ever before experienced.

From the porch, Capt. Chuck Scates gives me a one-man standing ovation. I can't help but laugh, partly from the jubilation of dueling with the infuriated trout and partly from this veteran fly fisher's shoreline antics. Still, he knows what's going on here. Another addict has entered the mesmerizing world of saltwater fly fishing, and life will never be the same.

Another lousy morning in Paradise at Redfish Lodge on Copano Bay. Fly-fishing ace and lodge manager Capt. Chuck Scates mans the bow and sight-casts to tailing reds while Capt. Brian Holden—another whiz at "fishing on the fly" maintains position from the poling platform of the Hewes Redfisher.

Scates epitomizes the coastal fly caster. Lean as a strip of beef jerky with light blue eyes and a suntan that's equally dark, excepting the give-away "coon face" that comes from wearing polarized sunglasses on the water day after day, he looks every bit the part. Furthermore, he has the credentials to back up the image.

Back on July 8, 1989, Chuck Scates broke the IGFA 2-pound-tippet speckled trout world record with an 8-pound, 11-ounce sow he took from the Lower Laguna Madre. I think about that while snatching the still-struggling speck from the water and carefully easing the fly—a shrimp pattern that Scates personally designed as part of the Hank Roberts "Premier" fly series—out of the wiggling fish's purple-tinged jaw.

Here I am with a 2-pound trout taken on a 10-pound tippet, showing off for a fellow who has caught a near-9-pounder and numerous other heavyweights on spiderweb 2-pound-test line. I can't even imagine the fight, much less the finesse and skill required to pull it off.

The trout disappears in the inky black water as I set it free and, dragging my feet ever so slowly, shuffle my way back to shore. Earlier this afternoon, a group of bank fishermen caught a half-dozen stingrays from this same stretch of hard sand bottom while chunking natural bait. I imagine a submerged squadron of attack rays lurking at my feet, waiting like swimming land mines for a fast and painful shot at an unprotected Achilles tendon, and a shiver not borne by the evening chill scampers up my spine like a cat squirrel on a finger-thin pine limb. At long last out of the water, I drop the wade fishing belt on the sand and join Scates on the porch.

"Congratulations," he says while handing me a cold one. "Now you've *really* done it." Indeed I have. A quick toast, and I can't ask questions fast enough. That I'm going to make a habit of this is not up for debate. *How* I'm going to do it, however, is.

There is a conception among the general public that fly fishing is an elite sport. I recall the numerous lodges I've visited in Costa Rica, where tarpon fishermen in $250 worth of Patagonia fishing togs sip Brandy Alexanders and smoke Havana cigars while swapping tales of monster *sabalo* landed on 10-weights. Sitting there quietly with my Ambassadeur 6500C and medium-action Fenwick popping rod, I felt about as out of place as a handgun instructor in Sarah Brady's living room.

That sense of separation, Scates tells me, is sheer poppycock.

"The more you do it, the more you're going to enjoy it and the more you're going to succeed," he says. "Heck, Bozka, you already have most of the battle won."

"What the hell are you talking about, Scates?"' I asked. "This is all about as good as Greek to me."

"Mechanics-wise, maybe so," he responds. "But that part, with practice, is fairly easy to master. You have the tough part down—being able to read the water. That's the majority of the challenge. If a fisherman can go out on the flats and understand what's happening—in essence apply the same knowledge required to wade or drift fish with baitcasting or spinning gear and artificial lures—the rest of it is just not that big a deal."

"How so?"

"Knowing where to put the lure is 90 percent of it," Scates replies. "If you've fished lures with conventional tackle in shallow water you're gonna take that same method of fishing and apply it to your fly fishing. The prerequisite is that you need quality gear.

"I'd like to be able to tell you otherwise," he comments, "but you simply *cannot* cheat when it comes time to buy a fly rod. The rod makes you or breaks you. They're expensive; there's no doubt about it. But," he continues, "they're expensive because a good rod will almost throw the fly by itself. Plus, if you spend the money on a quality rod you can afford to go with a cheaper reel."

In Scates' estimation, the beginning saltwater fly fisher can't go wrong if he or she starts out with a 9-weight rod. "The heavier weight makes a big difference," he explains, "because of the winds we have to deal with along the coast. Not only can you penetrate the wind with a 9-weight; you can throw the fly a little bit farther because it 'loads up' better."

The aspect of "loading up" is critical. Unlike baitcasting, in which the weight of the lure carries the cast, fly casting is a matter of casting the line.

"The rod actually 'shoots' the line," Scates explains. "Doing it right is a matter of practice. If you've ever pulled back a bow and shot an arrow, that's exactly the way a fly rod should feel when you let go on the forward cast and the rod shoots the line."

Unlike casting lures, casting fly line calls for almost no use of the wrist. "Pretend you have a hammer in your hand and a post in front of you," Scates instructs. "It's the same action you would employ to drive an 8-penny nail into a board with about six or eight hits. Hit that 'nail' on the head every time, and you'll shoot enough fly line to cover almost every flats fishing scenario you encounter."

According to Scates, the normal cast at a redfish is usually going to span 40 to 60 feet. "With a little practice and a quality rod, it's very easy to attain that distance with no more than three false casts," he explains. "But remember, the longer you keep the fly line in the air, the more apt you are to make a mistake."

Fly line, of course, must be stripped out first so that it'll fly freely when the caster shoots the line. "Strip out 30 to 40 feet of line before making the cast," advises Scates. "Then, as you see that you might need a little more, after you have your rhythm down, you can pull off more line and keep it looped in your hand."

Modern fly rods have gotten to the stage in development where a beginner can count on any of the mid- to upper-level models to do a more than adequate job. "People like Chico (Fernandez) or Lefty (Kreh) can tell the difference," Scates expounds, "but for someone who's just starting out a 9-foot, 9-weight rod is all it takes to reach a sufficient level of competence."

Likewise, most of today's fly reels will perform admirably in saltwater provided they're washed and lubricated after every trip. "An inexpensive $75 to $150 reel will last you a lifetime, as long as you rinse it off," says Scates. "The reel should hold about 100 to 150 yards of 20-pound-test dacron backing on top of the 87 to 90 feet of fly line that's the standard packaged length."

There are two different types of dacron—micro and standard. "The micro dacron might allow you an extra 20 to 30 yards of backing," Scates notes. "The backing is there as insurance, just in case you get that one real feisty redfish that runs off 100 feet of fly line plus another 20 to 30 yards of backing. But in the 16 years I've been fly fishing on the Texas Coast, I might have gotten into my backing a total of 40 times. Almost invariably," he says, "that's been with large redfish and large black drum."

Because of the shallow water in which most fly fishing is done, Scates recommends the use of floating fly lines. "The standard leader length is 9 feet," he says, "so there's really no reason to have a sinking line unless you're specifically fishing for flounder or perhaps are fishing over a 5- to 6-foot-deep shell reef. On windy days I'll cut it back to 6 feet. Both ways, the leader usually tests between 8 and 15 pounds."

The delicate presentation of a shrimp-imitating fly is virtually irresistible to a flats-cruising red. However, the ability to accurately place the fly in front of the fish is absolutely essential.

There are various line conditioners on the market, and some contend it's best to use a specially formulated fly line conditioner. In Scates' opinion, however, the best way to keep a floating line coated and lubricated is with a conventional vinyl treatment like Armor All. The coating makes it easier for the line to slip through the fisherman's hands and also enhances its buoyancy. It should be applied at least once a month.

Perhaps the most intimidating aspect of getting started is the myriad assortment of knots utilized by fly casters. What's necessary on Montana trout streams where the fish are shy of stout leaders, however, isn't normally necessary on the Texas Coast. The only possible exception, Scates points out, might be skittish black drum in clear and super-shallow water.

"Normally, redfish are not leader-shy fish," says Scates. "Neither are speckled trout. I use a regular Surgeon's Loop to tie my backing to the fly line. You can run a stretch of 15-pound-test mono all the way to the fly. A standard Improved Clinch or Palomar Knot is all you need to attach the fly," he notes. "The only specialized knot you need to learn is the Nail Knot. That's the knot you'll use to attach the leader to your fly line. It clinches down on the fly line and makes for a very strong and yet subtle connection." (See Chapter 13 for the complete rundown on knots.)

There is an inherent advantage to fly casting that I immediately noticed during my nighttime trout fishing experience. Fish surface at different distances and angles. With baitcasting or spinning gear, the only way to re-present the bait to a different fish is to reel in as quickly as possible and then make another cast. With fly tackle, all you have to do is pick up the line, make a couple of false casts in the direction of the sighted fish and let the line fly.

Furthermore, a shrimp- or mullet-imitating fly makes an incredibly delicate landing on the water surface. Contemporary plugs, spoons and jigs seem like depth charges when compared to saltwater flies, and the fish appreciate the difference.

I strongly advise anyone who's considering taking up the sport to invest in fly casting lessons before hitting the water. It's much simpler to learn the proper technique right up front than it is to start out on your own and then have to shed bad habits later. Scates, who manages Redfish Lodge with his wife, Lynn, is an excellent instructor. Usually, visitors to the lodge spend their first day simply learning to cast.

There is no shortage of fly fishing instructors, not only in the state of Texas but also throughout the Gulf Coast to Florida. As the popularity of the sport continues to swell (which, from all current indications, it certainly will) the number of teachers will grow accordingly. There are, as well, a plethora of good fly fishing videos on the market. (For more information on Redfish Lodge on Copano Bay and getting started in coastal fly fishing, call Chuck and Lynn Scates at 1-800-392-9324. And while you're at it, ask 'em about Chuck's new fly fishing book. A collaboration with writer and long-time fly fisherman Phil Shook and award-winning photographer David Sams, it's a "must" read for all aspiring saltwater fly casters.)

Above all, buy quality gear. A good rod and reel combo will cost around $350 to $400 or more, which again, compared with the cost of the typical rifle-and-scope combination is not an immense investment. Take the time to learn all the mechanics you can beforehand. Spend whatever free moments you have practicing in the back yard. Drop in at local sporting goods stores that sell fly fishing gear and saltwater fly patterns and ask questions of the locals. Take lessons, rent videos, read books and do anything else you can to give you an edge when the time comes that you finally stalk your way into a trio of redfish nosing along the bottom in only a foot of water.

When that precious moment finally arrives and you get that long-anticipated hook-up, it'll be a landmark event. Make it the best memory it can be, because you'll keep it for a lifetime.

Chapter Nineteen

A Guide for Learning:
How to Hire a Pro

Let's assume that the cookie jar stowed away in the top shelf of your kitchen cabinet now holds a grand total of $350. Let's also assume that the money contained therein is intended for fishing, and fishing only.

So, how do you best invest it toward furthering your fishing enjoyment? A new rod and reel, perhaps? A complete new assortment of spoons, plugs, and grubs? Thirty quarts of live shrimp?

Wait a minute! How about a guided fishing trip?

You hesitate. That money got there in increments of one, five and 10, and it's been a long while in the gathering. Seems like a real gamble to venture it on a one-day guided fishing trip.

Think again.

Depending upon which guide you choose, a chauffeured day on the bay can be one of the best investments you'll ever make as an angler—especially for the novice, or someone who wants to learn the layout and seasonal tendencies of unfamiliar waters.

The $350 figure mentioned here is a rough average at best. Guide fees vary according to who's doing the guiding and what services are offered. For the typical bay fishing guide, though, you won't often pay more than 50 bucks (more

Guides like veteran operator Capt. Gary Clouse of Rockport haven't made guiding a decades-long pattern of success by taking their professions lightly.

or less) than the aforementioned $350. Usually, that fee covers at least two, and in a few cases, three fishermen.

What can those anglers expect in return for the hard-contemplated layout of hard-earned cash? To some extent, that depends upon the fishermen themselves.

It's a widely-accepted assumption that fishermen pay guides to put them on fish—*lots* of fish. Reputable bay guides realize that fact, and as a result spend around three out of every four days on the water keeping up with what the fish are hitting and where they're doing it. Party or no party, any fishing guide worth his salt is going to aggressively seek out the action, day after day after day, in order to stay on top of his game.

He has to. That's what he's being paid to do. And, when he does his job and the party returns home with a heavy Igloo cooler, everyone's happy.

That's fine, and it makes for some great bragging pictures and fish stories. However, for the fellow who wants more out of a guided trip than a fillet-filled freezer, fish steaks are only part of the story—and a very small part at that.

The rest is knowledge.

More can be learned from one day on the bay with a knowledgeable fishing guide than the average angler will get from a month of trial-and-error in his own boat. And when you consider the hire-a-guide equation from that perspective, a guided excursion suddenly becomes very cost-efficient.

The key, in essence, is to treat the day like an expensive and accordingly valuable on-the-water seminar. So, *pay attention*. Ask questions. Take notes. Carry along a tape recorder, and use it. However you do it, pick the expert's brain, and keep his advice on record. Doing so can make one heck of a difference in the next trip you make, wherever it is.

Most guides, approached in a polite manner, are more than willing to give advice to learning fishermen. Don't expect them to hand you a pencil-marked map of their favorite holes or a detailed list of hotspot GPS coordinates; those places wouldn't stay productive for long if they did. What I'm talking abut here is general information. Things like seasonal tendencies of the fish in the bay system, what lures work best at which time of the year and underwater obstructions to watch out for.

Don't underestimate the importance of the latter. Hand-held GPS units have become very affordable, while at the same time gaining more and more electronic sophistication and overall utility. Invest the $200 or so it takes to buy one, and then use it to plot your guide's path from the dock to various holes. Let him know you plan on doing this before you make the trip; if he has a problem with it, find another guide.

Sure, you can peg the exact coordinates of productive coves, reefs and sloughs. But it's the safety element that ranks foremost. Even if a given "leg" of your trip is not a treacherous one, you'll be very happy that you have it plotted and (literally) on-hand when heavy fog sets in or you are for some reason forced to navigate at night.

The learning experience doesn't stop there. Unless requested to do otherwise, most guides fish right alongside their parties. Some claim this is because they want to keep and enhance their fish-catching reputations, and know that they can best do it by fishing themselves. Perhaps, in some instances, that's indeed the case. Despite what you might hear, a very real—and in some respects, very unfortunate—competitive comparison takes place when fishing guides off-load their day's catch on the local cleaning table.

Pride runs deep among professional anglers.

Far as I'm concerned, it really doesn't matter whether a guide fishes due to pride or practicality. What matters is that he fishes. If you're smart, you'll *encourage* him to—and not, I might again add, because you'll take home more fish as a result.

Here again, the benefit is one of knowledge.

You may be a real whiz with a quarter-ounce weedless Johnson Sprite, but that doesn't mean that watching how your guide works his rod tip won't give you just a little more insight into the fine art of spoon-feeding redfish and trout. The same goes with any type of lure or, for that matter, even live bait fishing.

Little things are important when it comes to fishing technique, and no one knows those things better than the guys who make a living by putting 'em to use. They use every method they can to increase their chances of success, from modifying their fishing tackle and custom-rigging their lures to changing the interior of their boats. Paying attention to such things invariably pays off. Show me someone who's spent a day on the bay with a top-notch guide without learning anything and I'll show you a fisherman who operates with his mouth open and his eyes and ears shut.

So, exactly how does one go about finding a "top-notch" bay guide?

Simple. Ask around.

Word of mouth does a whole lot to further the cause of quality fishing guides. The angler who has been there can tell you what kind of fellow to expect, and what kind of services he offers—or perhaps more importantly—*doesn't* offer his clients.

If you're short on friends who have recently fished with a guide, then check with your local newspaper or magazine outdoor writers. Newspaper (and radio) reports are admittedly exaggerated a bit at times by overzealous bait camp operators, but for the most part I think you'll find those reports to be credible—especially if the guide working out of that marina has been operating for several years or more.

Many guides operate independently, but their phone numbers can usually be obtained through nothing more than a call to your local outdoor writer or—easiest of all—a check of *Texas Fish & Game* magazine's "Discover Texas/Team TF&G" section. If a fishing guide is serious enough to fork over the dollars for continuous magazine advertising, odds are good that he's in it for the long run.

When you've selected the guide you think you want, be sure to query him over the phone—and query him *thoroughly*—before booking the trip. Find out what kind of boat he runs, whether or not he provides fishing tackle, bait and lunches, and how many people he will allow in one party. Always get an exact fix on the specific charges for extra fishermen. Find out if he's strictly a lure fishing specialist, a live bait enthusiast, or both.

If you prefer wade fishing, drift fishing or any other specific style of angling, make sure that he's willing and able to fish the way you want to. Ask if he's amenable to the idea of taking along kids, and if so, how old a child must be before boarding his boat. Eliminate all the potential "gray areas." Doing so can save a lot of unnecessary confusion, and possibly even some hard feelings.

Not all doctors are good doctors, and not all fishing guides are good fishing guides. Ditto for lawyers, construction contractors, accountants, teachers and yes, even outdoor writers. I have fished with literally hundreds of guides since I began my career in the mid-'70s, and with the exception of one fellow who comes immediately to mind, all have been a pleasure to fish with. That one individual, however, taught me all I need to know about how painfully miserable a day on the water can be with a "pro" who isn't up to the task.

It was, in a word, *awful*.

I'd say it might have been because this man simply didn't like me, or perhaps had read something I'd written in the past that turned him sour on me. After all, he surely wouldn't have been the first—nor the last—fishing guide to take exception with my opinions.

But there was another fellow dealing with this guy that same day, a long-time buddy of mine who redefines the word "friendly." After a long, and I do mean *long* day of trying to get along with our so-called "guide," he left the boat ramp scratching his head in wonderment—primarily, wonderment as to why this obviously unhappy man wasn't doing something else with his time.

Capt. Dennis Jochen shows off a fat 8-pound speckled trout taken from the oyster reef-laden flats north of Rockport. Jochen is a serious, full-time pro, and if you're planning on booking a trip with a fishing guide, I strongly recommend that you do so with one who does it as a career–not a hobby.

Not five minutes into the trip, he made it very plain to us that guiding fishermen wasn't something he especially cared to do. He told us that he was drawing a healthy retirement pension, and didn't really need the money. He also told us that his favorite days were the ones on which his parties canceled out and thereby allowed him to fish alone.

His "motto," he proudly told us about a dozen times that day, was "I don't

give a ----."

Go figure.

Guiding, I assure you, involves a lot of bother. Pro guides often have to put up with tons of unmitigated crap from arrogant and abrasive individuals who they don't even remotely know. They get ridiculously little sleep. Broken equipment, rude and incredibly demanding clients with outrageously unrealistic expectations, unpredictable weather that regularly

Capt. George Knighten hands over the stringer to Capt. Dennis Jochen while Chuck Bosone, owner of Bosone's Automotive in Seabrook, admires the morning's catch. Any guide worth his salt will work as hard as possible to put you on fish, but there are never any guarantees.

turns on them like a rabid dog, frustrating days that despite even superlative conditions fail to produce a single fish, being relentlessly "bird-dogged" by boaters who follow them day after day from spot to spot—fishing guides put up with all of this and more.

But—

It's their job. And they do it because it is what they have chosen to do.

Nobody makes them charge money to take people fishing. What they do is a business, and—especially in light of the amount of money being charged—it should be treated as such. You'll find out real fast if that's the case with your chosen pro.

Which is why, in my estimation, you should always ask a guide for a couple of references and check with those folks before you commit to a trip. And you should focus your efforts on full-time guides, not those who run trips on the week-ends to pay their boat notes or get a day off from the fire station now and then and use it to make some extra cash. Some such folks might be excellent fishermen; no doubt about it. But bear in mind here, what you're looking for is an excellent *guide*. You're much more likely to find one if you stick with full-timers.

You should also make sure that your chosen pro is U.S. Coast Guard licensed. If he is not, then he's in violation of the law.

Be as up-front as possible, ask all the questions that come to mind, and then—after having carefully, and I do mean *carefully,* made a choice—forget all that and focus on having a great time on the water with a person who is much more likely than not a bona fide first-class individual. Treat your guide with respect, and you'll almost invariably receive the same.

For most of us, a $350 to $450 fee (not counting the customary tip) is no small sum to pay for a one-day fishing trip. However, when you consider that much of the money is going toward the guide's operational expenses and basic overhead—and especially when you compare it with the cost of owning, maintaining, insuring and storing your own boat—it's really

The smartest thing you can do when fishing with a guide is to pay very close attention to exactly what he's doing. Consider it an on-the-water education. Capt. Mike Sydow of Rockport landed this 26-inch red while casting a red/white tail Mr. Wiffle soft plastic shadtail along the outside beach of Traylor Island in April 1996.

not a bad deal at all.

No guide, no matter what he tells you, can guarantee you a successful trip. Still, most will work like the dickens to see to it that you have one. These guys catch fish more often than not; again, if they didn't they wouldn't stay in business for long.

You may have been at this game of coastal fishing for many, many years. You may have your spots picked out, your patterns established, your techniques perfected.

Or, you may not.

If that's the case, and if you'd like a good chance at catching a mess of fish while learning some new tricks and reinforcing some old ones, it may just be time to dig into the cookie jar.

Chapter Twenty

Back to the Future:
The Need for Conservation

I'll never understand why, but the Texas Parks and Wildlife Department chose to send an inland fisheries biologist from West Texas to represent the department at the public hearing being held at the Galveston County Courthouse that hot summer night in 1980. Maybe they were short-staffed; perhaps the biologist from the Coastal Fisheries Division called in sick. Or maybe it was just plain old stupidity.

I doubt the latter. Although the TPWD is just like any other government bureaucracy—prone to sometimes make decisions that make sense to them and no one else—on the whole it is what I consider to be the finest state fish and wildlife agency in the entire nation.

But whatever the case, they really screwed up on this one.

The young lady was bright and articulate, extremely knowledgeable about freshwater species like largemouth bass, crappie and stripers. Catch was, she didn't know squat about redfish, and the commercial fishermen representing the PISCES lobbying organization were chewing her up like a bull red munching mullet.

The harassment grew worse as the evening drew on, and although the hearing director was repeatedly asking for "order in the court" he wasn't getting it. The poor girl got more and more flustered, and the netters got more and more abusive, so when my time to testify finally came I'll admit that my own attitude had deteriorated somewhat.

I was 23 years old, fresh out of college and working as the editor of GULF TIDE magazine and chapter coordinator for the fledgling Gulf Coast Conservation Association. With me at the hearing was a small cadre of sport fishermen and about half the GCCA staff.

You have to understand; for us this was not a job. It was a *mission*. Come hell or high water, we intended to get House Bill 1000—the "Redfish Bill," as it was commonly referred to—passed into law. But first we had to go through these hearings, and this one was not going particularly well.

I had spent the past several years learning everything I could about red-fish—population densities, spawning habits, migrations, "escapement," you name it. The fish were getting hammered. In 1979 alone, TPWD game wardens confiscated enough illegal monofilament gill net from Texas bays to stretch a nylon web all the way from Houston to Dallas. The wardens would burn the nets; then the commercials would retaliate by burning the cabins or slashing the tires of sport fishermen on Baffin Bay and the Laguna Madre.

They didn't call it "The Redfish Wars" for nothing. And this particular battle was going downhill fast.

So, I swaggered to the podium with the imagined demeanor of Chuck Norris rescuing his district attorney girlfriend from yet another group of bad guys who had locked her up in some dank basement. I was—and still am—no fisheries biologist, but I knew enough about it to get up on the stand and present a viable case as to why it was a bad idea to keep netting our redfish and speckled trout into oblivion.

I explained to the crowd how it takes a redfish at least three or four years to become capable of reproduction, and how the unbridled illegal harvest of so many hundreds of thousands of pounds of 5-pound-class reds was ringing a death knell for the species all the way from Beaumont to Brownsville. The Laguna Madre was hardest hit—especially during the wintertime, when the fish were particularly susceptible to being corralled into gill nets strung along the mouths of narrow-necked coves. I told them that there was a reason we stopped annihilating buffalo in the late 1800s, and that that reason applied no less aptly to the declining state of the Texas red drum fishery.

In essence, I told 'em it was time to find another job.

Ironically, a bunch of them eventually did—as professional fishing guides.

From left to right, TPWD Executive Director Andrew Sansom, Chief of Staff Gene McCarty and Houston Chronicle outdoor writer Shannon Tompkins, conducting an interview at the then-still-in-construction Sea Center Texas in Lake Jackson. The state-of-the-art hatchery and research facility is the result of many years of hard work and funding provided by CCA volunteers and the sport fishermen of Texas, not to mention the generosity of Dow Chemical Co.

The netters-turned-guides—the late Howard Brown of Rockport comes immediately to mind—turned out to be some of the best fishing guides in the business. Some still are. A man can learn a bay system pretty well after years of being chased at high speeds through meandering and shallow, reef-laced flats by hot-in-pursuit game wardens in the middle of the night. But at this point, these guys weren't quite ready to give up the business of netting. They were—at least some of them—a pretty rough crowd.

In retrospect, I believe that if the majority of the commercials had stuck with the law, they might to some degree still be in business today. Trouble was, the law-abiders weren't willing to rat on the law-breakers, and as the harvesting process became more and more efficient, the whole group ultimately paid the price.

They broke the camel's back.

But this night, at this point in a process that would require hard work in two consecutive legislative sessions, the "Redfish Bill" was anything but a done deal.

I finished up my presentation, and stepped down from the podium as my comrades cheered and the commercial fishermen cut through me with stares that would kill charging rhinos. As I walked to the rear of the courthouse to join my friends, I heard one mutter.

"That's the SOB we need to get," he told his friend, who somberly nodded in unabashed agreement. "Maybe we ought to burn that fancy four-wheel-drive he has parked out on the lot."

I knew these boys; they operated out of Smith Point—located at the intersection of East Galveston and Trinity Bays—and they hated my guts. We'd faced off a time or two before. I'd received a few phone calls in the past several months to the effect that someone was going to inflict serious bodily harm upon my person (*"whip my ass,"* I believe they said), and though I couldn't prove it, I suspected these guys were the ones doing the calling.

At any rate, the situation was tense and all eyes were focused on Yours Truly in anticipation of the forthcoming retaliation. Then I got to thinking about the aforementioned "fancy four-wheeler." It was a '78 Blazer that looked really great—coal black paint, headers and dual Cherry Bomb mufflers, amber KC Hi-Liters on the brush guard, an interior roll bar, super-stud six-speaker Craig Power Play stereo and 14/32/15 Mickey Thompson off-road tires with rubber lugs the size of small bricks. Yep, it looked outright studly.

However, mechanically it was a piece of junk. The monthly maintenance bills on the thing—just to keep it running—were enough to send my local mechanic's kid to Harvard.

"Tell you what," I told my bearded, wild-eyed adversary. "I hate that damned truck. It's costing me a fortune. But, it is insured. Here's what we'll do."

I pulled my keys and a cigarette lighter out of my jeans pocket and in jest offered them to him.

"There's a bar just down the street from here. I'm going to walk over there and have myself a few longnecks. Meanwhile, if you guys would drive that stinking clunker somewhere way out of the way and set it on fire, I'll catch a ride home with one of my buddies and be forever indebted to you. And I promise, I'll never say a word about who did it."

My friends thought it was real funny; the duo from Smith Point—to put it mildly—did not. The bearded one looked over at his buddy and said, "Like I told you, *we need to get that son of a bitch.*"

Obviously, they never did or you wouldn't be reading this book.

In retrospect, this stuff is amusing. At the time, it was as serious to us as a blown powerhead 60 miles offshore.

Then there was the Great NBC Television Interview of Spring '81.

The entire GCCA staff had taken a bus to Austin, where we were met at the Capitol building by a huge contingency of angry commercial fishermen wearing body placards that read "Commercial Fishermen: Farmers of the Sea." In tow were their children, all dressed in tattered jeans and shirts that made the little girl selling match sticks in the snow look like a Tommy Hilfiger model.

It was a compassionate image for the half-dozen or so television crews who were on hand to record the event.

I learned a whole lot that day about "media slants" and the fine art of "spinning." Excuse me if the wording is not exact, but author Hunter S. Thompson once described the television business as *"a long and shallow money trench, where pimps and thieves roam freely while good men die like dogs."* Thompson had apparently been interviewed a few times himself—perhaps by the guy who late that afternoon—after interviewing a half-dozen desperate-looking netters and their starving waifs—decided to have his cameraman turn the big glass eye on me. (I don't mean to sound discompassionate, but a bunch of these folks were making a hell of a lot more money than they wanted the public—much less the IRS—to know. And frankly, the fact that their daddies, and their daddies before them, had proudly worked as commercial fishermen, didn't make a rat's ass to me.)

"We don't want a GCCA staffer," the reporter told then-GCCA Executive Director Dick Ingram—incidentally, one of the finest men I've ever had the privilege to work for. "We want a *fisherman*."

(Like the people who worked for GCCA weren't.)

In December of 1980, I had left the GCCA to become editor, and eventually publisher, of *Texas Fisherman* magazine. I'd only been away from the job for a few weeks, but hey; fact was, I wasn't a GCCA staffer any more. So Ingram sent the reporter over to talk with me.

"Are we running?" he asked the cameraman, who nodded that indeed he was. Then he put on his "extremely concerned about the welfare of downtrodden poor folks being run out of business by uncaring and incredibly rich sport fishermen" face and began the interview.

I remember it almost word-by-word.

"Do you think it's fair to put these poor people out of business?"

"Do you think it's fair," I responded, "to the resource if we allow them to net these fish out of existence?"

Not the answer he wanted, I gathered.

"These people are just trying to make a living," he answered. "They are the FARMERS OF THE SEA, and you want to put them out of business."

"Sir," I said, "despite what those placards say, these people are not farmers. They're *rapists*."

Reporter Man turned white in the face, but the camera kept rolling.

"A farmer," I said, "shepherds the land and then harvests his crops. He tills the soil, fertilizes it and plants seeds. His plants grow, he nurtures them, and when they're mature, he harvests them. Then he does it all over again. Commercial fishermen, on the other hand, do nothing but harvest. And worse yet, what they're harvesting is a public resource."

He used about five seconds of my little diatribe that night on the 10 p.m. news, the part about "fairness to the fish." The "rapists" part never made it past the edit suite.

I didn't get to see the segment, though I heard about it the next day from a few of my friends. Because a series of interviews with various legislators kept us late, *TIDE* magazine Editor Larry Teague, *Houston Post* outdoor writer Ken Grissom and I missed the bus and were forced to spend the next several hours in a night club listening to jazz music and downing Long Island Iced Teas while waiting for the next Austin-to-Houston bus run. We arrived at the Houston bus station at around 4:30 a.m., at which point we were rescued by Teague's wife—who as I recall, wasn't exactly ecstatic about the situation. Can't say as I blamed her.

PISCES had an ally in the Texas Restaurant Association (TRA). TRA adamantly opposed the Redfish Bill, and spent a lot of money in Austin trying to keep it from getting to the Senate floor. Many restaurateurs contended that taking redfish and speckled trout off their menus would ruin their businesses, and they donated a lot of dinners to the cause of "educating" legislators who were undecided about HB1000. Today, many of those same restaurateurs still have redfish on their menus; catch is, the fish are pond-raised via aquaculture.

Aquaculture—though it, too, has its problems, especially when effluents and possibly even exotic viruses from shrimp farms are released into estuaries and rivers—is indeed farming. Yanking wild-roaming redfish out of our bays with gill nets is not. Not even close.

There's still a little illegal activity going on, but it's virtually nothing compared to what transpired during the 70s. The ones that anger me the most are the "sport fishermen" who sell their catches through the back doors of willing fish markets. It isn't easy for them to do, and it's not being done a lot, but some still do it and get away with it. And as far as I'm concerned, anyone convicted of doing so should lose the right to buy a fishing license for the rest of his life.

In Louisiana, measures to that effect have already been enacted. There, too, thanks largely to CCA and its volunteer corps, gill netting is now illegal. And the Cajuns, a few years afterward, are learning that their waters will indeed grow 8- and 10-pound trout—but only if they're given the chance to do so.

It reminds me of the deer hunting scenario in Lavaca County, Texas, where my family owns a small ranch. "This country won't grow big bucks," a local once explained to me. "*We don't have the genetics.*"

I asked our local biologist about it, and he laughed. "You may not realize this, he said, "but the average age of a buck killed in this county is 14 to 16 months. It ain't genetics that's keeping you from getting a big deer off this place, son; it's *bullets.*"

Everywhere along the Louisiana Coast, anglers are catching more 5-pound speckled trout than they've ever imagined. On Lake Calcasieu, adjacent to Sabine Lake on the Texas border, the relatively small saltwater "lake" has become to Louisiana what Baffin Bay is to Texas.

When I made my first trip there in spring '86 with veteran waterfowling outfitter and fishing guide Capt. Terry Shaughnessey of Hackberry Rod & Gun Club, the numbers of small fish were incredible. However, wallhangers were relatively rare. Now, Texas trophy trout hunters flock to Calcasieu

The future literally in-hand—a 5-inch long fingerling speckled trout— or, as the biologists call them, "spotted seatrout." The passage of a law which increased the minimum legal size to 15 inches in Texas waters made a remarkable difference in the quality of the state's trout fishery.

Croakers, sand trout, whiting or sheepshead—it really doesn't matter to a kid, as long as there's some action. Fifteen-year-old Jason Arebalo of Seabrook was plenty happy to snatch this bigger-than-average Atlantic croaker from the base of the Pelican Island Bridge near Galveston.

like *muy grande* buck hunters on their way south to Webb County.

Once Joe Doggett's topwater-duped 10-pounder made the outdoor section of the *Houston Chronicle*, Calcasieu suddenly became the new Big Trout Mecca—home of the Spotted Grail. (Doggett is still kicking himself because he wasn't registered in the Louisiana CCA S.T.A.R. Tournament.)

None of this would have happened, through, if a small group of well-heeled sport fishermen hadn't gotten their bellies full of not catching fish. They garnered the support of thousands of Texas anglers who were feeling the same frustration and—after a hellish battle to get it accomplished and one failed effort behind them— finally got House Bill 1000 introduced to the Texas Legislature on February 11, 1981, by State Reps. Stan Schlueter and Hugo Berlanga. The bill passed the house on April 9.

It went from there to the Senate Natural Resources Committee. The floor votes were there to get it passed, but—under no small amount of pressure from PISCES and the TRA—the Committee refused to submit it. Then, at considerable political risk, then-Lt. Gov. Bill Hobby stepped in with a procedural maneuver that sent the bill to the Economic Development Committee.

On May 14, HB1000 passed via a floor vote. And on May 19, 1981, then-Texas Gov. Bill Clements signed it into law.

"What about the people who want to eat redfish and trout at their favorite seafood restaurant?" he was asked by a reporter.

Clements responded with a retort I'll never forget.

"Let 'em eat catfish."

My friend Sam Caldwell, sporting artist par excellence and a kamikaze supporter of CCA since its infancy, is currently working on a book entitled "Change of Tides." It will explain in much better detail than I have here how and why redfish and speckled trout were eventually protected from the ravages of monofilament gill nets. If you find any of this stuff interesting, I suggest you buy it when it comes out. You'll not only get a great book that profiles perhaps the most interesting chapter in the nation's sport fishing history; you'll also be supporting CCA. And I promise you, that's a good thing.

Don't take today's great fishing for granted. Commercial boats would be dropping purse seines in the Gulf at this very moment if they had half a chance. Louisiana netters are now complaining to the state's Legislature that netting needs to resume because—get this—the redfish—a "pestilence," as they call them—*are eating all the crabs*. Don't laugh; these people *aren't* kidding.

So join and support the Coastal Conservation Association. OK? This deal is way too good to mess up. Saltwater fishing along the Western Gulf Coast is as strong as it's been since baitcasting reels came without anti-reverses.

It didn't get that way by happenstance.

Today, Texas redfish hatcheries—most recently, Sea Center Texas in Lake Jackson—are pumping 30 million-plus redfish fingerlings into the state's bays every year. Dow Chemical Co., who donated the land, CCA, and the people who continue to support it, deserve much of the credit for that astounding accomplishment. The "cause" has not disappeared.

Perhaps my friend Gene McCarty, Chief of Staff and former Director of Coastal Fisheries for the Texas Parks and Wildlife Department, put it best.

"*A little bit of ethics*," he said, "*goes a long, long way*." So does a little bit of catch-and-release.

The Gulf of Mexico and its inland estuaries, we now finally realize, contain a finite resource. The bounty of the bays is not infinitesimal; despite its incredible resilience, it is not forever self-sustaining.

And there's no reason that in order to enjoy it, we must also destroy it.

For information on CCA, contact:

> Coastal Conservation Association
> 4801 Woodway, Suite 220 W
> Houston, TX 77056
> Phone: 713-626-4222
> Fax: 713-961-3801

There's one other entity out there that deserves mention, the Webster, Texas-based Galveston Bay Foundation. Aside from water quality sampling and intensive public education programs, these folks are working hard to see to it that some of our most precious waterways—bayous and creek bottoms fringed with hardwoods and wildlife habitat—are not transformed into sterile, concrete-banked drainage ditches.

For information on the GBF, contact:

> Galveston Bay Foundation
> 17324-A Highway 3
> Webster, TX 77598
> Phone: 281-332-3381
> Fax: 281-332-3153

Afterword

It was early Saturday morning, about two weeks before this book was slated to go to the printer, when Mike Haring called me at the house.

"Bozka," he said, "I'm going to drop something by later on today. I thought you'd like to be the first writer to see it."

Comments like that get my attention. Haring, 36, is a manufacturer's representative for Mainstream Marketing. He's been in the business of marketing and selling sporting goods for 20 years, and today he reps some of the more notable saltwater lure, tackle and outdoor accessory lines—to name a few, MirrOlure, Mustad, Stearns and Bass Assassin. After committing me to absolute secrecy, he told me about a hot new bait that at this writing is being developed by the folks at Bass Assassin. "It is," Haring said, "unlike anything else you've seen."

And indeed it was. Just when you think the lure wizards have exhausted their alchemy, they come up with something new. This time it was a transparent, slug-like soft plastic that—much like the MirrOlure and many other hard baits—contains a reflective insert. It was rigged with a 5/0 Mustad Mega-Bite wide-gap single hook—yet another bass-oriented creation that after three years in the largemouth bass domain has suddenly found utility in the world of coastal angling. Playing with the lure, I could already see the thing darting about like a spooked finger mullet among the tide-flooded saltgrass of Christmas Bay's south shoreline, a weedless wonder that—just looking at it, even in the rough-edged prototype stage—I could somehow sense would be a first-rate fish-catcher.

"We don't have a name yet," Haring said, "so we could use some suggestions."

Mary and I spent a half-hour or so coming up with possibilities—the "Shiny Slug," or maybe the "Sea Shiner."

"Looks like an icicle," I added. "Hey, how 'bout the Bass Assassin 'Icicle?'"

"Yeah, right," she answered in a less-than-impressed tone. We passed on that one.

Before we were done we'd added a few other potential monikers to the list—among them, the "Flashback," "Sparkle Shad," "Sea Darter" and "Moonshiner." My personal favorite is the Flashback, but the final call is up to Bass Assassin's Robin Shiver, who owns the Mayo, Florida-based lure company and came up with the design.

According to Haring, the Flashback—or whatever it's going to be called—will hit the shelves in August '98. The new downsized and still-unnamed version of the MirrOlure Top Dog (the "Top Dog Junior," or maybe the "Walkin' Puppy" or "Walkin' Pup?")—another "secret prototype" that Haring sent me in early April—won't see the store racks until January of '99.

I used the Top Dog almost exclusively during the "Four Amigos Rockfest" in the early part of May—a first-time event sponsored by MirrOlure, All Star Rods, Numark Manufacturing and *Texas Fish & Game*. George Knighten caught a 28-inch trout on the lure the first day of the event—which for Rockport waters (or most anywhere else, for that matter), is an exceptionally big speck—and the rest of us also cashed in on lots of solid trout with a lure that I now consider to be the biggest "no-brainer" "walking bait" on the market. I'm sure that the new down-sized Top Dog will be no less potent.

So what, you no doubt wonder, is the point of this seemingly insignificant anecdote? Simple. Without the support of helpful individuals like Mike Haring, I'd be at a dire disadvantage. Knowledgeable sources and the information they provide are the bloodstream that keeps a writer alive, and over the years I have relied on people like Haring countless times. Their relationships, as well as their friendships, are precious to me. The sportfishing community is a close-knit clan.

Since 1976, I've written for a major metropolitan newspaper, edited three major outdoor magazines and freelanced for a dozen others, hosted a television show, produced and co-hosted a radio show, published three books and conducted state-wide multi-media seminars and too many "fishing clinics" and speaking engagements to recall. It took a lot of help from a lot of people to pull it all off.

It would be all too easy to fall back on the old cliché, *"You know who you are."* However, that would be a world-class cop-out. At risk of almost certainly forgetting more than a few deserving individuals, I'd like at this point to give credit where credit is due.

First of all, a huge thank-you to Ken Grissom. Today, Grissom is Boating Editor for *Texas Fish & Game* and writes outdoors and legislative coverage for a large chain of newspapers in Louisiana. Around 20 years ago, he was the outdoor writer for the *Houston Post*, and in that capacity allowed a 21-year-old kid who thought he could write to go ahead and write anyway. In my last two years at the University of Houston, while my journalism professors were telling us to just "try to get something published, *anything, anywhere,* even your church newsletter," Grissom allowed me to crank out photo features for the Post on a weekly basis. My profs took the credit, and I, of course, let them. Fact was, though, if Grissom hadn't given me the leeway I would have had a much tougher time working my way into this incredibly competitive business.

Check the "Help Wanted" listings in your local paper, and I daresay you won't find anyone looking for a full-time outdoor writer. When you're starting out, your portfolio is all you have, and Ken Grissom made it possible for me to build one that in the years to come would get the attention of publishers who were looking for someone at least twice my age.

Three days after I graduated from UH, I moved into an office off of Houston's West Loop and became editor of the GCCA's *Gulf Tide* magazine. Today, it's the CCA, and the magazine is simply called *TIDE*. But some of the guys who were there then are still there today, most notably artists Sam Caldwell and Ben Kocian and board members (and now fishing guides) Chuck Naiser and Jim Atkins, and I didn't know until years later just how hard those guys—Caldwell in particular—lobbied to help me get that job. It was a good one, and I stayed there until December of 1980, when I got a call from Bob

Gray at Cordovan Publishing.

Gray, who at the time also published the *Houston Business Journal*, *Horseman*, *Jet Cargo News* and *Western Outfitter* magazines, had the foresight in May of 1973 to start a brand-new magazine called *Texas Fisherman*. It was the bible of fishing for me and 80,000-plus other Texas anglers, and when Gray called to tell me that—despite his reservations about my age—he had decided to hire me on as editor, it was one of the most exciting moments of my life. It was, he later told me, the aforementioned *Houston Post* portfolio and the issues of *Gulf Tide* I had left with him that prompted his decision.

In the years since, that portfolio has grown in accordance with the list of friends and associates I have repeatedly called upon with the never-ending need for information and advice. Again, my friends in the "repping" business have been real Godsends.

Among them: Rick Stovall, Dave Richards, Wyndall Lansford, Neill McKinney, Mike Mills, Jerry Moon, Mel Carter, Tom Murski, Jimmy Clapp, Billy Murray, Brad Locker, Bob Knopf, Fonda Shawver, Barkley Souders, Mike Fine, Bill Cork, Ken Syphrett, Mike Thompson, Matt Bell, Phil McClain, Gary Grant, Dave and Blanche Holder, Mike Michalec and Herschell Ivey.

Thanks, too, to the many manufacturers, large and small, and the company representatives and agencies who have kept me appraised of industry happenings throughout the years:

Connie Coble of Costa Del Mar; Ken Chaumont of Bill Lewis Lure Co.; Brett Crawford and Lonnie Scott of All Star Rod Co.; Eric Bachnik of L&S Bait Co./MirrOlure; Craig Weber of Rapala/Blue Fox; Darrell Lehmann of Texas Tackle; Mark Nichols of D.O.A. Lures; Holly Hagler of 10X; Pam and Roger Parks of Parks Mfg./Blue Wave Boats; Bill Kenner of Kenner Boats; Jesse Simpkins of Plano Molding; John Storm and Sharon Andrews of Storm Lures; Louis Russo, Kirk Shipley and Victoria Kearns of Wrangler Rugged Wear; Mark Davis and Gary Remensnyder of Shakespeare Fishing Tackle; Tom Bedell, Gary King, Dennis Stulc, Karen Anfinson, John Prochnow, Keith "Doc" Jones, Bob Lawson, Richard Rabe, Linda Rubis, Barry Day, Clay Norris, Steve Grice and the entire crew of Outdoor Technologies Group (Berkley, Abu-Garcia, Red Wolf and Fenwick); Gary Dollahon of Zebco/Quantum/Motorguide; Fred Epperson and Thomas Newlin of NuMark Mfg.; Jack Stazo of Flex-Jig; Wayne Vinton of Vinton Mfg.; Ted Sheridan of Tidewater Lures/Mr. Wiffle; Eric Cosby of Top Brass Tackle; Paul and Pat Perrin of Fish-N-Hunt, Inc.; Bruce Stanton, Gary

Hughes and Joe Hughes of PRADCO; Larry Colombo of Humminbird/Techsonic Ind.; Lisa McDowell Hughes of the Sportsman's Outdoor Network; Jerry Jones and Dave Brundage of Clear Concepts (makers of the Clear Catch Bait Net); award-winning taxidermist Joe Lesh of Sportsman's Gallery in Spring, Texas; Darrell Lowrance and Steve Schneider of Lowrance Electronics; Ray Murski, Phil Marks and Doug Minor of Strike King; Dan Schaad and Ben Jarrett of Mercury Marine; Mark Gostisha of Frabill Nets; Tony Gergely of Sure-Life Labs; David Kinser of Oxygenation Systems of Texas; Alan McGuckin of Terminator Spinnerbaits; Gary Enders of Enders Rod Co.; George Calhoun and Matthew Gregory of Wade-Aid Enterprises; Cliff Shelby and Bobby Standifer of Ranger Boats; Thayne Smith of Jayco Motorhomes; Randy Vance of Bass Pro Shops; Al Kavalauskas of Fieldline; Davis and Karen Gordon of El Pescador Boats; Alvin Fogleman of Wright McGill/Eagle Claw; Jim White of Magellan Systems Corp.; John Mazurkiewicz of Catalyst Marketing; Pete and Cheryl Johnson of Johnson Communications; Karen Lutto of Lutto & Associates, Inc.; Kenny Bradshaw of Family Boating Center, Houston; John Topping of Avis Sports; Tim Irwin of Trillium Creative; Kevin Howard of the Farrell Group; Bruce Bear of Kodiak Communications; Jep Turner of Ball Mfg.; Sam Heaton and John Morlan of Johnson Worldwide Associates, parent company of Minn-Kota, Johnson Fishing, Mitchell and Spidercast tackle and SpiderWire fishing line; Kim Harbinson of Carmichael Lynch Spong advertising agency; Dave Burch of Berry Braiding; Ron Ballanti, Francis Feild and Jim Hendrix of Bear Advertising; and Mike Walker and Dennis Phillips of the Walker Agency.

Thanks too, to some special people who have put me up over the years—or perhaps better put, have put up with me:

Allen Ray and Betsy Moers of the Surf Court Motel in Rockport, and Rockport-Fulton Chamber of Commerce President Diane Probst; Richy Ethridge and J.C. Frerichs of Kontiki Condos in Fulton; Sam Rayburn "Fishin' Schools" instructor Will Kirkpatrick and his wife Vicki, James "Macky" McIntyre of Bieri Lakes near Angleton; Forrest and Jimmy West of Los Patos Lodge at Gilchrist; Capt. Terry Shaughnessy, his wife Martha and sons Bobby, Kirk and Guy of Hackberry Rod & Gun Club on Lake Calcasieu, La., Capt. Erik Rue (who also guides on Calcasieu); Capt. Tom Holliday, his wife Ruby, Tom "Capt. Floppy" Turner (the most incredible Cajun chef I've ever met) and all the wonderful folks at Cocodrie Charters in Cocodrie, La.,; Capt. Chuck and Lynn Scates, and guide Brian Holden of Redfish Lodge on Copano Bay; Calvin and

Jan Canamore of Wild Horse Lodge on Baffin Bay; and Capt. Jim Atkins and his floating "Church" on Baffin Bay—one of my favorite places on the planet. There's nothing like waking up knowing that there are very likely 30-inch-long speckled trout and schools of tailing redfish cruising the waters only a few hundred yards away from where you're having your morning cup of coffee.

On the tournament fishing scene, hats off to Don Farmer and veteran Baytown, Texas, fishing guide Capt. Mickey Eastman of Gulf Coast Troutmasters. Take note of this operation; you'll be hearing a lot more about it. If you enjoy friendly (and lucrative) competitive coastal fishing, then Troutmasters is definitely for you. On the freshwater side (and quite possibly, the saltwater arena in the near future), likewise kudos to Bob and Donna Sealy of Sealy Enterprises in Jasper. (Sealy also puts on a first-class whitetail contest every year called "Megabucks." If you're a deer hunter, it's well worth checking out.)

On the conservation scene, special thanks to David K. Langford, Executive VP of the Texas Wildlife Association (a San Antonio-based group that does a wonderful job—among other things—of protecting the rights of private landowners); Linda Shead, executive director of the Galveston Bay Foundation; Kevin Daniels, Bill Kinney (head honcho of the annual S.T.A.R. Tournament), Capt. Pat Murray and the entire staff and volunteer corps of the Houston based Coastal Conservation Association (CCA); and at a place that's very special to my heart (to the tune of 35 million baby redfish a year), Sea Center Texas' Hatchery Manager Camilo Chavez and Assistant Hatchery Manager Connie J. Stolte in Lake Jackson.

I also don't know what I would have done all these years without the incessant support of Alan Allen, executive director of Austin-based Sportsmen Conservationists of Texas (SCOT). Alan keeps the Texas Legislature on its toes like no one else. He's a kind and considerate friend who—when it comes time to defend sportsmen's rights in the hallowed halls of the Capitol building—attacks with the unfettered tenacity of an unleashed pit bull.

Thanks also to my friends on the radio airwaves for helping spread the word, too: Bob Stephenson, Jr. and Bob Stephenson, Sr. on KILT in Houston; Jim Harris of WOAI in San Antonio; Mike Leggett on KVET in Austin; Harold Gunn on KKTL-FM in Houston and KLVI-AM in Beaumont; and Steve Coffman of Texas Radio in Hallettsville.

If you're ever passing through Lavaca County, turn that dial to 92.5 FM or 99.9 FM. Thanks to Coffman, an inveterate outdoorsman with an impeccable taste for Lone Star talent, you'll hear a homegrown genre of Texas-bred tunes that haven't been blessed with airtime since Willie, Waylon and David Allan Coe were Austin "outlaws" back in the mid-'70s. Way I see it, the only thing as uplifting as fishing and hunting is the music you listen to on the way to the blind or the boat ramp. A little Robert Earl Keen, Jr. goes a long way when you're half-asleep at the wheel and the bay is still two hours away.

In TV-land, we've had some help along the way from Keith Warren of Texas Angler and Thom Dickerson of KTRK-TV Channel 13 in Houston. *Muchas gracias, amigos.*

Speaking of "airtime," thanks much to pilot Mike Hyde of Cliff Hyde Flying Service in LaPorte, who last fall took us up for a spin over East Galveston and Trinity Bays. The aerial shots you see in this book were taken by Wife Mary while I was hanging a video camera out the window. Until you've seen a bay system from 2,500 feet, you haven't seen it, and we have the footage and film to prove it.

Talk about *"reading the water."*

There are so many others to whom I am indebted–Capt. Doug Corry of Pasadena, a U.S. Coast Guard Auxiliary Master Captain who works in the computer business with Greg Westerman of Westerman & Associates in Houston and who, with Westerman, has pulled me through many a late-night cyberemergency; my fishing buddy Dennis Holland of Avant Hair in Seabrook, who sees to it every time I head out to host a television spot or make a speaking engagement that I don't look like the poster boy for bad hair days; Chuck Bosone of Bosone's Automotive in Seabrook who, despite its propensity to break down at inopportune times, keeps my four-wheeler in good running condition; my old friend Al Hillmeyer of Conroe—a man who I have long ranked as the best fish taxidermist in Texas; Denny Rosenfeld, who greatly helped us out with the use of his video projection units during the production of the *Texas Fish & Game* Multi-Media Seminar Series; and last—but as they say, certainly not least—the entire team at *Texas Fish & Game* magazine.

Roy and Ardia Neves and Ron and Stephanie Ward are not just our partners; they're our friends. Each and every one of them makes this job the fun undertaking that it's supposed to be.

Thank you, Roy, for believing in this project and doing so much to help make it become a reality. My sincere appreciation to Wendy Kipfmiller and Anna Campbell for their tireless efforts to help get it through the production department, and lastly, a huge thank-you to Assistant Editor Judy Rider—who read and proofed the entire text not once, but twice, and who helps me out in countless ways as part of her position as my right-hand support person.

There's one other person who, over the past 15-plus years, has been not only one of my best friends and closest confidantes, but who has also time and again provided me with incredible artwork–Friendswood, Texas, artist Mark Mantell. Wife Mary shot a photo of Yours Truly that Mantell transformed into the unique colorized line drawing that graces the cover of this book. There are other examples of his talents contained herewithin; he also pens the rib-tickling line drawings that complement humorist Reavis Worthham's "Open Season" column in Texas Fish & Game®.

Mantell, however, does "how to" illustrations and whimsical line drawings in his sleep. His fine artwork rivals anything being produced by the nation's top sporting artists, and today, his original watercolors, acrylics and oils go for $5,000 and up. Art collectors and galleries take note: Mark Mantell is a rising star in the galaxy of sporting art, and you'll be seeing more of his work and limited-edition prints as time goes on–much of which will be proudly portrayed within the pages and on the covers of Texas Fish & Game®.

Lastly, my love and appreciation to my 15-year-old son and budding world-class fisherman Jimmy, who has lugged enough fishing tackle, camera gear and duffel bags to last him a lifetime—not to mention unloading the truck in the middle of the night countless times and patiently standing side-by-side with me in knee-deep water when the fish absolutely refused to bite—and to my wife and best friend of 17 years, Mary.

I was extremely fortunate to marry a woman who loves not only me, but also God's Great Outdoors. Like she says, *"It's the going and the doing."*

Neither would have been near as good without her.

Index

M